MW00638492

PUBLISHED BY CLEVELAND LANDMARKS PRESS, INC.
14189 WASHINGTON BOULEVARD, CLEVELAND, OHIO 44118
WWW.CLEVELANDLANDMARKSPRESS.COM
(216) 658-4144

ISBN: 978-0-936760-41-4
LIBRARY OF CONGRESS CONTROL NUMBER: 2020914965
BOOK DESIGN BY JOHN YASENOSKY, III
PRINTED BY BOOKMASTERS, ASHLAND, OHIO

# RESISTING SEGREGATION

## SUSAN KAESER

# CONTENTS

# ACKNOWLEDGMENTS

Beginning in 1964, determined residents of Cleveland Heights, Ohio created five new organizations to challenge powerful interests that denied African Americans the right to decide where to live. Over the next dozen years, their persistence and that of African Americans willing to live in a potentially hostile neighborhood, resisted the forces of segregation and transformed Cleveland Heights from an elite all-white suburb, into a vibrant and viable racially integrated community – a seemingly impossible achievement. They also established a culture of civic activism that continues to engage residents, strengthen the community, and enrich life.

Cleveland Heights continues to defy historic norms that made segregated living normal and integration unsustainable. As we know all too well, racism has not been extinguished and integration is always tenuous. It can't be taken for granted.

I initiated this project to celebrate the community elders whose courage and determination made housing choice a reality, and to make sure that residents today and in the future know and appreciate the unique history of the community that belongs to them. I hope as they know more about the role of residents in shaping the community, they too will want to sustain and strengthen the community by joining with others to challenge entrenched power and address difficult problems.

This account is dedicated to the courageous African Americans who during the civil rights movement resisted the humiliation of racism and the second-class citizenship it bestowed upon them. Their courage and determination are as inspiring today as they were then, and appear to be no less relevant. Their message – and the bravery they exhibited to convey it – inspired Cleveland Heights activists to end passive acceptance of institutional racism and to resist the norms and behaviors that thwarted full citizenship for African Americans and denied people of all races the chance to live together.

I started my research in earnest in 2012. I dug into the archival record and interviewed more than 30 people who participated in the organizations that were instrumental in making change. My research produced hundreds of pieces of a large, complicated human puzzle, and slowly but surely, over several years and through many efforts to explain this period, the image and story came into focus. It has been a labor of love, completely engaging, and immensely rewarding and uplifting. I never tired of the project and as I learned more, was even more inspired by the actions of my fellow residents of Cleveland Heights.

I want to thank everyone who shared their experiences with me and thousands more who decided to pursue justice. What a message and legacy. I am grateful to each person I interviewed who helped shape my understanding of the details of making change, the cost and rewards, their strong values and principled thinking, and the cultural norms that they challenged. They were generous with their time and insights, reflective and humble, and often expressed regret for what they had not achieved. Their stories added the human dimension to this history, one full of passion, concern, and commitment to fairness. Every interview helped me understand and appreciate how important having a vision of what should be is to activism.

I took immense pleasure from ferreting out newspaper accounts and documents created during this unique moment in history. It was a magical treasure hunt that brought me understanding and inspiration. Holding flyers, meeting minutes, newsletters, brochures, mailing lists, sign-in sheets, and position papers produced more than 50 years ago literally put me in touch with the past and offered compelling evidence of the nuts and bolts of social change. I couldn't get enough of these artifacts of a moment in time and commitment to social justice.

I am grateful to Marian Morton, my neighbor and friend, for introducing me to the joys of archival research. She took me on field trips to the Cuyahoga County archives and the Western Reserve Historical Society, and shared folders of relevant materials from her Cleveland Heights history research. Her coaching helped me access amazing materials and information. I am an anthropologist and city planner by training, and journalist and local activist by experience. This background helped, but what I needed to create a well-documented history was found in the archives that she made accessible to a novice.

I am also indebted to Doris Allen, Carl Campbell, Ned Edwards, Gerda Freedheim, Betty Nelson, and Diana Woodbridge, who not only told me about their activism but dug out of their basements and closets folders full of materials from this era. The story would have lacked detail, tone, and accuracy without them. Joan Dowling's nearly complete collection of the Heights Citizens for Human Rights newsletters revealed the evolution of this pioneering grassroots organization, and its thinking, disputes, language, and strategies over ten years. The cardboard box she handed me also included a small black notebook with her notes, contacts, and lists. When I touch that notebook, I have my hand on the pulse of her 1960s activism.

The photography department and the online newspaper collection of the Cleveland Public Library and the Cleveland Catholic Diocese archives were also goldmines for this project. I want to thank Phil Haas, who during my visits to the Diocese archives, welcomed me with stacks of relevant files, made copies, and even reminded me to feed my parking meter. Staff at the Cleveland Public Library, Forest Hill Church, Cleveland Heights-University Heights Board of Education, and the City of Cleveland Heights were gracious and helpful. I am also grateful to Mark Souther, director of the Center for Public History and Digital Humanities at Cleveland State University and a Cleveland Heights resident, who encouraged me to undertake this project and helped record many of my interviews and made them available through the center.

Through this process I gained a much deeper understanding of a story I thought I knew and was awestruck by the foresight and courage of the residents of Cleveland Heights who made possible the quality of life that I enjoy today. I repeatedly discovered that organizations with which I had been affiliated and people whom I knew had been the pivotal players in creating the community that I cherish. I was lucky to learn more about people who I already respected.

I debuted my research findings on August 28, 2013, the 50th anniversary of the March on Washington for Jobs and Freedom. It was a "Civil Rights History of Cleveland Heights" bike tour, organized by my friend Joy Henderson and sponsored by the Heights Bicycle Coalition. This was the first of several public presentations, each of which was rewarding and helped me increase community knowledge of our history. I appreciate the hosts who invited me to speak to members of the Cleveland Heights Historical Society, students at Cleveland Heights High School, members of Forest Hill Church, documentary filmmakers for the Heights Community Congress, the staff at Fairfax Elementary School, and the staff of the Cleveland Heights-University Heights school district. Greta DeMeyer applied her creative computer skills to arm me with great visuals to accompany my presentations.

It was finally time to write. Unlike my lectures, the written record is permanent and can reach people now and in the future. Each word had to be carefully chosen. I wrote and rewrote the manuscript at least a dozen times over three years as I worked through my understanding. Many people provided encouragement and validation through that process as well as editing help. My first readers were my long-time writing partner Louisa Oliver, and my life-long friend Sarah Cooper who for years collected materials for the social action collection at the State Historical Society of Wisconsin. I turned to Kermit Lind, a patient informant and expert on fair housing law and history, to assure me that the story I told matched the reality that he lived. Phil Lammers cleaned up my distracting punctuation problems. All of them made my writing better and more accurate.

At last, I was ready to look for a publisher. Suzanne DeGaetano, owner of Mac's Bacs, unlocked this door for me. She read an early draft, encouraged me to publish, and advised me about who might be interested in the story. After a false start in 2018, in 2019 I connected with Greg Deegan and Cleveland Landmarks Press for the final leg of the journey. He responded to my writing and was enthusiastic about the chance to publish this untold history. I have enjoyed working in collaboration with him to produce a final manuscript and a finished product. Thanks to Peter Harvan for his editing expertise and to John Yasenosky for his cover and book design.

My husband Jerry Blake has supported me every step of the way as I disappeared into the research and writing that created this book. He has always been my best supporter and that has freed me to pursue my interests. I am also grateful to our children George and Sarah Blake who continue to teach us about social justice. Their understanding and commitment, shaped largely by growing up in Cleveland Heights, are living proof that the struggle to end segregation changed lives for the better.

I am fortunate to have had the time and opportunity to bring an idea to fruition. I hope that readers will share my excitement and regard for grassroots activism and will understand that we all share responsibility for shaping our world so more people can live the lives that they want.

# FOREWORD

## My Beloved Community – Cleveland Heights, Ohio

My first encounter with the civil rights movement was in the spring of 1968, when as an aspiring photojournalist, I documented and participated in the Poor People's Campaign in Washington, D.C. I was deeply affected by this historic moment in a spectacular period of citizen activism and courage. I witnessed the power of grassroots action and knew that I wanted to be part of it. However, it would take another decade for me to figure out my exact role.

In August 1976, on my 29th birthday, I moved to Cleveland, Ohio to begin a career as a city planner. Cleveland was grappling with the demise of its manufacturing economy, along with concentrated poverty, unstable neighborhoods, and hyper-segregated public schools. The chance to work on these issues with Planning Director Norman Krumholz made it my ideal job.

I moved to an airy, older apartment in Ludlow, a successfully integrated eastside neighborhood that straddled Cleveland and Shaker Heights. I joined the Ludlow Community Association, one of the region's first neighborhood groups created to advance racial integration, and the board of the Neighborhood Housing Services program for the Buckeye neighborhood, and went to work at Cleveland City Hall, where I focused on neighborhood preservation.

My first assignment was to figure out why school-aged youth were roaming their neighborhoods during school hours. The district's superintendent was suspicious of my interest and lobbied the mayor. As a result, I was soon called off the issue. After a year as a city employee, I joined the staff of a nonprofit organization, the Citizens Council for Ohio Schools, and continued searching for solutions to education for alienated youth.

One evening, a living room wall in my aging apartment collapsed. The landlord's disinvestment had caught up with him and displaced me. Despite my deep distaste for suburban life, I jumped at the chance to sublet a spacious apartment on Euclid Heights Boulevard in Cleveland Heights. In 1979, I moved to a suburb, and it changed my life.

I fell in love with Cleveland Heights. This first-ring suburb embodied many of my best hopes for a just and equitable society. It was integrated by race, religion, and class, and the civic culture expected involvement. A variety of nonprofit organizations gave residents an opportunity to solve problems and shape their community. City Hall embraced integration as the community's best asset and invested resources to market diversity and preserve integration.

Integration made Cleveland Heights unique and exciting – but also fragile. Vigilance was required to maintain its distinctive character. Committed residents were essential to hold the line against segregation and construct a new reality of respect, understanding, opportunity, and mutual responsibility. I wanted to be part of this process! In 1982, my husband Jerry Blake and I found a house on Compton Road. By March we moved in, ready to contribute to our community and learn from it, raise our family, and live our ideals. We are still here.

I had finally found my place in the movement for social justice. By putting down roots in Cleveland Heights, a racially diverse community, I was living my beliefs. From this position, I could throw myself into shaping my community.

I became a school volunteer and served on the boards of two integration support organizations: the Heights Community Congress and the Home Repair Resource Center. In 1989, a handful of other public school supporters and I founded Reaching Heights, a nonprofit organization to mobilize community ownership for the success of the Cleveland Heights-University Heights City school district and its students.

I directed Reaching Heights between 1991 and my retirement in 2008. This final chapter of my work life allowed me to pursue my commitment to social justice by working closely with other residents who cared deeply about our schools and community. Our work was part of my community's ongoing commitment to civil rights. This special work gave my life purpose and connected me to my community. Much like the experiences of community activists in this story, it taught me what citizens working together can do to create a community that works for its residents – despite challenging odds!

Retirement provided me the time to investigate and capture the story of how residents of Cleveland Heights, inspired by the civil rights movement, challenged housing segregation. They fostered an amazing civic culture and created an inclusive and racially diverse community that endures to this day. These exceptional qualities – the reason I made Cleveland Heights my home – didn't appear out of thin air. I hope that by telling the story of how community members united to transform Cleveland Heights, new generations of residents will have a deeper appreciation for this place and will be inspired to add to its continued success.

I started my research in 2013, the 50th anniversary of the March on Washington, and finally, by the 50th anniversary of the 1968 Fair Housing Act, I had written much of what I learned from the community elders who put themselves on the line for social justice. As you read this account of how Cleveland Heights activists challenged an entrenched system to make meaningful integration an enduring reality, I hope you will share my sense of awe for their foresight, courage, and determination.

The story is also a case study in local activism and the power of citizens working together to successfully tackle almost any complex issue. It's a hopeful story that can motivate all of us to make a difference.

*Susie Kaeser*

# INTRODUCTION:

# GRASSROOTS RESISTANCE TO A NATIONAL PROBLEM

*"Above all, the King years should serve as a bracing reminder
that citizens and leaders can work miracles together despite
every hardship, against great odds."*
*– Taylor Branch,* The King Years [1]

In the winter of 1964, at the height of the civil rights movement, a handful of young white women met in the Cleveland Heights home of social worker Barbara Roderick. That day, this small group of women committed themselves to a long-term quest to transform an all-white suburb of 61,000 residents into an enduring, racially integrated community. The meeting would lay the groundwork for Heights Citizens for Human Rights, a grassroots civil rights organization devoted to transforming Cleveland Heights. They organized because they knew their elected leaders would never lead such a social revolution. It would be up to them.

Courageous African Americans, the "foot soldiers" of the civil rights movement, inspired grassroots involvement in unlikely places such as Cleveland Heights, an elite white suburb. Galvanized by these African-American role models, Roderick and her group rejected white supremacy, racial discrimination, and segregation, along with the limits they imposed on the lives and opportunities of those for whom race defined housing choices. They supported the movement and were ready to do their part where they had best chance of making a difference – their community.

At the time, discrimination was legal, and residential segregation was nearly universal. Starting with the first wave of the Great Migration of African Americans departing the South during World War I, white property owners in northern cities imposed racial separation. The white real estate industry demonized African Americans as "undesirable" and "inharmonious." These powerful gatekeepers defined the presence of one black person in a neighborhood as a drain on property values and a destabilizing force on the community. Segregation, enforced with restrictive covenants and intimidation, was their solution.

Segregation was further etched across the American landscape by the New Deal, whose federal housing policies fueled the growth of suburbs and segregation. During the post-World War II housing boom, only single-race neighborhoods were eligible for public funds to finance the development or purchase of suburban housing, making segregation federal policy.

Interracial neighborhoods were characterized as "not a legitimate part of the system; they were assumed to be in a state of pathological transition," between all-white and all-black.[2] This destructive real estate myth ignored the reality that racial turnover was profitable to realtors, and that real estate practices like blockbusting and racial steering made integration transitional.

Segregation was carefully guarded by the real estate industry and policy makers and endorsed by the racial prejudice of property owners and white neighbors. In 1960, it was so prevalent – and barriers to integration so powerful – that interracial living was nearly nonexistent in the United States. In Cuyahoga County, race defined housing opportunities for 1.6 million people, including the residents of one of its oldest suburbs, Cleveland Heights.

Could good-hearted citizens, focused on their local community, make real headway against such deeply seated odds?

Segregation was national in reach, and experienced in neighborhoods – the logical place to create change. Residents of a street have a vested interest in the success of their neighborhood, as well as significant power to inflict harm or promote harmony. Neighbor to neighbor engagement proved to be a powerful way to strengthen communities and promote stability.

Cleveland Heights activists rejected the rationale for segregation and embraced integration as the hallmark of a desirable community. For them, an open housing market, one in which ability to pay was the only variable that should affect access, was essential to promoting black civil rights and equal opportunity, thereby healing racial division, and taming white supremacy.

Sensing the inevitability that African Americans would find ways to escape overcrowded city neighborhoods, and believing that this was desirable, activists mobilized to improve their community by ending segregation. They were ready to use their time, connections, and determination to achieve a seemingly audacious goal – ending racial segregation. However, there was neither a roadmap for creating change, nor any real evidence they could succeed. Nevertheless, they believed "integration was possible if people worked at it."[3]

Over the next twelve years, hundreds of Cleveland Heights residents worked through five different local organizations which had been formed to build a stable and inclusive integrated community. In 1976, a critical piece of the puzzle was completed when a municipal ordinance outlawed discrimination, blockbusting, and racial steering, and city council adopted a nine-point strategy to maintain demand for interracial living and guarantee its stability. Local elected officials committed public resources to integration, and from this point on, integration became a selling point for living in this older, first-ring suburb.

Building this stable, integrated community was achieved in two phases. The first created integration and the second defended it.

The first section of this story describes the initial challenge: recruiting African Americans to a nearly all-white community. Between 1964 and 1970, Cleveland Heights residents working through Heights Citizens for Human Rights and a variety of regional fair housing organizations recruited and supported African Americans who were willing to move to a potentially hostile neighborhood. This involved circumventing resistant realtors and organizing neighbors to welcome outsiders. They engaged in a variety of activities to promote among their neighbors respect for African Americans and their rights, and acceptance of racial change. They also mobilized the community to rebuke violence and embrace integration when, in a handful of incidents, newly arrived black residents experienced intimidation.

By 1970, the city had achieved some level of integration, and the federal fair housing law was in place. This marked the start of the second phase: defending integration. Despite progress, realtors and home owners continued to discriminate, and community comfort with integration was tenuous. The new challenge was to protect integration from white fear and persistent pressure from lenders and realtors to make neighborhoods all-black, a challenge that remains today.

In the second section of this account, I focus on the period between 1970 and 1976 when Cleveland Heights residents created four additional organizations to build upon and defend nascent integration. It ends in 1976 when city government adopted its Nine Point Plan to support integration as the community's greatest asset.

These four organizations were: Forest Hill Church and its housing arm, the Forest Hill Church Housing Corporation; Committee to Improve Community Relations; St. Ann Housing Action Committee; and the Heights Community Congress.

These community-led projects were motivated by a commitment to social justice and a conviction that massive white flight would be costly and disruptive. Their impact demonstrates the amazing power of grassroots groups to challenge the status quo.

# CIVIL RIGHTS ERA ORGANIZATIONS THAT ADVANCED INTEGRATION

## Cleveland Heights Integration Organizations

Heights Citizens for Human Rights: 1964 – 1974
Forest Hill Church Housing Corporation: 1971 – present
Committee to Improve Community Relations: 1971 – 2000
St. Ann Social Action Housing Committee: 1972 – 1973
Heights Community Congress: 1973 – present

## Regional Fair Housing Partner Organizations

Fair Housing Inc.: 1962 – 1971
Fair Housing Council: 1965 – 1971
Operation Equality: 1967 – 1976
Suburban Citizens for Open Housing: 1968 – 1980s
Cuyahoga Plan: 1974 – 2003

Activism did not spring out of thin air. Only a handful of people established these citizen-led organizations; but because they focused on an issue of significance, they succeeded in mobilizing a large constituency. As a result, these groups provide inspiring evidence of how the leadership of individual community members can animate important social change. For that reason, this book includes an account of each group's unique origins and the strategies they employed to accomplish their ultimate goals.

For integration to endure, realtors had to relinquish control over where people lived, residents had to accept change, and race had to subside as a variable affecting choice. Advocates used a variety of strategies – from personal appeal, education, cooperation, local laws, and legal action – to reign in realtors who engaged in the highly profitable practices of racial steering and blockbusting. Community organizing grew as a means to address fears, solve problems, strengthen community loyalty, and develop a sense of agency among residents that would make staying in Cleveland Heights desirable and integration viable. A new organization to support housing maintenance, and a new ordinance to require it, addressed another issue that could undermine stability. Also, regional fair housing organizations took the pressure off of integrated communities by pressing for new communities to open their doors and encourage African Americans to seek housing in many suburbs.

After the initial work to recruit African Americans to Cleveland Heights, city government marketed the community to both black and white prospective residents and invested in local services that would keep the community attractive. Private programs offered incentives for homeownership that would support integration. The Committee to Improve Community Relations, an African-American organization, played a critical role in changing white attitudes and white institutions to promote successful interracial living. This combination of civic involvement, municipal laws, and city investments was highly effective.

The early and sustained work by enthusiastic and determined citizens paid off. They successfully created a firm foundation to make integration viable and enduring, despite the odds. Leadership by tenacious residents made integration a virtue and turned the definition of a successful community upside down. They built a strong partnership between city government and new, nonprofit organizations that shared responsibility for providing a full range of resources to make integration work. Together, they built a vibrant community that was stronger because it was diverse.

They made Cleveland Heights a place where civic engagement was possible and citizen activism was the norm.

Racial justice was also advanced by national leaders. In 1963, President John F. Kennedy declared civil rights a moral issue and called for the nation to advance racial equality. He introduced the first civil rights legislation since the Civil War. After President Kennedy's assassination, President Lyndon B. Johnson brought the legislation to fruition with the 1964 Civil Rights Act. He also provided essential leadership for the Voting Rights Act of 1965 and the Fair Housing Act of 1968. These laws revived commitment to equal citizenship and made it enforceable.

At the height of his political leadership, President Johnson made clear his commitment to equality as something more than rhetoric by stating "It is not enough just to open the gates of opportunity. All our citizens must have the ability to walk through those gates . . . We seek not just equality as a right and a theory but equality as a fact and equality as a result."[4]

Richard Nixon, who became president in 1969, did not share President Johnson's commitment to results. Nixon believed discrimination should end, but he was not willing to alienate suburban voters by supporting a proactive role for the federal government.[5] Instead, he opted for local control, leaving responsibility for meaningful change in the hands of communities.

Luckily, grassroots organizations in Cleveland Heights and other communities had already stepped in to advance integration. In May 1970, Barbara Roderick represented Cleveland Heights at the first meeting of National Neighbors, a new federation of 33 grassroots organizations dedicated to multiracial living. The meeting included representatives from many previously white, city neighborhoods that had recently experienced racial change with the arrival of blacks who had been displaced by urban renewal. Other member organizations, like Heights Citizens for Human Rights, were from integrated suburbs where building integration was intentional.

Members came from as far west as the Crenshaw neighborhood in Los Angeles, and as far east as Jamaica Plain in Boston. The meeting, held in Dayton, Ohio, included relatively new groups along with groups established in the 1950s like the Ludlow Neighborhood Association in Shaker Heights, the Hyde-Park Kenwood Community Conference from Chicago's south side, the West End Community Conference in St. Louis, and Neighborhood Inc. in Washington, DC. Neighborhood groups from suburbs of Chicago, Newark, Philadelphia, Baltimore, Denver, Detroit, and Rochester were also there. Ohio was well represented by Toledo's Women of the West End, and groups from Trotwood-Madison, Akron, and Cincinnati. By 1981, National Neighbors had 125 members in 25 states and had begun securing foundation grants and federal contracts.[6]

Nevertheless, despite persistent grassroots action to maintain integration, National Neighbors closed its national office in 1985. Fair housing had lost its edge, national policy was in retreat, and funders turned away from community organizing. After limping along for a few years with board member Chip Bromley guiding its work from Cleveland Heights, it merged with the National Community Reinvestment Corporation, bringing to an end a golden era of community-led initiatives to advance multiracial living.

The Cleveland Heights story unfolded at the high point of the civil rights movement, when federal commitment to social justice and proactive strategies to challenge residential segregation were at their peak. The early federal retreat from President Johnson's vision for achieving civil rights confirmed what activists had known from the start: elected officials would not create a social revolution. It was up to them.

Unfortunately, some communities had not acted soon enough or prevailed long enough or they lacked sufficient firepower to resist this retreat. Other communities lacked the amenities needed to attract diverse buyers. But suburbs like Cleveland Heights, Shaker Heights, Oak Park, Evanston, and Hyde Park prevailed. They proved that with substantial, long-term attention, interracial living was achievable, preferable, and worth the effort.

More than 150 years after the abolition of slavery, white supremacy continues to thwart opportunity and divide society. Neither laws nor civic action have fully extinguished its incendiary power. Nonetheless, Cleveland Heights provides inspirational evidence that citizens working together can confront barriers to equality, change attitudes and behavior, make the political system more responsive, and create lasting social change.

As was true in the King years, citizens and leaders can work miracles together, against great odds. It is still true today.

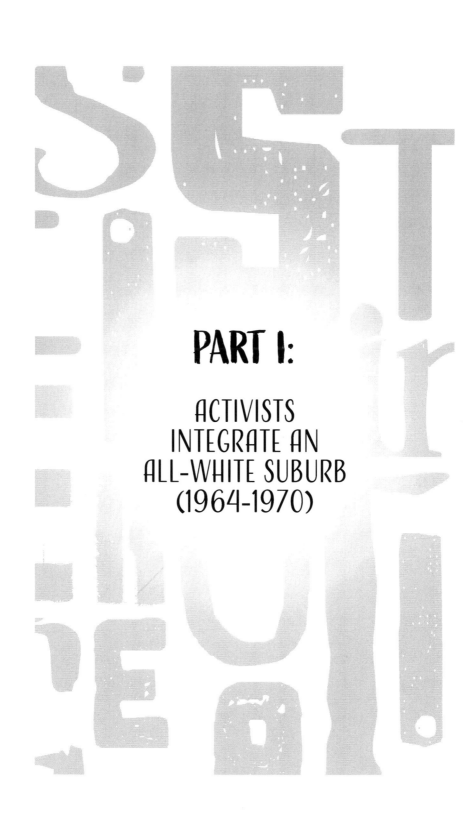

# PART I:

## ACTIVISTS INTEGRATE AN ALL-WHITE SUBURB (1964-1970)

# CIVIL RIGHTS DEVELOPMENTS AT THE NATIONAL AND LOCAL LEVELS 1954-1969

**(L)** LOCAL          **(N)** NATIONAL

**54**
(N) MAY 17, 1954 – SUPREME COURT DECIDES BROWN V. BOARD OF EDUCATION AND MAKES SEGREGATION IN PUBLIC SCHOOLS ILLEGAL.

**55**
(N) DECEMBER 1, 1955 – ROSA PARKS REFUSES TO LEAVE HER SEAT AND IGNITES YEAR-LONG MONTGOMERY BUS BOYCOTT. MLK BECOMES A CIVIL RIGHTS LEADER.

**60**
(N) FEBRUARY 1, 1960 – GREENSBORO, NC STUDENTS BEGIN LUNCH COUNTER SIT-INS.

**61**
(N) MAY 14, 1961 – MOBS ATTACK FREEDOM RIDERS IN ANASTON, ALABAMA. JOHN LEWIS IS A FREEDOM RIDER.

**62**
(L) JUNE 5, 1962 – THE OHIO CIVIL RIGHTS COMMISSION HEARING IN CLEVELAND FINDS WIDESPREAD REALTOR DISCRIMINATION.

(N) SEPTEMBER 20, 1962 – JAMES MEREDITH ATTEMPTS TO INTEGRATE THE UNIVERSITY OF MISSISSIPPI. FEDERAL TROOPS ARE CALLED IN.

(N) OCTOBER 11, 1962 – VATICAN II OPENS IN ROME.

**63**
(L) JANUARY, 1963 – THE OHIO COMMITTEE FOR CIVIL RIGHTS LEGISLATION BEGINS ITS DRIVE FOR A FAIR HOUSING LAW.

(N) 1963 – THE 175TH GENERAL ASSEMBLY OF THE PRESBYTERIAN CHURCH USA COMMITS TO "PURGE ITS OWN HOUSE OF THE UNCLEAN PRACTICE OF COLOR PREJUDICE."

(N) APRIL 3, 1963 – THE SOUTHERN CHRISTIAN LEADERSHIP CONFERENCE (SCLC) LAUNCHES PROJECT CONFRONTATION IN BIRMINGHAM, ALABAMA.

(N) APRIL 16, 1963 – DR. MARTIN LUTHER KING, JR. WRITES "LETTER FROM THE BIRMINGHAM JAIL."

(L) MAY 5, 1963 – FOREST HILL CHURCH, PRESBYTERIAN INSTALLS REV. NED EDWARDS AS PASTOR FOR CHRISTIAN EDUCATION.

(L) MAY 14, 1963 – DR. MARTIN LUTHER KING, JR. SPEAKS AT ST. PAUL'S EPISCOPAL CHURCH IN CLEVELAND HEIGHTS.

(L) JUNE 3, 1963 – CLEVELAND NAACP CONVENES 50 CIVIC AND RELIGIOUS GROUPS AND FORMS THE UNITED FREEDOM MOVEMENT.

(N) JUNE 11, 1963 – ALABAMA GOVERNOR GEORGE WALLACE BLOCKS INTEGRATION OF THE UNIVERSITY OF ALABAMA.

(N) JUNE 11, 1963 – PRESIDENT JOHN F. KENNEDY CALLS CIVIL RIGHTS A MORAL ISSUE OF SIGNIFICANCE TO THE WHOLE NATION.

(N) JUNE 12, 1963 – NAACP LEADER MEDGAR EVERS IS ASSASSINATED IN JACKSON, MISSISSIPPI.

(N) JUNE 18, 1963 – PRESIDENT KENNEDY
INTRODUCES CIVIL RIGHTS LEGISLATION.

(L) JULY 13, 1963 – GOVERNOR RHODES PROHIBITS
DISCRIMINATION IN OHIO STATE GOVERNMENT.

(L) JULY 14, 1963 – MORE THAN 25,000 PEOPLE PARTICIPATE IN A
UNITED FREEDOM MOVEMENT (UFM) AND CONGRESS OF RACIAL
EQUALITY (CORE)-SPONSORED CIVIL RIGHTS MARCH IN CLEVELAND.

(N) AUGUST 28, 1963 – DR. MARTIN LUTHER KING, JR. DELIVERS HIS
"I HAVE A DREAM" SPEECH AT THE MARCH ON WASHINGTON
FOR JOBS AND FREEDOM.

(L) SEPTEMBER 1963 – THE UFM BEGINS CAMPAIGN
TO END OVERCROWDED SCHOOLS IN GLENVILLE.

(N) NOVEMBER 22, 1963 – PRESIDENTS KENNEDY
IS ASSASSINATED IN DALLAS, TEXAS.

(N) NOVEMBER 27, 1963 – PRESIDENT LYNDON B. JOHNSON
ADVOCATES FOR THE CIVIL RIGHTS ACT.

(L) JANUARY, 1964 – FAIR HOUSING INC. OPENS AS A REGIONAL FAIR
HOUSING REAL ESTATE FIRM. STUART WALLACE IS THE DIRECTOR.

(L) FEBRUARY 25, 1964 – JOAN DOWLING AND DOROTHY SCHIFF
URGE THE CH-UH BOARD OF EDUCATION TO CREATE A LAY
COMMITTEE ON HUMAN RELATIONS.

(L) WINTER, 1964 – BARBARA RODERICK CONVENES WOMEN
TO CREATE A CIVIL RIGHTS ORGANIZATION TO INTEGRATE
CLEVELAND HEIGHTS AND UNIVERSITY HEIGHTS.

(L) APRIL 3, 1964 – MALCOLM X DELIVERS "BALLOTS VS. BULLETS"
SPEECH AT A CORE-SPONSORED FORUM.

(L) APRIL 7, 1964 – REV. BRUCE KLUNDER IS KILLED IN A DEMONSTRATION
TO BLOCK CONSTRUCTION OF STEPHEN HOWE ELEMENTARY SCHOOL.

(L) APRIL 12, 1964 – MORE THAN 250 ACADEMICS SPONSOR
AN ADVERTISEMENT IN THE CLEVELAND PLAIN DEALER
CONDEMNING THE CLEVELAND BOARD OF EDUCATION AND
CALLING FOR INTEGRATION.

(L) MAY 27, 1964 - VANDALS DAMAGE THE HOME OF KENNETH
COOLEY, 3670 MONTICELLO BOULEVARD, CLEVELAND HEIGHTS.

(L) SPRING 1964 – THE CH-UH BOARD OF EDUCATION
APPOINTS A LAY COMMITTEE ON HUMAN RELATIONS.

(L) JUNE 10, 1964 – A PLANNING GROUP HOLDS A PUBLIC MEETING
AT THE JEWISH COMMUNITY CENTER TO LAUNCH HEIGHTS
CITIZENS FOR HUMAN RIGHTS (HCHR).

(L) JUNE 15, 1964 – FOREST HILL CHURCH ISSUES
ITS SEVEN-POINT POSITION ON RACE.

**L** — SUMMER 1964 – CH-UH SUMMER SCHOOL INCLUDES 10 AFRICAN-AMERICAN CHILDREN FROM CLEVELAND.

**N** — JUNE 21, 1964 – THREE CIVIL RIGHTS WORKERS ARE MURDERED IN MISSISSIPPI DURING FREEDOM SUMMER.

**N** — JULY 2, 1964 – PRESIDENT JOHNSON SIGNS THE CIVIL RIGHTS ACT OF 1964.

**N** — MARCH 7, 1965 – ALABAMA TROOPERS ATTACK VOTING RIGHTS MARCHERS ON "BLOODY SUNDAY" IN SELMA, ALABAMA.

**N** — MARCH 15, 1965 – PRESIDENT JOHNSON INTRODUCES THE VOTING RIGHTS ACT.

**L** — MARCH 1965 – THE HCHR URGES MEMBERS TO LOBBY FOR STATE FAIR HOUSING LEGISLATION.

**L** — MARCH 18, 1965 – GERDA FREEDHEIM ADVOCATES FOR FAIR HOUSING LEGISLATION IN A LETTER TO THE EDITOR OF THE CLEVELAND PLAIN DEALER.

**N** — MARCH 21, 1965 – MORE THAN 4,000 VOTING RIGHTS ACTIVISTS RESUME MARCH FROM SELMA TO MONTGOMERY.

**L** — MAY, 1965 – THE HCHR SURVEYS REALTORS AND DOCUMENTS REALTOR RESISTANCE TO FAIR HOUSING.

**L** — MAY 13, 1965 – THE HCHR STARTS OUTREACH TO LOCATE HOME OWNERS WILLING TO SELL ON THE OPEN MARKET.

**L** — JUNE 1965 – CH-UH SUMMER SCHOOL INCLUDES 115 AFRICAN-AMERICAN STUDENTS FROM OTHER SCHOOL DISTRICTS.

**L** — JUNE 6, 1965 – 12 HCHR VOLUNTEERS JOIN A PROTEST TO PRESSURE GOVERNOR RHODES TO PRESS FOR FAIR HOUSING LEGISLATION.

**L** — JULY 23, 1965 – THE OHIO LEGISLATURE PASSES A FAIR HOUSING LAW.

**N** — AUGUST 6, 1965 – PRESIDENT JOHNSON SIGNS THE FEDERAL VOTING RIGHTS ACT.

**L** — OCTOBER 19, 1965 – TWO RACIALLY MOTIVATED BOMBINGS DAMAGE HOMES OF ROGER SAFFOLD, 2624 EUCLID HEIGHTS BOULEVARD, AND BERNARD DIRENFELD, 2352 EDWARDS COURT.

**L** — OCTOBER 28, 1965 – CLEVELAND HEIGHTS CITY COUNCIL INCREASES PENALTIES FOR VANDALISM.

**L** — OCTOBER 30, 1965 – THE OHIO FAIR HOUSING LAW TAKES EFFECT.

**L** — NOVEMBER 1, 1965 – THE FAIR HOUSING COUNCIL (FHC) OPENS. HCHR VOLUNTEER BARBARA HEALD IS THE DIRECTOR.

**N** — DECEMBER 8, 1965 – VATICAN II CLOSES WITH CALLS FOR GREATER ATTENTION TO SOCIAL JUSTICE MISSION OF THE CATHOLIC CHURCH.

**L** — FEBRUARY 9, 1966 – HCHR MEMBERS APPROVED A CODE OF REGULATIONS AND AGREE TO INCORPORATE.

MAY 1966 – BARBARA RODERICK IS NAMED INTERIM DIRECTOR OF THE FHC.

JUNE 28, 1966 – THE HOME OF MR. AND MRS. CHARLES GARD, 2604 E. OVERLOOK, IS BOMBED.

JUNE 29, 1966 – 250 ATTEND HCHR RALLY AT ST. PAUL'S CHURCH TO PROTEST THE BOMBING AND CALL FOR CITY ACTION.

JULY 6, 1966 – MARY BOENKE DELIVERS HCHR DEMANDS TO CITY COUNCIL. MORE THAN 280 SUPPORTERS MARCH TO HEIGHTS TEMPLE TO PLAN A FOLLOW-UP.

SEPTEMBER 20, 1966 – AN HCHR-SPONSORED "OPEN DOOR" AD APPEARS IN THE SUN PRESS.

OCTOBER, 1966 – THE HCHR LAUNCHES ITS "HOME SELLER PROJECT."

NOVEMBER 2, 1966 – THE URBAN LEAGUE RECEIVES FUNDING FOR OPERATION EQUALITY.

NOVEMBER 21, 1966 – CLEVELAND HEIGHTS CITY COUNCIL REJECTS HCHR POLICY REQUESTS.

DECEMBER 10, 1966 – THE CH-UH BOARD OF EDUCATION APPROVES A NEW HUMAN RELATIONS POLICY.

WINTER 1966-67 – THE HCHR REPORTS 76 NEGRO FAMILIES IN CLEVELAND HEIGHTS LIVING ON 41 DIFFERENT STREETS; 10 IN UNIVERSITY HEIGHTS.

1967 – PRESIDENT JOHNSON APPOINTS THURGOOD MARSHALL TO THE SUPREME COURT.

1967 – PRESBYTERIAN CHURCH USA REVISES THE BOOK OF CONFESSIONS TO CONDEMN DISCRIMINATION.

FEBRUARY 1967 – SHAKER HEIGHTS LAUNCHES SUBURBAN CITIZENS FOR OPEN HOUSING.

APRIL 1967 – MORE THAN 50 LIVING ROOM MEETINGS ARE HELD TO DISCUSS RACE AS PART OF HCHR'S NEIGHBORHOOD DISCUSSION PROJECT.

MAY 13, 1967 – THE HOME OF NEWTON HILL IS BOMBED. MORE THAN 700 PROTEST THE NEXT NIGHT AT A HCHR RALLY AT ST. PAUL'S.

MAY 16, 1967 – THE HEIGHTS MINISTERIAL ASSOCIATION ISSUES STATEMENT ON OPEN HOUSING.

JUNE 5, 1967 – HCHR PRESIDENT RALPH BRODY ASKS CITY COUNCIL TO TAKE A "MORE VIGOROUS STAND ON INTEGRATING OUR SUBURB."

SEPTEMBER 27, 1967 - HCHR PRESIDENT BRODY TESTIFIES IN OPPOSITION TO THE CITY'S BAN ON SIGNS.

DECEMBER 3, 1967 – THE HCHR PARTNERS WITH OPERATION EQUALITY FOR OPERATION HOUSE SHOP.

**68**

**FEBRUARY 25, 1968** – THE HEIGHTS REALTORS ROUND TABLE SPONSORS A PANEL ON OPEN HOUSING IN THE SUBURBS.

**APRIL 4, 1968** – MARTIN LUTHER KING, JR. IS ASSASSINATED IN MEMPHIS.

**APRIL 30, 1968** – CLEVELAND HEIGHTS CITY COUNCIL ISSUES AN OPEN LETTER TO THE COMMUNITY ASKING SUPPORT FOR A STABLE COMMUNITY.

**MAY 20, 1968** – FOREST HILL CHURCH SESSION APPROVES A STATEMENT ON OPEN HOUSING.

**MAY 21, 1968** – CONSTRUCTION OF RESURRECTION CITY BEGINS ON THE NATIONAL MALL TO HOUSE PARTICIPANTS IN THE POOR PEOPLE'S CAMPAIGN.

**JULY 23, 1968** – THE "GLENVILLE SHOOTOUT" BETWEEN CLEVELAND POLICE AND BLACK MILITANTS LEAVES SEVEN PEOPLE DEAD.

**OCTOBER 6, 1968** – FOREST HILL CHURCH BEGINS "OPERATION OPEN MIND," A FOUR-PART SERIES TO EXAMINE RACIAL PREJUDICE.

**DECEMBER 1968** – ISAAC HAGGINS OPENS A FOR-PROFIT, OPEN HOUSING REAL ESTATE COMPANY IN CLEVELAND HEIGHTS.

**69**

**JANUARY 1, 1969** – THE BOARD ON CHURCH AND SOCIETY BEGINS AT FOREST HILL CHURCH.

**1969** – AUXILIARY BISHOP WILLIAM COSGROVE AND FR. DAN REIDY DEVELOP THE COMMISSION ON CATHOLIC COMMUNITY ACTION.

**1969** – SIXTEEN CLEVELAND HEIGHTS-BASED JEWISH INSTITUTIONS FOUND CLEVELAND HEIGHTS ASSEMBLY TO PREVENT JEWISH FLIGHT.

**FEBRUARY 14, 1969** – ISAAC HAGGINS REALTY COMPANY AT 2221 N. TAYLOR ROAD IS BOMBED.

**FEBRUARY 23, 1969** – MORE THAN 2,500 PEOPLE SIGN A REGISTRY TO CONDEMN VIOLENCE AND SUPPORT ISAAC HAGGINS.

**MAY 1969** – MORE THAN 2,000 PEOPLE PARTICIPATE IN HCHR'S FOUR-PART BLACK HERITAGE SERIES.

**JUNE 20, 1969** – THE AMERICAN JEWISH COMMITTEE AWARDS THE ISAIAH AWARD TO HCHR FOR BLACK HERITAGE SERIES.

**OCTOBER 1969** – FOREST HILL CHURCH BEGINS FOUR WEEKLY SESSIONS ON, "DYNAMICS OF COMMUNITY CHANGE."

**OCTOBER 26, 1969** – AUXILIARY BISHOP COSGROVE REQUESTS FUNDING FOR "ACTION FOR A CHANGE."

# CHAPTER 1

# CHALLENGING
# DIFFICULT ODDS

Cleveland Heights is located on a plateau on the eastern boundary of the city of Cleveland in Cuyahoga County, Ohio. One of Cleveland's first three suburbs, it was developed at the turn of the 20th century as an elite, white community – an identity that 1960s civil rights activists reshaped as an integrated oasis.

By 1960, there were 60 municipalities in Cuyahoga County. White residents were welcome in all of them. By contrast, black residents, regardless of their financial capacity, were confined to a few overcrowded and highly segregated neighborhoods in Cleveland.

Residential segregation was historic, intentional, and massive. As the population of the Cleveland metropolitan area grew and suburban development flourished, so did racial separation. At the onset of mass suburbanization, realtors and lenders saw integration as destructive to property values and used this rationale to enforce segregation. During the New Deal, the federal government advanced segregation on a grand scale with policies designed to prevent foreclosures and restart construction employment. Laws reduced the cost of home ownership, but imposed racial exclusion as a requirement of program funds. Finally, individual prejudices reinforced racial separation.

When Cleveland Heights residents would eventually confront

segregation in the 1960s, they took on the results of persistent systemic racial discrimination that enshrined inequality and established segregation as normal, nearly universal, and seemingly impossible to change.

The challenge was enormous, but high-minded activists were determined to change a system that was dehumanizing, denied African Americans equal rights as citizens in violation of the 14th Amendment, and, by barring access to suburban living, fostered a long-lasting wealth divide. They were not deterred by the scale of the problem, the difficulty of the challenge, or the degree to which discrimination was institutionalized in the levers that controlled housing opportunity. They were ready to tangle with racism, the underlying cause. Like all civil rights activists, they defied deeply rooted forces that created and protected inequality.

## Cleveland's Early Growth Leads to the Urban-Suburban Shift

Cleveland traces its founding to 1796 when Moses Cleaveland surveyed the area for the Connecticut Land Company and opened the door to white settlement. By 1830, Native Americans had given up their rights to the land, and this tiny western outpost, well-situated on the Cuyahoga River and Lake Erie, was home to about 1,000 of the 10,000 inhabitants of Cuyahoga County. By 1860 Cleveland had become a small city of more than 43,000. For the next 100 years, as the region continued to grow, most of the population lived in the urban center. The city's dominance was gradually eroded however, with the development of suburbs. By 1970, the majority of Cuyahoga County residents lived in the suburbs.

After the Civil War, Cleveland's population and its industrial base mushroomed. Limited transportation options required that Clevelanders live close to their work, making the city the center of employment and population. In 1880 Cleveland's 160,000 residents accounted for 81% of the county's population. Twenty years later, the city had grown to 381,000 people, the seventh largest city in the country.

Cleveland's booming industrial economy brought with it crowded living conditions, congestion, pollution, social problems, but also a burgeoning wealthy class. The invention of the electric streetcar in the 1880s made it possible for people who worked in the city to live as far as ten miles away, making suburban living feasible for those who could afford it. Developers were ready to build housing for the elite in locations outside the city and away from its many problems. They began to convert undeveloped rural areas into exclusively residential communities.[1]

At this time, East Cleveland Township bordered the City of Cleveland close to East 55th Street. Late 19th century developers had their eyes on Glenville, Collinwood, Collamer, and Cleveland Heights – unincorporated sections of East Cleveland Township that were popular summer retreats for Cleveland's wealthy class. After Cleveland annexed Glenville and Collinwood, developers, anxious to control suburban expansion, convinced residents to incorporate the remaining sections of the township into independent villages.

In 1895, the residents of Collamer incorporated East Cleveland, creating Cleveland's first suburb. In 1901, residents of Cleveland Heights and Lakewood voted to incorporate as hamlets. In 1903 Cleveland Heights became a village. These new, independent communities were built as residential suburbs and as escapes for the urban elite. They set the stage for the long-term shift in residential living from the city to the suburbs.

Suburban population growth was constant after 1910, but not so for African Americans. Table 1.1 tracks the total population of Cuyahoga County from 1910 to 2010 and the share of the county's population that lived in the city. Table 1.2 tracks that change for African Americans. In 1910 Cleveland had more than 573,000 residents who accounted for 90% of the population of the county, an all-time high that steadily declined over the next 100 years as suburbs grew. Cleveland's population peaked in 1950 at nearly one million residents but suburbs grew faster. Fueled by federal funds and pent-up demand, the post-war housing boom added nearly 300,000 more suburbanites to the region between 1950 and 1960. This was the largest decade of suburban population growth in the 20th century but only included 1,100 African Americans. As the suburbs grew, the city's share of the county population decreased every decade. But for African Americans this did not change until 1970.

This urban/suburban shift intensified racial segregation. In 1910, before segregation had become the norm, 97% of the county's African-American population lived in Cleveland. Over the next 50 years, both the black and white population of Cuyahoga County increased, but blacks were predominantly confined in the city. In 1960, Cleveland was home to 98% of the county's African-American population but only 53% of the total population. It was not until 1970 that this long-lasting pattern of black exclusion from Cleveland's suburbs began to change.

## TABLE 1.1: DISTRIBUTION OF THE TOTAL POPULATION BETWEEN SUBURBS AND CITY OF CLEVELAND 1910 – 2010

| CENSUS YEAR | CUYAHOGA COUNTY | CITY OF CLEVELAND | REST OF COUNTY | CLEVELAND RESIDENTS AS % OF COUNTY |
|---|---|---|---|---|
| 1910 | 637,425 | 573,872 | 63,553 | 90% |
| 1920 | 943,495 | 806,368 | 137,127 | 85% |
| 1930 | 1,201,455 | 902,471 | 298,984 | 75% |
| 1940 | 1,217,250 | 878,336 | 338,914 | 72% |
| 1950 | 1,389,532 | 914,808 | 474,724 | 66% |
| 1960 | 1,647,895 | 876,050 | 771,845 | 53% |
| 1970 | 1,721,300 | 750,879 | 969,956 | 43% |
| 1980 | 1,498,400 | 573,822 | 960,578 | 38% |
| 1990 | 1,412,140 | 505,616 | 906,524 | 36% |
| 2000 | 1,393,845 | 477,459 | 916,386 | 34% |
| 2010 | 1,280,122 | 396,815 | 883,307 | 31% |

*Sources: U.S. Census, Population of States and Counties of the US, 1790 to 1990;*
*Howard Whipple Green, Census Facts and Trends by Tracts;*
*Rich Exner, Cleveland.com, March 9, 2011.*

## Table 1.2: DISTRIBUTION OF THE BLACK POPULATION OF CUYAHOGA COUNTY BETWEEN CITY AND SUBURBS 1910 - 2010

| CENSUS YEAR | CUYAHOGA COUNTY | CITY OF CLEVELAND | REST OF COUNTY | CLEVELAND RESIDENTS AS % OF COUNTY |
|---|---|---|---|---|
| 1910 | 8,763 | 8,560 | 203 | 97% |
| 1920 | 35,347 | 34,611 | 736 | 98% |
| 1930 | 74,827 | 72,469 | 2,358 | 97% |
| 1940 | 87,145 | 84,504 | 2,641 | 98% |
| 1950 | 151,187 | 147,847 | 3,340 | 98% |
| 1960 | 255,310 | 250,818 | 4,492 | 98% |
| 1970 | 328,614 | 287,841 | 40,578 | 88% |
| 1980 | 340,827 | 251,084 | 89,743 | 74% |
| 1990 | 350,185 | 235,406 | 114,779 | 67% |
| 2000 | 392,902 | 249,192 | 143,710 | 63% |
| 2010 | 380,198 | 211,672 | 168,526 | 56% |

*Sources: U.S. Census, Race and Hispanic Origin for Selected Cities and Ohio Places, Table 36;*
*Howard Whipple Green, Census Facts and Trends by Tracts.*

## Segregation and the City of Cleveland

Cleveland has always been home to a diverse population. In his book, *A Ghetto Takes Shape, Black Cleveland 1870 to 1930*, historian Kenneth Kusmer reports that the first African American arrived in Cleveland in 1809. By 1880, Cleveland's 3,000 black residents "enjoyed a significant degree of racial equality."[2] Churches, schools, hospitals and other institutions were integrated. Most of the black population lived on the east side of the Cuyahoga River; however, it was widely dispersed with no areas where blacks made up the majority of residents. Housing choices were defined by income, not race.

World War I production demands and a halt in foreign-born immigration created a labor shortage in Cleveland and other northern industrial centers that triggered the first large-scale wave of Southern blacks moving north. The Great Migration of 1916-19 ended the relatively open housing market enjoyed by black Clevelanders, who by 1920 numbered 34,000. By this time, white property owners and realtors had begun using violence, intimidation, racial discrimination, and restrictive covenants to limit the housing options of black residents.[3]

African American poet and author Langston Hughes graduated from high school in Cleveland in 1920. He described the housing problem for African Americans in his memoir, *The Big Sea*:

> It was difficult to find a place to live. White people on the east side of the city were moving out of their frame houses and renting them to Negroes at double and triple the rents they could receive from others. An eight-room house with one bath would be cut up into apartments and five or six families crowded into it, each two-room kitchenette apartment renting for what the whole house had rented for before.

> But Negroes were coming in a great dark tide from the South, and they had to have some place to live. The landlords and the banks made it difficult for them to buy houses, so they had to pay the exorbitant rents required.[4]

As the black population grew, neighborhood choices decreased, and crowded, all-black neighborhoods became the norm. Blacks were concentrated in fewer census tracts within the city and excluded from the ever-expanding suburbs.

According to the 1910 census, Cleveland's 8,500 black residents were widely dispersed. They lived in all but 17 of the city's 158 census tracts and did not constitute more than 20% of the population of any tract. Ten years later, the black population had nearly quadrupled, but housing options were more limited. The number of Cleveland census tracts without blacks increased to 38, while more census tracts had larger concentrations of blacks. In 13 tracts, 25% of the residents were black, and in two tracts they were the majority.[5] Housing segregation within Cleveland had taken root, and a growing African-American population had fewer residential options.

As the black population grew, segregation intensified. By 1950, 99% of Cuyahoga County's 151,187 black residents lived east of the Cuyahoga River, and 98% (147,847) lived in the city. Most of Cleveland's black population (92%) lived in 39 of the city's 206 census tracts where they accounted for 75% of the population of those tracts.[6]

The second wave of Southern blacks moving north following the end of World War II added more than 104,000 black residents to Cuyahoga County between 1950 and 1960. Despite this growth, 98% of Cleveland's 255,310 black residents still lived in the city. The closed system put tremendous pressure on Cleveland's black neighborhoods and increased the number of people affected by discrimination.

## Segregation and the Suburbs

The founding of new suburbs increased housing choices for white homeowners, but not African Americans. Not only were blacks confined to fewer city neighborhoods, they were not welcomed in the new suburbs. Discrimination made suburbs all white and large parts of the city all black. Integration was fleeting at best and mostly nonexistent.

The numbers are breathtaking. In 1960, the population of Cuyahoga County was 1.64 million. Between 1910 and 1960, the population of Cuyahoga County (Table 1.1) had increased by more than a million people, and 700,000 of those new residents lived in the suburbs. During the same 50 years, the black suburban population (Table 1.2) increased by only 4,289. In 1960, Cuyahoga County was home to 255,310 African Americans. They comprised 15% of the county population and .5% of the suburban dwellers.

In 1960, Cuyahoga County's 4,492 black suburbanites lived in 46 municipalities and did not have a significant presence anywhere. There were fewer than 50 blacks in 26 communities, and none in 13 communities. Only seven suburbs had more than 100 black residents. East Cleveland had 804 African-American residents, the largest concentration in any suburb, followed by Berea (450) and Shaker Heights (357). Maple Heights, Cleveland Heights, Garfield Heights, and Parma each had between 130 and 255 black residents.

Between 1960 and 1970, African-American pioneers and fair housing activists began prying open suburban doors with some limited success. The black suburban population grew nearly tenfold, reaching 40,578 in 1970. For the first time in 60 years, the proportion of blacks living in the city declined, dropping from 98% to 88%. Even though most African Americans were still confined in the city, they were finally part of the urban-to-suburban shift.

Black access to suburbs during this decade was concentrated in five communities, which raised concern about resegregation. East Cleveland added 22,392 African-American residents who accounted for 62% of the new black suburbanites. Another 32% of the increase took place in four suburbs – Shaker Heights, Warrensville Heights, Garfield Heights and Cleveland Heights – each of which added more than 1,000 black residents. Change was practically nonexistent everywhere else.

## Tools of Segregation

Institutionalized discrimination caused the nearly complete and long-term exclusion of blacks from suburbs and most urban neighborhoods. Realtors defined blacks as "undesirable" and "inharmonious" with whites, and a "threat" to property values. These prejudices were incorporated into the ethical positions and practices of the housing industry that governed the early development of suburbs. Realtors made segregation desirable and racially mixed neighborhoods undesirable. Those values produced widespread housing segregation.

Frequently, early stages of racial change were met by real estate practices to advance resegregation. The resulting instability was used to justify continued resistance to integration which was assumed to be a passing phenomenon and not a legitimate part of the housing market. Thanks to realtors, resegregation, though not automatic, was certainly typical.

Two New Deal housing laws that governed the post-war housing expansion that encouraged suburban living treated African Americans as unworthy of support and a threat to the value of white-owned property. Old neighborhoods suffered while suburbs flourished. Integration was devalued. The wealth divide increased. Blacks were marginalized.

Real estate agents began to play an important role in the development of Cleveland as early as the 1860s. In 1892, as land development was booming, about a dozen of Cleveland's 175 realtors formed the Cleveland Real Estate Board to set standards in the industry, encourage development, and influence legislation.[7] It was an all-white organization until 1968 when fair housing activist Joe Battle became the first African-American member.

Housing is first and foremost shelter, but realtors emphasized its significance as an investment to protect. In 1909, at its first meeting, the National Association of Real Estate Boards, a national lobbying organization representing local real estate associations, promoted the idea that blacks were a threat to property values. They defined African Americans as "undesirable." The organization recommended wording for deed restrictions to prohibit sales or rentals to "any person other than the Caucasian race."[8]

Real estate agents, appraisers, home builders, and lenders justified discrimination because property values would "experience a severe drop" with the arrival of black neighbors. Numerous studies of race and property values refuted this position, but real estate textbooks and realtor training spread the idea as fact.[9] This myth proved to be a powerful justification for segregation. It still defined housing opportunity when civil rights activists in Cleveland Heights challenged segregation 50 years later.

Many local real estate boards along with state legislatures adopted policies to expel members who sold property on a white block to a black buyer. In 1924, the National Association of Real Estate Boards declared it unethical to support racial mixing on a street proclaiming, "A realtor should never be instrumental in introducing into a neighborhood, members of any race or nationality whose presence will clearly be detrimental to property values in that neighborhood."[10]

Realtors found it unethical to introduce a black buyer into a white area because it would damage property values, but appeared unconcerned by practices that encouraged white flight from an integrated neighborhood. If, in the judgment of realtors, too many blacks occupied a white neighborhood, these realtors would resort to racial steering and blockbusting to stimulate rapid change. These techniques were common place before suburbanization began and were in use during the onset of integration in the 1960s. Mayor William Racek of Warrensville Heights, a Cleveland suburb that was facing rapid change in 1962 because of blockbusting, referred to this practice as "panic-for-profit."[11]

The real estate business operated as a dual system. The all-white Cleveland Real Estate Board only handled property sold by white owners to white buyers. African Americans were excluded from the white professional organization and denied access to white listings. One of the only options for black realtors to participate in white sales was when realtors triggered panic selling.

Banks and other traditional lenders served white customers in white neighborhoods, but for the most part, they denied loans to African Americans anywhere. So, old neighborhoods suffered while suburbs flourished. Segregation became nearly universal and impenetrable. This was Cleveland in 1960.

At a 1962 hearing held in Cleveland, the Ohio Civil Rights Commission focused on realtor practices. Sheldon Braff, a Cleveland Heights realtor, testified that his business would be hurt if he showed a "Negro buyer a house in a white neighborhood." James Funero, the Executive Secretary of the Cleveland Board of Realtors and an opponent of fair housing legislation, testified that "with the right to own property, you also have the right to dispose of it as you wish." Selmer Prewitt, a black broker, criticized the Cleveland Board of Realtors for "keeping an all-white block all white or – once broken into – deciding they must go all-Negro."[12] Albert Dillehey, who chaired the hearing, observed, "The pattern is clear. Realtors don't sell to Negroes in white communities, and white prospects are not shown houses that are shown to Negroes."

In March 1963, the Government Operations Committee of the Ohio legislature held a hearing on the topic. Black broker William Hamilton summarized ways in which discrimination affected black opportunities:

White realtors 'refuse to offer their services to members of minority groups;'

White lenders discriminate against blacks, refusing to make mortgages 'because no other member of the buyer's race lives in the immediate area;'

White homeowners who may be willing to sell to a minority buyer would not because they feared 'that their neighbors would tear them apart.'[13]

The housing industry promoted the dehumanizing belief that African Americans were undesirable, thus justifying discrimination, and excluding blacks from white neighborhoods. Until the civil rights movement forced passage of federal fair housing laws to prohibit discrimination, owners had no legal obligation to treat buyers fairly. Realtors were free to promote residential segregation, and they did.

While racist attitudes among white realtors, lenders, and owners drove the business practices of the real estate industry, they also permeated public policy. Richard Rothstein's exhaustive account of the causes of housing segregation, *The Color of Law*, places responsibility squarely on the shoulders of government at all levels: "Racial segregation in housing was not merely a project of southerners in the former slaveholding Confederacy. It was a nationwide project of the federal government in the 20th century designed and implemented by its most liberal leaders."[14]

The Home Owners Refinancing Act of 1933 and the National Housing Act of 1934 legally codified racist views of African Americans as "undesirable" and racial integration as a threat to property values. The legislation was, in one sense, progressive because it made mortgages and homeownership more affordable. However, it also fostered inequality and segregation because loans were only available in segregated neighborhoods and to owners who were white. These policies stimulated a dramatic increase in suburban living while expanding the footprint of segregation.

During the post-war housing boom, federal housing programs initiated as part of the New Deal were particularly instrumental in driving the development of white suburbs. Policies discriminated against older city neighborhoods and black citizens, essentially funded segregation, and fostered a serious wealth divide by prohibiting African Americans from purchasing homes in new communities where property values would appreciate.

The Home Owners Refinancing Act of 1933 established the Home Owner Loan Corporation (HOLC) to head off massive foreclosures in urban neighborhoods caused by widespread unemployment. At the time, home ownership was financed with short-term (five to ten year), high-interest loans. A missed payment could result in the forfeiture of the property and all payments. HOLC rescued homeowners by lowering the cost of monthly mortgage payments. The federal government purchased outstanding mortgages and then sold the property back to the owner with amortized mortgages at lower interest rates and a repayment period of 20 to 30 years.

When the Federal Housing Authority (FHA) was created the next year, it undertook a national project to assess where to invest federal funds. It was initially applied by the federal government to minimize defaults on loans made with federal funds. The project was led and designed by FHA's chief economist, Homer Hoyt, a Chicago realtor.

Hoyt saw ethnicity as key to predicting housing value. It was the dominant factor in his seemingly objective and systematic practice of evaluating risk.[16] As a doctoral student, Hoyt adopted from the eugenics movement, a "real estate desirability index" that ranked the value of residents by race and ethnicity. Eugenics attempted to use science to prove white superiority. As shown in Table 1.3 (p. 41), Negroes and Mexicans were at the bottom of the list. This list was incorporated in the risk assessment method.

Trained work groups, made up primarily of local realtors, assessed risk in 239 urban areas in this national project. They gathering data on the occupation, income, religion, and ethnicity of the inhabitants of each block, in addition to the age, type of construction, price range, sales demand, and general state of repair of the housing stock.[17]

The evaluation teams, guided by written manuals, used this data to grade each block on a scale of A to D. Each letter grade was color coded. The assessment was then used to create a "Residential Security Map" for that metropolitan area. An A or B neighborhood, where lending was encouraged, was colored blue or green. C areas, where caution was advised, were colored yellow. This frequently applied to older areas that had mixed land use which is typical of older, central cities. Red areas were too dangerous for lending, and African-American neighborhoods were automatically red. Thus began "redlining," the practice of withholding loans and thwarting investment in whole neighborhoods based merely on the racial composition of its residents.

The Residential Security Maps created a uniform national system that codified "discrimination against racial and ethnic minorities and against older, industrial cities" as official government policy.[18] The system excluded blacks from acquiring conventional loans, legitimized discrimination, guaranteed disinvestment in urban neighborhoods, and incentivized segregation. Historian Antero Pietila defined the practices as mapping bigotry.

HOLC was disbanded in 1939, but during its short existence, it had made more than a million loans. The program did soften the foreclosure crisis and improve lending by introducing long-term amortized mortgages. It also caused irreparable damage to housing choices and wealth development for African Americans.

Urban historian Kenneth Jackson, one of the first scholars to trace the impact of the Residential Security Maps on urban development, concluded that while the system was developed for government use, the real damage was created when lenders, appraisers, and realtors applied the maps and their assumptions to private lending decisions, even long after HOLC had folded.[19]

The Residential Security Map of Cuyahoga County was completed in 1939. The east side of Cleveland, home for 98% of the city's black population, was primarily yellow and red. Cleveland Heights, an upper middle-class, white professional community, consisted of blue and green neighborhoods, so it was clearly a good bet for lenders.[20] For a neighborhood to remain blue required the exclusion of blacks.

**National Housing Act of 1934 Mandates Segregation**

The National Housing Act of 1934 was the New Deal response to high unemployment in the housing trades. It created the Federal Housing Administration (FHA), and in order to stimulate home construction, gave the federal government a new role: to insure mortgages made by private lenders. Federal mortgage insurance was contingent upon lenders making long-term loans and following FHA guidelines for assessing credit worthiness. When the government assumed the mortgage risk, lenders could afford to charge lower interest rates and require smaller down payments. This combination added up to lower monthly payments, and thus, affordable homeownership for many more buyers. Housing starts boomed.

FHA insurance was available to individuals to finance home purchases and to developers to finance the construction of large housing developments. It restarted employment in construction, increased access to home ownership for the middle class, addressed the post-war housing shortage, and promoted a single-family suburban housing boom. Between 1934 and 1972, FHA-insured loans helped 11 million families buy homes. The percentage of households who owned homes increased during this period from 44% to 63%.[20] FHA lending also supported home improvement loans, but they were smaller and fewer in number, showing a preference for new construction over maintenance of older urban housing.

## TABLE 1.3: GRADATION OF NATIONALITY "DESIRABILITY" AS DEFINED BY HOMER HOYT IN 1933

1. English, German, Scots, Irish, Scandinavian
2. North Italians
3. Bohemians or Czechoslovakian
4. Poles
5. Lithuanians
6. Greeks
7. Russian Jews of the lower class
8. South Italians
9. Negroes
10. Mexicans

*Source: Pietila, Antero. 2010. Not in My Neighborhood.*

While FHA financing spurred the vast growth of new housing in undeveloped parts of Cuyahoga County in the post-war era, federal lending practices excluded African Americans from the developments they insured. FHA refused to insure integrated projects and recommended the use of restrictive covenants to perpetuate white ownership in all-white neighborhoods that received loan guarantees. A project financed by FHA almost guaranteed that it would be white.

> Reflecting the racist tradition of the United States, the FHA was extraordinarily concerned with 'inharmonious racial or nationality groups.' It feared that an entire area could lose its investment value if rigid black-white separation was not maintained.[22]

According to Jackson "no agency of the United States government has had a more pervasive or powerful impact on the American people over the past half-century than the FHA."[23]

Federal lending practices which did not affect the development of early suburbs like Cleveland Heights, defined the growth of Cleveland's all-white suburbs in the post-war era and spread segregation across even more of Cuyahoga County. In 1962, President Kennedy issued an executive order prohibiting the use of federal funds to support segregation, but by then the die was cast.

**Community Values Reinforce Segregation**

Prejudice was not the sole province of realtors, lenders, and federal policy makers. It also infected the white narrative about African Americans and the opinions of many suburban residents. In 1968, Cleveland Heights housing activists Gerda Freedheim and Martin Bloom developed a guide for human rights workers that outlined beliefs that were consistently used by white communities to reject integration.[24] The same views reinforced and drove the business side of segregation. Challenging these assumptions was a crucial part of the battle.

These six fears were the most frequently expressed reasons to oppose racial integration, as reported in a presentation by Barbara Heald, Cleveland Heights League of Women Voters and HCHR member:

1.  Property values decrease when minority groups move in.
2.  Negroes do not maintain their property.

3. Negroes will not be able to keep up their mortgages and will sell to a lower-class buyer.
4. Different racial groups cannot live together in harmony.
5. Negroes are less intelligent and more criminally inclined.
6. As soon as neighborhoods and schools become integrated, racial intermarriage results.

These unfounded and offensive beliefs were widely accepted.

## Cleveland Heights: An Elite White Suburb

Cleveland Heights was part of the problem. Its history as an elite suburb added to the severity of segregation that defined the region through the 1960s.

When Cleveland Heights was incorporated as an independent municipality in 1901, it was a rural community of about 1,500 residents. Proximity to Cleveland made it an ideal location for an alternative to the problems of urban living. In their 1966 description of Cleveland Heights, authors Mary Harris and Ruth Robinson report that as early as 1890, the area attracted the attention of some "forward-looking men" who "thought this quiet farming area overlooking the city and furnishing a glimpse of Lake Erie would make a fine residential area."[25]

Enterprising developers built comfortable housing for wealthy Clevelanders, people who could afford expensive estates as well as travel to work in the city. These entrepreneurs were pioneers of suburbanization. Their vision for the new suburb, an exclusive residential retreat from urban problems, was "a place where the elite could live near the city but distant from its industry and commerce, close to nature and persons like themselves."[26]

By 1900, more than 30 country estates had been built at the western end of Cleveland Heights, earning the community its identity as a home for the wealthy. A 1909 advertisement promoted the new development as "a restricted residential section, only 32 minutes from the square."[27] Developers transformed Cleveland Heights' rural landscape into a residential community with a diverse housing stock that included duplexes and smaller homes. The city's self-promotion as an "exclusive" community was a central selling point even as developers built a wide range of housing options that accommodated the needs of the "respectable middle class."[28]

All white was implied.

Frank Cain was elected mayor in 1915, and he led the city through its growth years until his retirement in 1946. His motivation: "I wanted a home town that attracted only the best people."

Table 1.4 (p. 45) shows that the population of Cleveland Heights grew from 2,955 in 1910 to 15,264 in 1920, making it eligible for city status, a designation that gave it even greater political autonomy. It became a city in 1922 and quickly adopted the first zoning ordinance in Ohio. The new law made the city a single-purpose residential community. This designation supported its identity as an elite suburb.

The decade between 1920 and 1930 was the boom time for Cleveland Heights. More than 7,000 new housing units helped accommodate the population that grew from 15,000 to 50,945. Half of all Cleveland Heights houses were built by 1925.[30] By the 1920s, the community included a growing Jewish population but, otherwise, lacked diversity. A small number of African Americans, most of whom were domestic servants, are reported in the 1920 census and in subsequent years.

The Great Depression and World War II slowed development. In 1960, the Cleveland Heights population peaked at 61,813, having experienced only a 5% increase during the previous decade while the rest of the suburbs grew by 62%. Whites occupied nearly every house on every block of Cleveland Heights. The city had 251 African American residents, the smallest number since 1910, and they made up only .4% of the community's population. They were among the 4,492 blacks who lived in Cuyahoga County suburbs.

Segregation was in place. It was widespread and buttressed by long-standing racist assumptions.

Could Cleveland Heights idealists overcome these barriers?

## TABLE 1.4: CLEVELAND HEIGHTS DEMOGRAPHICS 1910 - 2010

| YEAR | TOTAL | AFRICAN AMERICAN | WHITE | % AFRICAN AMERICAN |
|------|-------|------------------|-------|--------------------|
| 1910 | 2,955 | 37 | 2,918 | 1.2% |
| 1920 | 15,560 | 185 | 15,375 | 1.2% |
| 1930 | 50,945 | 573 | 50,372 | 1.1% |
| 1940 | 54,992 | 511 | 54,481 | .9% |
| 1950 | 59,141 | 438 | 58,615 | .8% |
| 1960 | 61,813 | 251 | 61,429 | .4% |
| 1970 | 60,767 | 1,508 | NA | 2.5% |
| 1980 | 56,438 | 14,061 | 41,192 | 24.9% |
| 1990 | 54,052 | 20,054 | 32,534 | 37.1% |
| 2000 | 50,769 | 20,873 | 26,229 | 41.1% |
| 2010 | 46,121 | 19,587 | 22,984 | 42.5% |

*Source: US Census*

# CHAPTER 2

# THE MOVEMENT
# INSPIRES ACTION

White supremacy has plagued American life since the time of slavery. As a result, white privilege, institutionalized in laws and practices, has stymied black social, economic, and civic inclusion.

Reconstruction after the Civil War, and the civil rights movement of the King years are the two periods when "the United States experienced major social movements which, at their core, expressed a powerful vision of multicultural democracy and human equality."[1]

In the post-Civil War Reconstruction era, 1865 to 1877, civil rights laws and three constitutional amendments advanced black rights. In December 1865, Congress ratified the 13th Amendment that made slavery illegal. In 1868, the 14th Amendment extended citizenship rights to African Americans along with due process and equal protection of those rights. The 15th Amendment, adopted in 1870, extended voting rights to African-American men.

This progress was short lived, however. Republicans who had advanced civil rights backed away from their commitment. In 1877, President Rutherford B. Hayes ended protection for freed slaves when he withdrew federal troops from the South. Voting rights and "the conditions of black life and labor deteriorated dramatically."[2] In 1883, the Supreme Court overturned the Civil Rights Act of 1875. This allowed southern states to subvert black rights by imposing black codes and Jim Crow laws and frequently enforcing them with unchecked terror. Then in 1896, the Supreme Court enshrined racial segregation with the *Plessy v. Ferguson* decision legalizing "separate but equal" treatment. Racial segregation thrived within this supportive legal framework, and it shaped American life with only minimal challenges until school segregation was ruled illegal in 1954.

The civil rights movement blossomed in the wake of the Supreme Court's 1954 *Brown v. Topeka Board of Education* decision that outlawed segregation in public schools, repudiating "a major pillar of white supremacy."[3] It unleashed a wide range of citizen challenges to white control and black exclusion, and it started to make real the rights guaranteed by the 13th, 14th, and 15th amendments. Starting with the 1955 Montgomery bus boycott that thrust Dr. Martin Luther King, Jr. into his leadership role and continuing even after his murder in 1968, grassroots activists challenged a deeply rooted and perverse system of racial inequality and white privilege that denied African Americans their rights as citizens. "Deprived of the right to vote, blacks mobilized the resource most readily available to them – they put their bodies on the line against racism."[4]

Often at the risk of losing their jobs or their lives, Southern activists demanded dignity, voting rights, economic opportunity, and an end to segregation in all of its forms. Whether boycotting segregated buses, sitting at segregated lunch counters, integrating bus and train stations or movie theaters, or attempting to register to vote, thousands of African Americans joined by white allies challenged the status quo.

Direct action was met with hatred and ridicule from bystanders. Mob violence was common, as was brutality inflicted by white authorities. It laid bare the inhumanity and horrific reality of enduring prejudice.

The movement made equal rights a moral cause and a national imperative. Civil rights activists pressured a reluctant federal government to protect the rights of African Americans. They argued for a change in societal attitudes and demanded equality and increased opportunities for African Americans.

Nonviolent protesters shined a light on injustice in a way the world could not ignore. Their strength and determination inspired people across the nation to challenge inequality where they witnessed or experienced it.

One of those places was Cleveland, Ohio, where in 1963, civil rights activists tackled overcrowding in the public schools in the Glenville neighborhood. The region's hyper-segregated housing market confined blacks to a few city neighborhoods, the result of which was overcrowded schools. The activists' cause attracted suburban allies from nearby Cleveland Heights, who, within a year, started their own civil rights organization to end residential segregation in their all-white, elite suburb less than two miles from Glenville.

Their activism supported the overriding message of the civil rights movement. Taylor Branch, author of three histories documenting Dr. Martin Luther King, Jr. and the civil rights movement, summarized it this way, "Above all, the King years should serve as a bracing reminder that citizens and leaders can work miracles together despite every hardship, against great odds."[5]

As in the Southern civil rights experience, grassroots activists in Cleveland Heights led the challenge and effected change despite difficult and seemingly impossible odds. Their tools were limited to moral authority, determination, face-to-face connections, and public criticism of segregation. Even after fair housing laws had been adopted, what actually influenced their enforcement were organized citizens demanding equal treatment. This was an amazing moment of civic vitality and awakening.

## Civil Rights Activism Comes to Cleveland

On May 15, 1963, in the midst of the children's crusade in Birmingham, Alabama, when authorities using attack dogs and fire hoses thrust the civil rights movement into the national conscience, Dr. King made a one-day fundraising visit to Cleveland. His first stop was St. Paul's Episcopal Church in Cleveland Heights, the only suburban event on his five-stop itinerary.[6] The meeting was sponsored by the local chapter of the Episcopal Society for Cultural and Racial Unity, an emerging national project to root out racism and end segregation within the Episcopal denomination. Many future leaders of the Cleveland Heights struggle were in the audience.

Taylor Branch described the visit: "Mobbed at the airport, King motorcaded like an astronaut through the streets of Cleveland to St. Paul's Episcopal Church for what amounted to the first white mass meeting of the civil rights movement."[7]

CHAPTER 2

Less than a month later, on June 11, 1963, the day that Governor George Wallace barred black students from integrating the University of Alabama, President John F. Kennedy delivered his history-making address to the nation that elevated civil rights from a Southern problem to a national imperative. On national television, President Kennedy asked every American to "stop and examine his conscience." He described the significance of civil rights in this way:

> We are confronted primarily with a moral issue. It is as old as the scriptures and as clear as the American Constitution. The heart of the question is whether all Americans are to be afforded equal rights and equal opportunities, whether we are going to treat our fellow Americans as we want to be treated.[8]

Predicting a great change at hand, in the same speech he admonished Americans "to make that revolution, that change, peaceful and constructive for all."

After midnight that night, civil rights organizer Medgar Evers was assassinated in his driveway in Jackson, Mississippi. A week later President Kennedy introduced the Civil Rights Act that was passed after his death and signed into law by President Lyndon B. Johnson in 1964.

A few weeks after Dr. King's well-received visit to Cleveland and days after the President's speech, the Cleveland chapter of the National Association for the Advancement of Colored People (NAACP) convened a meeting of more than 50 civic and religious groups to take up the civil rights challenge. They founded a new coalition, the United Freedom Movement (UFM). It included both the newly activated Congress of Racial Equality (CORE), an organization that was more confrontational than the traditional organizations, as well as the established black rights organizations like the NAACP and Urban League.[9]

The southern movement reenergized Cleveland's organized opposition to discrimination. A united black community, joined by white allies, came together to advance equality.

On July 14, 1963, UFM and CORE sponsored a freedom march and rally at the Cleveland Stadium, the largest civil rights rally in Cleveland history. More than 25,000 people heard speeches by civil rights leaders James Farmer and Roy Wilkins and carried posters declaring,

*Takes blacks and whites to make a piano*
*Segregated housing is unconstitutional*
*Better jobs*
*Back the Bill of Rights*
*Support civil rights*
*Police brutality must go*
*Defacto schools must go*
*Ghettoes must go*
*Freedom for all*[10]

On August 28, civil rights supporters from across the nation assembled on the National Mall for the March on Washington for Jobs and Freedom that connected civil rights with economic justice. Dr. King delivered his never to be forgotten "I Have a Dream Speech" that injected indelible emotion into the cause.

This was a historic moment. The courageous determination of marginalized citizens captured the attention of the nation and inspired people in communities across the country to take action – against great odds.

## School Segregation Focuses Cleveland's Agenda

In August 1963, Cleveland's United Freedom Movement launched an intense, year-long campaign to relieve overcrowding in public schools in the Glenville neighborhood – a problem caused by the region's hyper-segregated housing market.[11]

Back in 1956, more than 1,500 Glenville children were denied entry to kindergarten because of a lack of space.[12] To alleviate the overcrowding, the Cleveland Board of Education used relay classes – half the Glenville students attended school in the morning, the other half in the afternoon. However, parent opposition forced the Cleveland Board to find a better solution. In February 1962, the school district implemented a busing program that moved black children to underused schools in white neighborhoods.[13] Glenville students attended Brett, Memorial, and Murray Hill schools, where they were kept in their own classrooms, separated from white students. Busing had given students access to full-day schooling for the first time in five years, but it required segregation.

UFM joined with Glenville parents in 1963 to demand integration. In January 1964, after protracted negotiations, the Cleveland Board of Education offered to integrate 40% of the black children with their white peers for one hour of the day. The deal prompted a protest on Mayfield Road near Murray Hill School that disintegrated into violence as a white mob attacked Glenville parents while police looked on. The conflict revealed ugly white resistance to integration and a lack of leadership by elected officials.[14]

One white parent who was part of the mob complained, "We are looking for education for our children, not for Negro sons- and daughters-in-law. I don't want my grandchildren black. I am proud of my race. I want to stay white."[15]

Board President Ralph McAllister pushed for a solution that would intensify segregation: the district would build three new schools in Glenville and keep black children in their neighborhood. With more than 12,500 empty desks in Cleveland schools, critics charged this option was a waste of existing space, and that building schools to segregate students was illegal. The board president refused to meet with the opposition and negotiate new options. Construction of two buildings began in late March 1964.

On April 3, 1964, CORE sponsored a forum featuring African-American author Louis Lomax and Black Nationalist leader Malcolm X at Cory Methodist Church in Glenville. More than 2,000 people, many of whom were white, heard the rousing addresses. After Malcolm X delivered his famous "Ballot or Bullets" speech, a CORE member invited the audience to picket the construction site for Stephen Howe Elementary School on Lakeview Road at noon, the following Monday, April 6, 1964.[16] The evening ended with a torchlight tour of the controversial school construction sites.

Surrounded by hundreds of onlookers, about 50 protesters assembled on Monday to stop construction and force the district to reconsider its plan. In acts of civil disobedience, 13 protesters jumped in ditches to stop a power shovel. Police arrested twenty protesters.[17]

The next day civil disobedience turned to tragedy. Three people lay on the ground in the path of a moving bulldozer while CORE leader and Cleveland Heights resident Rev. Bruce Klunder lay down behind the machine. Unaware of the minister, the driver backed away from the demonstrators, and the 27-year-old father of two young children was killed instantly. Rev. Klunder became a martyr of the civil rights movement and is honored at the Civil Rights Memorial in Montgomery, Alabama.[18]

His death set off a night of community outrage, followed by a day of silent protests and severe public criticism of the Board for its failure to engage with the community. Rev. Eugene Carson Blake, the Presbyterian Church USA's executive director for Race and Religion, presided at Rev. Klunder's memorial service at the Church of the Covenant on April 9.

In a scathing editorial, the *Call and Post* blamed an unresponsive Board for the young leader's death: "The unfortunate death of Rev. Bruce Klunder, smears his blood upon the Cleveland Board of Education." The newspaper joined the call by the UFM and the Episcopal Society for Cultural and Social Unity for board president McAllister to resign.[19]

More than 250 faculty members from University Circle institutions, many Cleveland Heights residents, expressed support for the protesters in a *Cleveland Plain Dealer* ad that endorsed integration and criticized the Board of Education:

> We express our total commitment to the constitutional and moral right of the Negro to equality of educational opportunity. We feel that the construction of new schools in the midst of ghettos denies that right and perpetuates segregation. Cleveland cannot survive as a civilized community unless all of its citizens can move with complete freedom from one neighborhood to another, from one job to another, from one social level to another.[20]

Construction resumed on April 13.

The opposition continued on April 20 with a one-day school boycott. Despite threats by the board president to prosecute adults whose children participated for "contributing to the delinquency of a minor," an estimated 60,000 black children, about 85% of the district's black enrollment, and 900 teachers attended alternative "Freedom Schools" set up around the community.[21]

In a final effort to stop construction, the NAACP filed a suit in the U.S. District Court. The *Craggett v. Cleveland Board of Education* case argued that the schools furthered segregation. Judge Girard Kalbfleisch acknowledged that the schools, once built, would be segregated, but he denied the injunction, arguing that the plaintiffs had not established that the segregation was the result of a "deliberate design to segregate." The plaintiffs appealed the case but did not prevail.[22]

The issue resurfaced in 1973 when the Cleveland NAACP filed *Reed v. Rhodes*. The plaintiffs used as evidence the school district's 1964 decision to build segregated schools in Glenville. In 1976, federal judge Frank Battisti found the Cleveland school district guilty of racial discrimination, and in 1979, the district implemented a court-ordered desegregation plan.

### Cleveland Heights Activists Challenge Segregation

The face-off between integration advocates and the Cleveland Board of Education revealed intense establishment resistance to integration. It also highlighted an uncomfortable reality for white suburban allies: they were part of the problem. The 1960 census showed that 98% of African Americans in the metropolitan area were confined to the city of Cleveland. Cleveland Heights, the suburb adjacent to Cleveland and two miles from Glenville, counted 250 African Americans among its 61,800 residents.

Lacking a focused civil rights project in Cleveland Heights, idealistic suburban activists like Joan Dowling, Gerda and Don Freedheim, Barbara and Glenn Roderick, Lee and Naomi Wolin, and Rev. Ned Edwards, focused on the Cleveland schools. Most of these future leaders of the Cleveland Heights movement had not yet met one another, but each was connected to the Cleveland experience and was ready to address prejudice and discrimination in their white suburb.

As the school integration battle raged in Cleveland, a few daring Cleveland Heights women started two projects to promote integration in their own community. One promoted integrated experiences for school-aged children; the other focused on a more complete solution – ending housing segregation. Joan Dowling, an idealistic parent, was involved in both. Within months the two projects would merge.

### Starting an Integrated Summer School Program

"Things were simmering. There was a feeling that there was going to be integration," recalls Dowling, a Cleveland Heights resident who joined other young suburbanites pushing children in strollers at the Cleveland school protests and witnessing the death of Rev. Klunder. "We were young mothers with small children and strong feelings. We were wet behind the ears. We were bold, naïve, and lucky."[23]

Dowling grew up in a Jewish household in Philadelphia. Her grandparents and parents were progressive and were admirers of President Roosevelt. Her mother ran for public office. Her father, a businessman, organized camping opportunities to promote interaction among youth from white suburbs and black city neighborhoods. Her education at a Quaker high school and Earlham College also nurtured her civil rights commitment. She married Scott Dowling as a college student and followed him to medical school in Syracuse. By the time they moved to Cleveland Heights from California in 1956, three of their five children had been born.

Dowling was committed to integrated living and advancing interracial respect. As a parent of school-aged children, education was her priority. In the midst of her involvement in the Cleveland school integration battle, Dowling and two friends, Dorothy Schiff and Leatrice Madison, convinced the Cleveland Heights-University Heights school district to open summer school to black students from Cleveland starting in the summer of 1964. Integrated summer school was ideal for facilitating positive race relations, a significant goal in an era when social contact across racial lines was nearly as rare as integrated neighborhoods.

Dowling and Schiff were married to psychiatrists who were in practice together. Madison, a Cleveland school teacher, was a native of Washington, DC, and was married to Robert Madison, the architect of one of the disputed schools being built in Cleveland. The Madisons left Glenville in 1960 because the relay classes were an unacceptable educational option for their daughter.[24] Mr. Madison designed two houses on North Park after a white neighbor attempted to buy the lots in order to prevent the family from moving to the suburb.

In 1963, the Cleveland Heights-University Heights school district had opened its summer program to private school students. The district welcomed the idea of including black children from Cleveland in their 1964 summer program and ten participated. This was the beginning of Dowling's role as a driver of civil rights activism in Cleveland Heights, and the first of many projects to enrich learning in the Heights schools.

The summer school program took off in 1965. The elementary program held at Fairfax School included 69 black students from the city while the high school had 46 participants.[25] The engaging curriculum featured a team-taught class with one district teacher and one from the Cleveland system. Integration not only made summer school profitable for the district, it allowed for social interaction among black and white students.

Dowling and her team raised tuition scholarship funds and recruited children to the program. "We felt this was a very specific contribution which we could make, as individuals, as a school system, and as a community, to open paths in the area of human relations," they reported in the May 1965 edition of *Human Progress News*, the Heights Citizens for Human Rights newsletter.

John Vaughn, the principal for the elementary summer school program, described the experience as a "breakthrough." He urged the district to share the experience with other school systems so they would try "this kind of school integration."[26]

### Updating the School District Human Relations Policy

In February 1964, Dowling and Schiff undertook a second project to pave the way for integration. In a letter to Mrs. Sherman Dye, President of the Cleveland Heights-University Heights Board of Education, they urged the board to appoint a citizens' committee to update the district's 1950s human relations policy. The letter had more than 200 endorsers and stated:

> It is during children's formative years that so much can be done to help them realize there is a world beyond their own homogeneous neighborhood. We urge you to consider creating a lay committee on human relations. Much thinking is needed to anticipate and prepare for further integration in our cities, which will surely affect education.[27]

The Board created the new committee in the spring of 1964. Dye and Superintendent Theos Anderson were the co-chairs. Dowling was also among the 20 citizens on the interracial committee that included African-American civil rights leaders and Heights residents, Ernest Cooper, director of the Cleveland Urban League and Dr. Kenneth Clement, a founder of Fair Housing Inc., a nonprofit open housing real estate firm. Dowling threw herself into crafting the policy.

Updating the human relations policy was controversial. Before the vote was taken on the revised policy, opponents submitted a petition with 1,200 signatures urging the Board to reject it because they believed the existing policy was adequate and it was wrong for the Board to "act on community attitudes."[28]

In the same newspaper account of the meeting, former Board member John Connell argued in support of the change. "We are living in an entirely different world in 1966 than we were in 1955. The world has changed completely and we must change with it." Board member Dr. Daniel Bloomfield also supported action: "If we don't take the lead who will?" Superintendent Anderson concurred: "If we are not affecting our community for good, we are not doing our job."

On December 8, 1966, a united Board approved the policy that took nearly two years to draft. Passage was welcomed with applause. Dr. Bloomfield defended the decision by stating, "People seem to think this policy will open the door to everyone, particularly Negroes. No Negro is going to come to Cleveland Heights-University Heights because of the policy, but if he comes it may help him to be accepted."[29] The policy gave the Board of Education responsibility for creating "a climate within the schools which enhances the dignity and importance of each individual" and called for steps that "promote a feeling of understanding, trust and acceptance among those of differing races, creeds, and socio-economic backgrounds." It also called for teachers to address "ethnic, racial and religious strands that are a part of the American fabric" and to explore controversial issues.[30]

These two successful school initiatives came about because committed and insightful citizens worked with receptive school leaders. The results were a stark contrast to the Cleveland school fight of the year before, during which stubborn leaders refused to engage with citizens, much less consider changing their policies.

## Founding Heights Citizens for Human Rights

During winter 1964, when Dowling was at work establishing an integrated summer school program for Heights and Cleveland students, another idealist, Barbara Roderick, was thinking about how to integrate the community. Barbara Roderick was the daughter of missionaries and grew up in China. She met her husband, Glenn, at Hiram College, earned her social work degree at Western Reserve University, and practiced as a social worker for ten years before becoming a parent in 1958. After a second daughter was born, her growing family moved to West Richfield in

1961. Having two small children and no car, the Rodericks then decided to move to the more accessible Cleveland Heights in 1964 where they intended to work on housing integration.[31]

Roderick, a newcomer to Cleveland Heights, invited about ten women to her living room to talk about a seemingly audacious goal: integrating the two suburbs that were served by the Cleveland Heights-University Heights school district. She did not know Joan Dowling but was aware of her activism and invited her to the meeting. This small gathering set in motion a new volunteer organization to end housing segregation. After considering a variety of names, including Heights Integration League, Suburban Committee for Integration, and Action Committee for Human Relations, they settled on Heights Citizens for Human Rights.

The living room meeting was followed by a public event to introduce the idea to the rest of the community and recruit people to help shape the emerging grassroots organization. About 200 people attended the meeting at St. Paul's Church, the site where Dr. King had been welcomed the year before.

Phyllis Brody was there. Brody had grown up in Brooklyn and came to Cleveland in the mid-1950s to study social work at Case Western Reserve University. She met her husband, Ralph, also a social worker, on the first day of school. He was a Cleveland native who lived in the Glenville neighborhood until he was ten. His family was part of the Jewish flight to Cleveland Heights.

At the meeting, the couple was asked "to decide what kind of community we wanted." In response, the couple signed up. For the next ten years they became consistent sources of ideas, manpower, and leadership as HCHR evolved and created change. "It was a matter of conscience; you had to do something," says Brody.[32]

After this first meeting, a steering committee designed the structure and goals for the new citizen organization. Barbara Roderick and her good friend Mary Boenke co-chaired the housing group, and Maggie Weisberg and Pat Travis led the education committee. Joan Dowling led a nominating committee to recruit a slate of officers. A biracial committee composed of Will Irwin, Dave Austin, Ruth Clement, Lee Madison, Maggie Weisberg, and Dowling agreed to develop the organization's statement of objectives with input from the two committees.[33]

The new volunteer organization established two goals: to support a balanced integrated housing pattern in the Heights, and to prepare for and promote integration in the Cleveland Heights-University Heights school district. They were committed to giving African Americans choice in where to live, along with creating for themselves the chance to participate in an integrated community.

HCHR held an organizing meeting at the Jewish Community Center on Mayfield Road on June 10, 1964. Those who paid their $2 membership fee voted on the slate of officers who would guide the organization for the next year. Barbara Roderick was elected president. Other officers included Ruth Clement, vice president; Margaret Conti, recording secretary; Bernice Lott, corresponding secretary; and Don Adamson, treasurer. Clement and Lott were African American.[34]

The meeting concluded with a panel discussion titled, "It Can Be Done," featuring speakers from three nearby suburban communities where integration had begun. The speakers were Rev. Andrew White from East Cleveland, David Stoner of Warrensville Heights, and Stephen Alfred from Shaker Heights. David Austin, a faculty member at Western Reserve University who had signed the advertisement condemning the Cleveland Board of Education after Rev. Klunder's death, was the moderator.

The new civil rights organization was on its way. With Roderick at the helm, a leadership team in place, and a statement of objectives, the new group found a workable structure, recruited members, and waded into integrating their community.

HCHR's introductory brochure articulated a clear connection to the highly visible civil rights movement. The founders were determined to end enforced residential segregation and build an accepting, integrated community – where they lived:

> We identify ourselves with the just purpose of the over-all civil rights movement.
>
> Membership in the Heights Citizens for Human Rights is open to all residents of Cleveland Heights and University Heights who want to help the civil rights movement in Greater Cleveland by achieving integration within their own communities.
>
> We want our communities to assist and accept racial integration as they have accepted so many changes that enhanced and enriched the Heights area over the years ... with dignity and understanding.[35]

By the fall, HCHR had 250 dues-paying members, and by the first annual meeting in May 1965, more than 480 people belonged. Despite resistance to formalizing the organization, at their January 1966 meeting, the members voted to incorporate as an Ohio nonprofit organization. Over time, their ranks included more than 900 paying members and several thousand supporters who participated in rallies and other activities. As they helped blacks move to Cleveland Heights, HCHR recruited them to join their organization. This helped create an integrated, albeit white-dominated, civil rights organization.

The organization issued a monthly newsletter to keep its members informed about progress, current events, housing issues, strategy debates, and activities. The first edition came out in June 1964 under the title *Heights Citizens for Human Rights Newsletter*. Throughout 1965, it was called *Human Progress News*. Starting in 1966 and until its final issue in 1974, it was called *HCHR Newsletter*. The publication was mailed to its members and was a valuable tool for recruiting and mobilizing volunteers to carry out the initiatives that led to change. It was, and is now, a detailed record of the organization's concerns and accomplishments.

Roderick led HCHR for its first two years. At the May 1966 annual membership meeting, she summarized the organization's accomplishments. HCHR had already distinguished itself by actively working to create integration, not just prepare for it. But she was frustrated by the slow pace of change and the city government's lack of interest in working on integration. She believed HCHR could play a critical role in this environment:

> How we succeed as an integrated community depends on many complex factors, but I strongly believe that one important factor is a strong volunteer organization that is free to act in many areas in which government and other established institutions cannot.[36]

Inspired by the Southern civil rights movement, this all-volunteer group challenged the real estate industry's control over who could live in the two communities that made up their school district. At this time, discrimination was legal, racial prejudice was accepted, property rights were sacred, integration was assumed to be unstable: thus, segregation was complete. The challenge was enormous.

There were neither laws nor funds to support their work, and city government was indifferent to their cause. Nevertheless, they forged ahead, took a stand, challenged the players who perpetuated segregation, and searched for the good will in their neighbors to force change. Their moral outrage, determination, organizing skills, perseverance, and courage proved to be powerful tools for change.

Powerful forces had created and maintained segregation. Heights Citizens for Human Rights was to become the counterforce.

# BARBARA RODERICK

*In the winter of 1964, Barbara Roderick invited several women to a meeting in her living room at 3283 Meadowbrook Road in Cleveland Heights. This meeting was the genesis of what was to become Heights Citizens for Human Rights, Cleveland Heights' first grassroots organization to challenge housing segregation in this nearly all-white suburb. Thus began this remarkable woman's 15-year journey as a quiet and effective advocate for housing choice and durable integration.*

*Barbara Holroyd was born in Manchuria to missionary parents. She met Glenn Roderick at Hiram College, and they married in 1948. They moved to Cleveland to attend graduate school where Barbara earned a master's degree in social work at the Case Institute of Applied Science. She worked as a social worker for Cuyahoga County for ten years before the birth of her two daughters Carolyn in 1958 and Lee in 1961. Soon after, the growing family moved to Peninsula. But by 1964, the location was too isolated. The family relocated to Cleveland Heights, specifically to work on integration.*

*Her faith spurred her interest in racial justice. She volunteered at Heights Christian Church in Shaker Heights and served as the first woman to chair its board. She worked with the Greater Cleveland Interchurch Council as well. She was, as Susanna Niermann O'Neil observed, "a true believer," who felt that ending discrimination was truly a moral imperative.*

*The Roderick family lived integration. The children participated in the interracial offerings at Karamu House in Cleveland. Dinner conversations always included a civics lesson. Lee actually learned the alphabet by helping her mother prepare mailings for HCHR. But the couple's integration activism presented challenges. Lee recalls, "people stopped talking to us and there were some houses where we couldn't trick or treat." After the 1967 bombing*

BARBARA RODERICK LED FAIR HOUSING INITIATIVES AS A VOLUNTEER ACTIVIST AND CITY EMPLOYEE. SHE IS PICTURED HERE (FAR RIGHT FRONT ROW) WITH THE HOUSING SERVICE STAFF AT A BABY SHOWER FOR SUSANNA NIERMANN O'NEIL (STANDING, SECOND FROM LEFT) IN 1978.

*of Newton Hill's house, the Roderick family received an ominous phone message: "You're next." As a result, police were assigned to monitor their home, but Roderick refused to back down. This indomitable attitude served her well throughout her distinguished career.*

*Roderick's vision of creating an organization to challenge violations of black civil rights, specifically with regard to housing discrimination, would launch a career of exceptional leadership. She was one of a handful of activists who was instrumental during the inception of integration efforts, and then as her expertise grew and the challenge shifted, she remained engaged and effective in preserving her community's hard-won, integrated status. She was also one of the few activists from this period whose volunteer work to promote housing rights turned into a paid, professional position focused on the same goal.*

*Roderick clearly understood the importance of organized citizen activism, noting in her remarks to HCHR members, "one important factor is a strong volunteer organization that is free to act in many areas in which government and other established institutions cannot." As the first HCHR president, she was instrumental in establishing its strategies and identity as an effective volunteer resource for creating and maintaining integration. As the landscape changed, she was a key player in the design and implementation of an evolving set of initiatives that sustained the momentum for change.*

*Ironically, after leading a grassroots organization that compensated for the failure of city leadership to support integration, Roderick became the first full-time city employee to focus on making Cleveland Heights an enduring, integrated community. As a volunteer, her activism often antagonized a static city government that was generally unwilling to commit to neighborhood integration. In 1970, she evolved from an outside agitator to a city employee. Much to the joy of her HCHR friends and after compelling city government to take an active role in fair housing, she* was hired by Cleveland Heights to lead its efforts to address housing integration.

In September 1973, she represented the city as a founding trustee of the Heights Community Congress. Earlier that year, in July, the Businessmen's Interracial Committee and Cleveland Heights leaders asked her to develop a countywide fair housing agency. She convened and led the planning group that designed the Cuyahoga Plan which was implemented in 1974.

Neither her upbringing nor her activism was parochial. She served on the regional level as a board member and then interim director of the Fair Housing Council. On the national scene, she participated in the 1965 meeting of the National Committee Against Discrimination in Housing, she advocated with other Ohio activists who lobbied Congress for the 1968 Fair Housing Act, and she attended the 1970 founding meeting of National Neighbors.

In 1976, when the city-funded housing service became an arm of city government, Roderick was put in charge. HCC rental coordinator Susanna Niermann O'Neil and a few former HCC staffers went to work for her. Much to their relief, Roderick shared their priorities. Soon after, the city council approved the Nine-Point Plan the group had devised. Marketing the community and working with realtors also fell to Roderick and the staff she mentored and inspired. In 1979, after years of experience promoting social change, she resigned from city hall and public life.

Kermit Lind, one of many who benefitted from Roderick's efforts, recalls: "She was demure and approachable, patient and not committed to the status quo at city hall. Barbara emerged as a bridge between the more left-leaning radicals who were advocates for integration, and the conservatives who were frightened of any change, especially racial change. She opened doors to people who were not part of the 'establishment order' and introduced key persons of the established order to those who would become the order that followed."

*Barbara Roderick served as the linchpin in launching organized citizen resistance to racial segregation in Cleveland Heights. Not only did she take the first step by calling that informal, living room meeting that would lead to the creation of the community's first integration organization, but she faithfully stayed the course. Subsequent generations of civil rights activists would build on the foundation that she helped to create. After a lifetime of selfless activism, she died in 2004.*

THE RODERICK FAMILY MOVED TO 3283 MEADOWBROOK ROAD IN 1964.
THE FOUNDING MEETING OF HCHR TOOK PLACE IN THEIR LIVING ROOM. (SUSAN KAESER)

# JOAN DOWLING

JOAN DOWLING CONVINCED THE CLEVELAND HEIGHTS-UNIVERSITY HEIGHTS BOARD OF EDUCATION TO ADMIT BLACK CHILDREN FROM CLEVELAND TO THE DISTRICT'S SUMMER SCHOOL IN 1964 AND 1965. THIS WAS THE BEGINNING OF A LIFE OF GRASSROOTS LEADERSHIP AND ACTIVISM. (SUSAN KAESER)

*When the civil rights movement ignited activism in Cleveland, Joan Dowling enthusiastically joined the effort. Like many other sympathetic white suburbanites, she, with children in tow, showed up at the demonstration at the Stephen Howe Elementary school construction site on April 7, 1964 and witnessed the accident that killed another white activist, Rev. Bruce Klunder.*

*Dowling valued integration, and undaunted by the absence of any organized effort in her community to address segregation, created a local project to encourage interracial experiences for students. Unwilling to wait for a hyper-segregated housing market to change, Dowling and her friends Dorothy Schiff and Leatrice Madison convinced the Cleveland Heights-University Heights Board of Education to enroll black children from Cleveland in the district's 1964 summer school. They hoped children from segregated communities would learn together as* well as learn from each other. The program's enriching curriculum and talented teachers attracted students. School leaders welcomed the idea, and by the second year of the program, found it to be an overwhelming success.

When Barbara Roderick, another parent of young children, learned of Dowling's summer school project, she invited Dowling to join the living room meeting that launched Heights Citizens for Human Rights. School issues remained Dowling's special interest for the next two decades. From HCHR's first meeting until its last, Dowling adhered to her convictions and worked fearlessly through this organization to advance African-American opportunity.

Dowling, who was often seen by more moderate Cleveland Heights activists as radical, was raised in a family with a history of social activism. She grew up in a liberal German Jewish household in Philadelphia in which activism was the norm and social justice was a distinct value. Her grandparents and parents admired President Roosevelt and his progressive policies. Her mother worked for a union, and her father was a businessman. He promoted interracial understanding in the 1940s by organizing camping opportunities for youth that brought together urban blacks and suburban whites. This integration program remained a touchstone for Dowling, one she would later use as a model for her work in Cleveland Heights.

Dowling was educated at a Quaker high school and later at Earlham College. Both schools nurtured her ethics and sense of justice. She moved from California to Cleveland Heights in 1956, where she and her husband Scott Dowling would raise five children. Dowling later earned a degree in social work, and remained involved in many progressive causes.

*Through her activism, Dowling forged lasting friendships with people who shared her values, and she became particularly close to Phyllis and Ralph Brody, and Gerda and Don Freedheim. Some of these connections have gone beyond friendship. She and Phyllis Brody agree they are "like family."*

THE DOWLINGS MOVED TO 3436 BRADFORD ROAD IN 1956.

DR. MARTIN LUTHER KING, JR. SPOKE AT ST. PAUL'S EPISCOPAL CHURCH IN CLEVELAND HEIGHTS ON MAY 14, 1963. HISTORIAN TAYLOR BRANCH CALLED IT THE "FIRST WHITE MASS MEETING" OF THE CIVIL RIGHTS MOVEMENT. (CLEVELAND PUBLIC LIBRARY, COPYRIGHT WITH GETTY IMAGES)

PEDIATRICIAN DR. BENJAMIN SPOCK, A CLEVELAND HEIGHTS RESIDENT, JOINED UFM'S CAMPAIGN TO END OVERCROWDING IN PUBLIC SCHOOLS WITHOUT SEGREGATING BLACK STUDENTS. (CLEVELAND PUBLIC LIBRARY)

MRS. DAVID COHEN WAS ONE OF MANY YOUNG CLEVELAND HEIGHTS PARENTS WHO PROTESTED SCHOOL OVERCROWDING IN GLENVILLE CAUSED BY HOUSING SEGREGATION. (CLEVELAND PUBLIC LIBRARY)

ON APRIL 7, 1964, UFM ACTIVISTS ATTEMPTED TO BLOCK CONSTRUCTION OF STEPHEN HOWE ELEMENTARY SCHOOL ON LAKEVIEW ROAD IN CLEVELAND. REV. BRUCE KLUNDER WAS KILLED WHEN A BULLDOZER BACKED OVER HIM. (CLEVELAND PUBLIC LIBRARY)

REV. BRUCE KLUNDER IS ONE OF 40 CIVIL RIGHTS MARTYRS HONORED BY THE CIVIL RIGHTS MEMORIAL IN MONTGOMERY, ALABAMA. THE FINAL NAME IN THE CHRONOLOGICAL LIST IS DR. MARTIN LUTHER KING, JR.

REV. KLUNDER AND HIS FAMILY LIVED AT 1661 CREST ROAD IN CLEVELAND HEIGHTS. (SUSAN KAESER)

IN DECEMBER 1966, THE CLEVELAND HEIGHTS -UNIVERSITY HEIGHTS BOARD OF EDUCATION UPDATED ITS HUMAN RELATIONS POLICY IN RECOGNITION OF THE DISTRICT'S CHANGING DEMOGRAPHICS. BOARD MEMBERS FROM LEFT TO RIGHT ARE DR. DANIEL BLOOMFIELD, MRS. JEAN DYE, MR. WORTH LOOMIS, MR. LESLIE MONROE, AND MR. EDWARD FRIEDMAN. (1967 CALDRON, CLEVELAND HEIGHTS HIGH SCHOOL YEARBOOK)

AS HCHR VOLUNTEERS, PHYLLIS BRODY (LEFT) AND JOAN DOWLING (RIGHT) FORGED A LIFELONG FRIENDSHIP, THE LASTING REWARD FOR THEIR ACTIVISM. (SUSAN KAESER)

# CHAPTER 3

# ACTIVISTS OPEN UP
# A WHITE SUBURB

The 1966 publication, *The Proud Heritage of Cleveland Heights, Ohio*, sponsored by the Women's Civic Club of Cleveland Heights and written by Mary E. Harris and Ruth M. Robinson, captures life in what the authors call their "fine upper middle-class suburb." It offers an exhaustive description of their "fine residential community's" many assets and its civic life of garden clubs, service and patriotic organizations, street and youth clubs, and men's business groups like the chamber of commerce and the Heights Roundtable, a group dedicated to protecting the rights of property owners. The account makes no mention of the civil rights interests brewing among its residents.

The book ends with comments by city leaders about the future of Cleveland Heights. Only the superintendent of schools Theos Anderson focused on racial change. Thanks to urging by Joan Dowling and others, he had already started to address an updated human relations policy and an integrated summer school. He noted, "Somehow we must find better answers to the problems of the world in regard to man's relations to man."[1]

By contrast, Mayor Kenneth Nash expressed his commitment to the status quo. He proclaimed, "It cannot be over-emphasized that, although some changes and some redevelopment will occur, the basic face and character of the community is expected to remain unchanged."[2]

Heights Citizens for Human Rights (HCHR) activists had a different forecast. They rejected the community's elite and exclusive identity that depended on excluding African Americans. It was a violation of black human rights to block African Americans from living in Cleveland Heights. Their goal was to create "a balanced, integrated housing pattern in the Cleveland Heights-University Heights area." Their ideal was "widely dispersed" integration, a signifier of an open market and the best protection against resegregation.[3]

However, housing discrimination was both legal and widespread. To create housing choices for African Americans, they had to upend traditional beliefs that segregation was normal and beneficial, and that integration was neither desirable nor stable. Long-lasting integration first required opening segregated neighborhoods, and then depended on active resistance to forces that devalued integration and promoted resegregation. HCHR did both.

HCHR was not the first community group in Cuyahoga County to advocate for residential integration, but as an early leader, it did stand out as the most proactive. At HCHR's May 4, 1966 annual meeting, president Barbara Roderick congratulated the members: "HCHR is one of the few suburban groups actually seeking to integrate the community and this distinction has marked us from the beginning." She noted that other groups focused on stabilization or preparing for integration through education.[4]

HCHR had a three-pronged approach to integration that relied heavily on person-to-person connections: volunteers plunged into grassroots activities that created housing choices for African Americans and circumvented the resistant real estate industry; they welcomed new black neighbors; and they built community support for racial change.

This volunteer-led effort functioned without the benefit of a supportive city government or the leverage of public policy. Public support was also uncertain, but HCHR forged forward. Their actions exemplified the role, voice, and power of organized and committed citizens. The strategies they employed remained important even after laws were passed and regional fair housing organizations joined the process.

**Creating Integration: Advancing Choice**

HCHR's Neighborhood Committee took the lead on fair housing. At its first meeting, held on August 24, 1964, members outlined three goals: bringing African Americans to every street in their community; welcoming those new residents; and preparing to stabilize integration once blacks settled in the community. They accurately predicted that stability would be the long-term challenge.

Housing committee members recognized that their neighbors still feared that the "settling of one Negro family will result in the entire neighborhood becoming ghettoized," but set out to bring at least one black family to every street. They acknowledged the difficult challenge of creating integration "without the formation of new ghetto areas." They were optimistic that "effective and balanced integration could work, if it is worked at."[5] So they set to work.

Their top priority was expanding housing opportunities so that race did not limit where African Americans could live. While they embraced integration as a desirable benefit of unlocking housing opportunity, they recognized that the lack of choice was the actual civil rights violation; thus, creating choice had to be paramount.

In her article in the December 1965 *HCHR Newsletter*, just a year after the group first assembled, Maggie Weisberg captured the range of views held by HCHR members about their role in directing where African Americans should look for housing:

> Some felt we are so far away from this that we should not even discuss it. Others felt that Negroes should be strongly discouraged from moving into an area where there already were 'several' Negro families. Some felt we have no right to attempt to interfere with open housing in any way, no matter what the consequences.[6]

By October 1967, HCHR adopted a bold housing policy that both embraced integration and emphasized choice. It set the tone for how the community would approach these issues long after HCHR disbanded. It also distinguished Cleveland Heights from its closest peer, Shaker Heights, where community leaders chose to restrict black access to some neighborhoods in order to preserve integration. Shaker Heights prioritized racial balance while Cleveland Heights prioritized choice. The HCHR's principled policy stated:

> The primary goal of HCHR is the development of a truly open housing market which allows complete freedom of choice in

place of residence for people of all races and religions. We believe racial integration within an open housing market is essential to the fulfillment of an enriched, just and enlightened society.

In the pursuance of this goal, we will seek to educate people to the value of integration and open housing, but under no circumstances will we deny or discourage the purchase or rental of any dwelling on the basis of race or religion.[7]

The emphasis on choice guided their ten-year journey to create an open housing market. However, members continued to grapple with the tension between choice and fear of resegregation.

To increase black access to their suburb, HCHR had to reduce the impact of three substantial barriers: white realtors who embraced segregation and controlled 95% of all real estate transactions; black Cleveland residents who were hesitant to enter a potentially inhospitable housing market; and resistant white neighbors who could sabotage progress. Neighbors defined how blacks would be treated, if integration would be accepted, and whether the street would remain integrated. HCHR volunteers engaged in the personal, emotional, and moral work of persuading realtors and neighbors to accept housing integration.

**Circumventing Realtors**

The real estate industry created a significant barrier to an open housing market and stable integration. Realtors were the gatekeepers of every community. Their powerful role is clearly articulated in Gerda Freedheim and Martin Bloom's 1968 guide for human rights activists:

Through the important role they play in the sale of real estate, they have been able to manipulate and control the very composition of our communities. They are the directors and controllers of housing racism and a very important role of the Human Rights Worker is to educate or at least discourage the broker from this self-assigned task.[8]

Activists engaged in a variety of strategies to reduce realtor control and stifle owner acquiescence. After inviting realtors to help them promote integration but encountering profound resistance, HCHR established an alternative real estate program. They looked for white homeowners willing to sell to black buyers without going through a realtor, and lobbied for fair housing legislation to forbid discrimination by realtors.

African-American migration from Cleveland to the suburbs became more prevalent in the mid-1950s in the wake of urban renewal. Most urban blacks at this time moved to East Cleveland and Warrensville Heights, in addition to the Ludlow neighborhood that straddles parts of Shaker Heights and Cleveland. Each destination shared boundaries with black neighborhoods. When HCHR set out to integrate Cleveland Heights and University Heights, a handful of African-American families had already found their way without assistance. They did not need convincing nor did they need help blazing the path. Many of the pioneers acquired their property by circumventing realtors. They bought through an intermediary, at a sheriff sale, or by working directly with a willing property owner.

In May 1965, as a way to inform realtors of their existence and identify possible allies, an ad hoc committee of HCHR volunteers surveyed brokers who did business in Cleveland Heights. Their questionnaire elicited realtor attitudes about open housing and fair housing legislation pending in the legislature. HCHR volunteers approached all 44 of the local white realtors and interviewed 36 of them.

The results were dismal. Mary Boenke and Phyllis Brody reported their findings in the June 1965 *HCHR Newsletter*. Realtors were deeply committed to segregation. Of the 36 respondents, 15 were outright hostile to HCHR volunteers and their goals. All but four disapproved of fair housing legislation, calling it "unfair housing" or "forced housing" and defended the owner's rights as supreme. Several agents argued that segregation was the way to maintain a "happy, stable neighborhood," and ghettos were proof that integration doesn't work. Even those who expressed personal belief in equality were not willing to alter their practices to make it possible.[9]

Realtors clearly endorsed their industry's long-standing commitment to segregation. All but five said they would forfeit a commission if it meant "breaking" an all-white neighborhood, and would turn down a listing if the owner wanted it sold on the open basis, without regard to the race of the buyer. Many brokers reported that they would not work with Negroes in any situation, while some indicated they would cooperate if an area had a "certain saturation" level. Most reported they were obliged to inform a prospective buyer if Negroes lived nearby.

Discrimination also dominated the rental market. In August 1965, a black female teacher hired by the Cleveland Heights-University Heights school district looked for an apartment in the community and was rejected by 43 landlords, despite the help of more than 100 community members and elected officials. Explanations were reported in a review of the incident written by the school district's Human Relations Advisory Board member and HCHR volunteer, Barbara Heald.[10] She cited replies like: "Let us face facts, I would lose money;" "Look I have the pulse of my tenants and they'd vacate;" "I'm under orders not to show to Negroes;" "We don't rent to colored;" and "No."

White realtors controlled housing opportunities in Cleveland Heights, and they opposed integration. To get around this barrier, HCHR sought the help of Fair Housing Inc. (FHI), a real estate agency committed to, as its stationery explained, "the Principle of Non-Discrimination in Housing."

Modeled after a Quaker-backed group in Philadelphia, this idealistic enterprise existed to facilitate integration, compete with white realtors, and demonstrate that integration was profitable. The FHI Code of Regulations communicated its lofty goals and the value of integration:

> FHI shall be dedicated to the principle that the best interests of a free, democratic society, characterized by equal opportunity for all, are most adequately served by neighborhoods containing persons of varied races, religions and nationalities and by a real estate market in which homes are equally available to all persons of equal financial ability.[11]

Joseph Finley and Gilbert Seldin, white members of the Ludlow Community Association in Shaker Heights, and African-American surgeon Dr. Kenneth Clement of University Heights, signed the incorporation papers in 1962. All were members of Fairmount Presbyterian Church in Cleveland Heights. The new business became operational in January 1964 with Stuart Wallace, a white realtor, at the helm. The founders planned to disband the business as soon as the mainstream real estate industry operated on an open basis. FHI eventually closed in 1971 after the federal fair housing law took effect but long before housing discrimination ended.

To finance the extra time and effort required to find sellers willing to go against racial codes, FHI sold shares of stock. In 1965, Shaker Heights dentist Dr. Winston Ritchie, the African-American treasurer of the group, led a campaign to sell 6,000 shares at $10 a share. Joan Dowling spearheaded an effort to sell shares to HCHR members.

HCHR members hoped that FHI could achieve their integration goal for them, but integrative sales depended on listings in white neighborhoods, and FHI lacked properties to sell. Therefore, HCHR took on the critical challenge of finding white homeowners in Cleveland Heights who were willing to sell their homes without racial restrictions. This role, crucial to increasing black access to white spaces, became a signature activity even after fair housing legislation was approved.

Gerda Freedheim led the team of HCHR volunteers who engaged in the person-to-person work of finding houses that could be offered on an open basis. She described the work as "the most important grassroots job in opening up the community to all."[12] While private housing sales were a small part of the market, any change was significant in an environment where the addition of just one person of color on an all-white street was seen as integration.

Once HCHR identified cooperative white property owners, FHI agents showed the property to African Americans interested in the white suburban housing market. Unlike the Cleveland Board of Realtors, FHI was ready to serve black and white home buyers and sellers and to facilitate integrative moves.

A transaction report showed that by June 1965, FHI was involved in 30 sales. There were 13 in Cleveland Heights and University Heights, and of these, 12 were to black or interracial couples.[13] It was slow going, but during seven years of operation, FHI chipped away at segregation, selling 350 properties across Cuyahoga County. Clients included 199 African-American buyers in previously white neighborhoods. White clients helped stabilize integrated neighborhoods.[14]

Many clients, like the interracial couple Joyce and Bill Collins, moved to Cleveland Heights and promptly joined HCHR, helping to make it a more integrated organization. Joyce Collins joined the housing committee and took her biracial children with her to visit houses for sale in order to check realtor behavior before escorting a black buyer to the house. It was pioneering work.[15]

HCHR's search for listings started in 1964 when discrimination was still legal. The volunteer-led recruitment process targeted Cleveland

Heights and University Heights homeowners who were selling by "owner." The newsletter urged members to be on the lookout and "report any possible listings to Harriet Nadler." By 1965, each elementary school neighborhood had a coordinator. Members who found willing sellers reported them to the neighborhood coordinator who then deployed a local volunteer to talk to the owner. They were prepared to convince reluctant owners to sell on the "open basis," without racial restrictions.[16]

Volunteers were expected to convince their neighbors to support integration by selling their homes to African Americans. This could be an uncomfortable request. In Nina McLellan's report in the October 1965 *HCHR Newsletter*, the committee chair assured HCHR members:

> It may be of some comfort to know that it has been the committee's experience that almost everyone is polite and that a surprising number of people are very glad to talk to you. They feel selling on the open market is right in principle, but are afraid of critical reactions from their neighbors. They are glad to discuss their fears with someone and glad to know that there are neighbors who would support them.[17]

The conversations brought forth a few willing sellers, and by giving owners a chance to express support for integration, ended tacit approval of segregation. After the first three months of outreach to neighbors, the volunteers were happy to find seven positive responses out of 35 homeowners contacted.[18]

In her June 1966 president's report, Mary Boenke urged members to help recruit white homeowners to sell on an open basis:

> After much preparation, orientation, role-playing, and anticipating the worst, my husband and I finally made our first call. The couple we visited was quite willing to show their home to any qualified buyer, and we had a most pleasant conversation! Wouldn't you be willing to make a few similar calls and enjoy the surprises?[19]

The "Home Sellers Project Worksheet," a document prepared in 1966 and updated in 1968 by Gerda Freedheim and Martin Bloom, gave volunteers arguments to use to convince white homeowners to sell on an open basis. This information appeared in many subsequent publications as advocates made their case for change.

The worksheet assigned owners to one of three categories based on the kind of arguments that might be most compelling: patriotic, religious, or legal. It offered rebuttals for each of six concerns that owners typically used to oppose integration:

What will the neighbors think?
Will property values go down?
I don't want to rock the boat.
Isn't it true that whites won't buy after Negroes move in?
Isn't it true that Negroes don't keep up their property?
Isn't it better for people to live with their own kind?[20]

Starting in October 1966, Gerda Freedheim led the search for willing sellers in a new direction. Each week a team of six loyal volunteers combed the *Sun Press* want ads for houses for sale by owner. They sent each owner a letter urging them to offer their property without restrictions, along with a list of 45 prominent east side residents who endorsed open housing practices. They followed up with a phone call.

The HCHR factsheet, "Integration in Our Community Winter of 1966-67," reported on progress since their recruitment efforts began in 1964. They estimated there were now 76 "Negro families on 41 different streets in Cleveland Heights," and ten on seven streets in University Heights. Integration was dispersed, most Negroes had had a pleasant experience, and there had been no panic selling or blockbusting. In general, "the pattern has been one of acceptance, normalcy and adjustment."[21]

Unfortunately, the factsheet also reported that real estate brokers continued to discriminate. White brokers only showed black buyers property in integrated or all-black neighborhoods, and "Negroes attending open houses or responding to newspaper ads invariably are told that the home is already sold. Immediate follow up by white people shows that the house is still for sale."

The strategy then expanded to include homes for sale through a real estate firm. State law had now made discrimination illegal, so the phone callers asked home owners to pressure their realtor to comply with the law by offering their homes on the open basis. They had some success. A report on contacts made in December 1968 showed 40 of the 50 sellers they contacted were working with a realtor, and 20 owners were willing to follow the law and sell on an open basis.[22]

Freedheim praised the work of her volunteer team: "It is not a fun job. It must be done each week routinely. None of our telephoners has ever missed an assignment."[23]

In 1968, Freedheim earned a real estate license and joined the staff of Fair Housing Inc. Jack Browne, HCHR's president, was also on the FHI staff. HCHR had lost the full attention of the prime mover in their organized work to increase housing choice in Cleveland Heights. At this critical moment their strategy shifted to working with another nearby fair housing group, Suburban Citizens for Open Housing (SCOH).

In 1967, the Ludlow and Moreland neighborhood groups in Shaker Heights created SCOH to promote integrated moves in more eastern suburbs. Their goal was to increase the number of communities that included African Americans. Broader dispersion was essential to preserving the hard-won integration that they had established in these two neighborhoods. Cleveland Heights resident and HCHR member Cathie Wherley staffed the start-up project. HCHR became a SCOH partner. Anne Weiss was HCHR's local coordinator.

In 1970, Gerda Freedheim was elected board president of HCHR. That year Cathie Wherley joined the staff of the Isaac Haggins Realty Company on Taylor Road, and Freedheim succeeded her as director of SCOH. The first African American to own a suburban real estate firm, Haggins was determined to make fair housing a commercial success. It helped to have an integrated staff.

The search for housing that could be sold or rented on an open basis was the bread and butter of integration work, and volunteers across the region were asked to support the metropolitan effort to help disperse integration. HCHR was a willing and active participant working with SCOH and other new regional projects.

Unfortunately, progress remained slow; changing realtor behavior took time.

### Welcoming Blacks and Building Community Support for Integration

Making integration a positive experience for the residents of integrating neighborhoods – new and old, black and white – was important to realizing the benefits of integrated living. It was also critical to preventing violence, staving off white flight, and resisting realtor efforts to encourage panic selling. A second important HCHR activity was to sponsor events to welcome new residents and to "encourage a climate of acceptance of Negro families."[24]

To accomplish this, the HCHR Neighborhood Committee identified streets with new black residents and recruited "hospitality families" to reach out and welcome the new neighbors. HCHR tracked the arrival of new black families so the welcoming committee could pay a visit and host neighborhood coffees. The May 1965 newsletter reported the creation of a babysitting clearinghouse as a way to "welcome new Negro families" who were having trouble finding sitters. Connecting new neighbors remained an essential strategy through the 1960s.

White neighbors did not always welcome new black residents. For example, in 1965 when a black physician bought a house near the Freedheim's on Dartmoor Road, an upset neighbor called a street meeting. Hearing about this, Gerda Freedheim informed the doctor about the meeting. Shortly after the start of the gathering, the new resident knocked on the door and introduced himself to the host, saying "I understand you are having a meeting to talk about me, here I am, what do you want to know?"[25] The personal contact diffused the issue and led to a positive transition.

Street meetings became an important strategy for addressing white fears, quelling rumors, reducing anxiety about racial change, and enlisting white residents to make integration succeed. Three years into the integration process (spring 1967), HCHR initiated the Neighborhood Discussion Program to build community-wide comfort with racial change and open housing. More than 500 residents participated in 40 facilitated living room conversations held throughout the community during April and May 1967.[26]

HCHR stalwarts Maggie Weisberg and Phyllis Brody coordinated this massive project that was co-sponsored with the Heights Ministerial Association, the Catholic Interracial Council, the Cleveland Board of Rabbis, the League of Women Voters, and the PTA Council.

The letter to recruit hosts for the conversations explained their purpose: "These are aimed at nonbelievers with a view toward offering a forum for free non-aggressive discussion."[27] The meetings were a chance to ask questions, gather the facts, and air opinions in order to continue to make constructive progress. The host provided the house and the coffee, and the organizers provided the facts and the discussion leader.

A promotional flyer stressed the individual citizen's power and responsibility to shape his or her community. It stated, "Either by acting, or not acting, we are responsible for our community. This is why, today, we encourage frank, face-to-face dialogue about racial integration. As a good citizen of Cleveland Heights-University Heights, do take part!"[28] The flyer also stated that realtor resistance to showing houses on an open basis remained a problem despite growing interest among white property owners not to restrict access. In describing the street meetings in testimony before the Cleveland Heights City Council, HCHR president Ralph Brody concluded, "Many learned that their neighbors had no intention of moving should a Negro family move on their street."[29]

Community education was also an ongoing strategy. In 1967, HCHR formed a speakers' bureau and initiated a letter-to-the-editor campaign. HCHR was the coordinating organization for a June 1968 conference at John Carroll University for more than 50 religious leaders who pledged to work vigorously to make open housing a reality and to educate their congregations on this important issue. Barbara Roderick coordinated the event and Ralph Brody served as the moderator. These two HCHR activists and Gerda Freedheim had become local fair housing experts, and were often tapped to speak on the issue in similar forums.

Education programming took a new turn in April and May 1969 when HCHR produced the four-part "Black Heritage Series." A biracial committee that included Phyllis Brody and Barbara Heald, Bob and Juanita Storey, Marge Ball, Jack Browne, Ellie Weld, and Nancy Klein organized the series. Distinguished presenters and performers brought to life the theme for that evening: Africa, Slavery, Soul, and Protest.[30] The programs attracted more than 2,000 community members.

That June, the Cleveland Chapter of the American Jewish Committee gave HCHR its annual Isaiah Award for Human Relations, which honors voluntary projects that eliminate racial and religious discrimination. After receiving the award, HCHR was praised by the *Cleveland Plain Dealer* for its many contributions: "This fine civic group has promoted human rights in schools, government and community. Its outstanding efforts during the last five years make it most deserving of the Isaiah Award."[31]

Keeping members engaged and informed was another important objective of the organization. In 1970, HCHR began a series of soirees, or "parties with a purpose." Hosts welcomed HCHR members and interested community members to explore an important community issue during a social event. This was a key effort to build relationships, recruit new members, motivate action, and have fun.

Reassuring neighbors, facilitating positive interaction within the neighborhood, honoring black culture, and building support for African Americans' rights to choose where to live demanded constant effort. HCHR volunteers renewed their commitment and adapted their work over and over again as integration unfolded. In the wake of fair housing legislation, they took on new roles, new partnerships, and made a significant difference in their community.

## HEIGHTS CITIZENS FOR HUMAN RIGHTS LEADERSHIP: 1964–1974

| YEAR | PRESIDENT | NEWSLETTER EDITOR |
|---|---|---|
| 1964 - 65 | Barbara Roderick | Ann Dobelstein |
| 1965 - 66 | Barbara Roderick | Ann Dobelstein |
| 1966 - 67 | Mary Boenke | Sally Handelman |
| 1967 - 68 | Ralph Brody | Bernice Lott* |
| 1968 - 69 | Jack Browne* | Iris Masotti |
| 1969 - 70 | Dudley McConnell* Nina McClellan | Harriet Tishkoff |
| 1970 - 71 | Gerda Freedheim | Harriet Tishkoff |
| 1971 – 72 | Albert Cunningham* | Harriet Tishkoff |
| 1972 – 73 | Pippa Kiraly | Harriet Tishkoff |
| 1973 – 74 | Bob Klein | Harriet Tishkoff |

*African-American leaders

# GERDA FREEDHEIM

GERDA FREEDHEIM WAS A RELENTLESS ADVOCATE FOR HOUSING CHOICE. SHE DESIGNED AND IMPLEMENTED HCHR'S PIONEERING WORK WITH PROPERTY OWNERS TO FIND HOUSES TO SELL TO BLACKS. (SUSAN KAESER)

*Between 1964 and 1974, Gerda Freedheim applied her peerless organizing skills, her intense sense of justice, and her fearless determination to spearhead citizen efforts to thwart realtor control over black housing opportunities. More than any other volunteer in this story, she drove the painstaking effort required to open up to blacks white spaces deeply protected by white realtors and property owners. She was there from the very beginning, and remained throughout the difficult period when protecting integration became a pressing challenge.*

*Don Freedheim, Gerda's husband, grew up in Cleveland Heights and the couple returned to the community from Boston in 1960 when he was hired at Case Western Reserve University. They were denied housing in the Roxboro neighborhood because they were Jews. "I couldn't believe people would be treated like this," remembers Gerda. This firsthand experience propelled her activism.*

*As housing chair and then board chair of HCHR, and later as director of the regional fair housing organization, Suburban Citizens for Open Housing, she shaped the strategies that mobilized citizen volunteers to facilitate integrative moves. Along with Martin Bloom, she authored a powerful guide for human rights workers to assist them in challenging white resistance to integration.*

*She understood that realtors had acquired far too much control over communities. So she relentlessly challenged them in face-to-face encounters at homes available for sale, accompanying African Americans in the market who had been told houses were not available to them. She challenged discrimination daily, but unfortunately, it eventually wore her down. In 1974, she finally retreated from her daily encounters with this kind of dehumanizing racism: "I got to the point where I would look at a white person and see a racist."*

*As a Heights Citizens for Human Rights housing committee volunteer (1964-69), a realtor with Fair Housing Inc. (1968-1970), the HCHR board president (1970-71), an executive director and board member of Citizens for Open Housing (1970-74), a delegate to the Jewish Community Federation (1970-73), and a community organizer with the Legal Aid Society (1972-74), she tirelessly advanced racial equality. She became a local and national expert on housing discrimination and ways to fight it, and frequently spoke about her work and trained others.*

*Joan Dowling, her friend and HCHR colleague observed, "unlike most women of our generation, she was unafraid to say what she thought." She was like a "steamroller," remembers Phyllis Brody, who always managed to get things done.*

*After "retiring" from housing advocacy in 1974 and spending a year in Israel, she completed a master's degree in social work and embarked on a long career at the Federation for Community Planning (now known as the Center for Community Solutions), a regional organization directed by her HCHR colleague and long-time friend, Ralph Brody.*

AFTER BEING DENIED ACCESS TO A HOUSE IN THE ROXBORO NEIGHBORHOOD GERDA AND DON FREEDHEIM PURCHASED THIS HOME AT 2617 DARTMOOR ROAD IN CLEVELAND HEIGHTS. (SUSAN KAESER)

FAIR HOUSING INC. SOLD SHARES OF STOCK TO FUND THE EXTRA COST OF FINDING HOUSES TO SELL WITHOUT RACIAL RESTRICTIONS. LIKE MANY HCHR ACTIVISTS, THE FREEDHEIMS INVESTED IN THE FIRM. (GERDA FREEDHEIM)

CLEVELAND HEIGHTS MAYOR KENNETH NASH (SECOND FROM RIGHT) WAS PART OF THE WHITE ESTABLISHMENT THAT IGNORED AND RESISTED RACIAL CHANGE. HE IS PICTURED HERE AT THE MARCH 5, 1962 GROUNDBREAKING FOR SEVERANCE SHOPPING CENTER. WHEN INTERVIEWED IN 1966 ABOUT THE CITY'S FUTURE HE PREDICTED NO CHANGE. (CLEVELAND PUBLIC LIBRARY)

SUPERINTENDENT THEOS ANDERSON WELCOMED THE SCHOOL DISTRICT'S 1966 REVISED HUMAN RELATIONS POLICY. WHEN INTERVIEWED ABOUT THE MOST PRESSING COMMUNITY CHALLENGE HE RESPONDED, FINDING "BETTER ANSWERS TO THE PROBLEMS OF THE WORLD REGARDING MAN'S RELATIONSHIP TO MAN." (CH-UH BOARD OF EDUCATION ARCHIVES)

AS AN ACTIVE HCHR VOLUNTEER, JOYCE COLLINS TOOK THEIR BIRACIAL CHILDREN WITH HER TO TEST REALTOR RESPONSES PRIOR TO ESCORTING A BLACK HOME BUYER TO AN OPEN HOUSE. LISA AND ERIC COLLINS ARE HEIGHTS HIGH GRADUATES AND IN THE DISTRICT'S HALL OF FAME. (JOYCE COLLINS)

BILL AND JOYCE COLLINS PURCHASED THEIR HOME AT 2304 WESTMINSTER ROAD THROUGH FAIR HOUSING INC. IN FEBRUARY OF 1965. (SUSAN KAESER)

IN 1968, ON BEHALF OF HCHR, BOARD PRESIDENT JACK BROWNE PRESENTED A CHECK TO CLEVELAND HEIGHTS LIBRARY STAFF FOR BOOKS TO ADVANCE RACIAL UNDERSTANDING. (CLEVELAND HEIGHTS-UNIVERSITY HEIGHTS LIBRARY PHOTO COLLECTION)

A Statement of Objectives
by Heights Citizens for
Human Rights, Inc.

HCHR HAD WELL DEFINED OBJECTIVES AND STRATEGIES TO GUIDE ITS ACTIVISM. THIS BROCHURE, DESIGNED BY PHYLLIS BRODY, WAS ALSO USED TO MARKET THE ORGANIZATION.

# CHAPTER 4

# FAIR HOUSING LAWS ADD LEVERAGE

A moral imperative drove Cleveland Heights civil rights workers headlong into tackling the injustice of housing segregation. This volunteer effort proceeded without the support of local government or the leverage of fair housing laws. HCHR's person-by-person efforts to bring one black family at a time into their white community was profound, but more was needed to create systemic change. Making it illegal to discriminate was essential to large-scale and lasting impact. Their agenda included both advancing fair housing laws and using them.

Cleveland Heights activists joined the state and national push for fair housing laws. After an ill-fated effort in 1963, citizens mobilized two years later and in 1965 the Ohio legislature approved fair housing legislation. On the federal level, pressure from the civil rights movement, including from HCHR activists, resulted in the Fair Housing Act of 1968. This prohibition on housing discrimination, also known as Title VIII of the Civil Rights Act of 1968, took effect on January 1, 1970. Passing a local fair housing ordinance took longer. Despite persistent advocacy by Cleveland Heights residents, it wasn't until 1976 that the Cleveland Heights City Council passed a fair housing ordinance.

To their disappointment, open housing advocates discovered that making it illegal to discriminate did not end discrimination. Fair housing legislation changed the playing field, but advocacy remained essential. Now, with the law on their side, advocates acquired new partners and developed new strategies.

Violence directed at blacks became another variable during this period. It energized advocates to demand that city government defend, and fully embrace, all of its residents and their civil rights.

The 1964 Civil Rights Act, the 1965 Voting Right Act, and the 1968 Fair Housing Act were tangible victories for the civil rights movement. These federal laws made discrimination illegal and provided new tools to force change among those who thwarted civil rights. Federal protection was especially important in the South where Jim Crow-era state and local laws mandated segregation and created impenetrable roadblocks to voting and opportunity.

The 1968 civil rights law prohibited discrimination in lending and in the sale or rental of housing, and created an enforcement mechanism for violations. It also required that the federal government promote integration. The law was especially important given the federal government's history of mandating segregation in public housing and in housing funded with federally insured loans.

## Ohio Legislation Makes Discrimination Illegal

Housing segregation in Ohio was not mandated by law, but it existed because it was legal for property owners to discriminate, and they did.

To advance equal housing opportunity, Ohio activists pushed for state legislation to end discrimination. In January 1963, the Ohio Committee for Civil Rights Legislation advocated for a state law to prohibit racial or religious discrimination in the sale, rental, or financing of housing.[1] Despite a statehouse rally and lobbying efforts, by June, just as the United Freedom Movement (UFM) was taking shape in Cleveland, the legislation was stalled in committee. In an attempt to advance the bill, UFM members Rev. Bruce Klunder, Bruce Melville, and Ruth Turner participated in a sit-in inside Governor Rhodes' office. Despite this protest, the bill died in committee.

Two years later, a second try eventually succeeded. HCHR endorsed the legislation. Gerda Freedheim organized HCHR-sponsored coffees to inform the community and encourage Cleveland Heights voters to write letters to Governor Rhodes, Cuyahoga County's six state senators, and the newspapers. Several members joined a Cleveland delegation that testified in Columbus to support the proposed bill. "Those of us who believe in equality for all people need to be heard in support of Fair Housing Legislation" read the call to action in the March 1965 *HCHR Newsletter*. In a letter to the editor to the *Cleveland Plain Dealer*, Freedheim compared the heartbreaking cruelty of overt white prejudice that she had witnessed while recruiting blacks to live in Cleveland Heights to the Bloody Sunday violence in Selma a few days before:

> I wonder which is a harder blow – the physical one inflicted by the bully policeman turning back a mass of people or the spiritual one felled by an upstanding real estate man who refuses a Negro admittance into a house he has opened for public inspection? Given the choice, I think I would take my chances and join the crowd in Selma.[2]

On June 6, 1965, a dozen HCHR members joined 100 protesters at a UFM-sponsored demonstration at a Republican dinner in downtown Cleveland. Their purpose was to pressure Governor Rhodes to get the stalled bill out of committee for a vote. HCHR volunteer Maggie Weisberg reported on her picketing experience in the July *HCHR Newsletter*: "Our group was evenly divided between whites and Negroes. Many of the whites were suburban home owners and new to picketing." Afterwards state representative Carl Stokes, a sponsor of the law, thanked the group and reported that the demonstration had made a difference.

Finally, the Ohio General Assembly passed a compromise fair housing law on July 23, 1965. It took effect on October 30. The law made discrimination illegal and provided a complaint process to force compliance. "At Last!!!" read the headline in HCHR's October newsletter. "HCHR can be pleased that our first foray into political activity has met with some measure of success," reported Barbara Roderick.[3]

Just days before the new law took effect, David Lawrence, the executive director of the President's Committee on Equal Housing Opportunities, spoke at a fair housing rally in Cleveland sponsored by the Ohio Committee for Civil Rights Legislation. He warned the crowd that three challenges would limit the success of the new law: the prejudice of white suburbanites, Negro fears, and the cynicism of the housing industry. He pressured blacks to play their part by stating, "All qualified Negroes have the responsibility to seek housing in white neighborhoods and to help dispel prejudice by living example."[4]

Despite the new legislation, realtors continued to resist housing integration. A poll taken by the Ohio Association of Real Estate Boards of 300 realtors, released the day the law took effect, indicated "96% said action should be taken to abolish the new law."[5] Less than a year later, Ann Dobelstein observed in the *HCHR Newsletter*:

> Our experience in Ohio certainly indicates that the existence of a law does not immediately guarantee open housing, but the law provides a foundation from which to work for adequate, open housing for all people.[6]

Making discrimination illegal reframed the battle. It made fair housing both a moral and legal imperative. Nonetheless, most real estate agents didn't budge. There would be no shortcut to creating housing choice.

Fair housing advocates could not take a "wait and see" approach to the new law. They pressured realtors to sell on an open basis, mobilized blacks to seek housing in new locations, and monitored realtor behavior for equal treatment. Progress depended on tireless advocacy by both activists and brave black consumers who confronted and pressured the key players. These steps gave life to the law and made it useful.

## HCHR Partners with Regional Fair Housing Organizations

In the wake of Ohio's 1965 fair housing law, two new regional organizations, Fair Housing Council and Operation Equality, added new strength to the existing efforts by Fair Housing Inc., SCOH, and local grassroots activists in advancing open housing in Cuyahoga County. The new metropolitan groups mobilized African Americans to look for housing in the suburbs, investigated complaints of mistreatment, and helped clients file complaints with the Ohio Civil Rights Commission. These organizations utilized paid staff and relied heavily on white volunteers to achieve their goals, including monitoring fair treatment.

HCHR continued to bring blacks to their community, welcome them, and build local support for integration among their neighbors. They also joined forces with these regional allies and provided invaluable leadership and manpower to both metropolitan groups as they worked to change the region.

Housing discrimination was difficult to eliminate, and segregation built over decades across whole communities and regions was even harder to dismantle. Immediate results were hard to achieve, and sustained effort was essential.

## Fair Housing Council

In the fall of 1964, the Ludlow Community Association, the region's first integration-focused community organization, held a workshop for fair housing organizations working in the area. They formed the Greater Cleveland Federation of Integrating Communities. This informal network faded within the year, but it provided the core for a new coalition, the Fair Housing Council (FHC).

The FHC opened its doors on November 1, 1965, the day after Ohio's fair housing law took effect. Its purpose: to make sure the law ended discrimination. It had funding from the Greater Cleveland Associated Foundation. The FHC made Barbara Heald its first executive director. Heald was a HCHR member, a Fair Housing Inc. board member, and was active in the Cleveland Heights League of Women Voters. This early fair housing leader shared office space with the nonprofit realty firm, Fair Housing Inc. and was supervised by its director, Stuart Wallace.[7]

In December 1965, Heald and her funders asked Mary Boenke, HCHR's real estate committee chair, to convene like-minded groups to learn about the FHC and contribute to its work. More than 75 representatives from 32 groups attended two meetings held on January 10 and February 1, 1966, during which they hammered out exactly how they would work together.[8]

The Fair Housing Council educated the public, realtors, and landlords about the law and helped blacks search for suburban housing. They provided volunteer escorts to help smooth the way at open house events and organized white "checkers" to visit open houses to monitor whether or not black and white shoppers experienced the same treatment. If black clients experienced discrimination and wanted legal relief, the FHC helped them file a complaint with the Ohio Civil Rights Commission. The FHC's member organizations provided the volunteer manpower needed to do this important law enforcement work.

Sara Hunter, a Cleveland Heights resident whose husband Joe Hunter served as the regional director of the Ohio Civil Rights Commission, mobilized volunteer escorts and checkers for the FHC. Her notes from a January 4, 1966, volunteer training meeting indicate that 38 people from six suburban groups attended. They represented the Euclid Society for Interracial Understanding, Hillcrest Citizens for Human Rights, Ludlow Community Association, Warrensville Heights Neighborhood Forum, West Side Interfaith Fair Housing Committee, and Parma Area Human Relations Association.

HCHR volunteers were a driving force in creating the FHC and in carrying out its work. Barbara Roderick, who served on its governing board, reported to the members in May 1966: "Fair Housing Council has found HCHR the most willing and able group to assist them and has relied heavily on our volunteers in finding apartments, escorting, and checking. Progress is slow but perceptible."[9] At the time, 60 HCHR volunteers were active with the FHC, and even more were needed. A few months later, Roderick took over as the FHC's interim director, filling in for Barbara Heald who left the country for a year.

Less than six months after the FHC had opened its doors, 173 individuals had contacted them for help because realtors did not follow the law. Barbara Heald reported, "I know of no voluntary compliance in significant areas."[10] The regional Ohio Civil Rights Commission office that served 20 northeast Ohio counties was swamped. Their impact on realtor resistance was limited by the lack of staff and the inability to initiate complaints.

In April 1967, Rev. W. Scott Hengen became FHC's permanent director and led their activities to coordinate the work of more than 40 fair housing groups in Cuyahoga County.[11] The FHC operated through 1971.

## Operation Equality

The existence of Fair Housing Inc., Fair Housing Council, SCOH and numerous volunteer-led, community-based integration organizations made Cleveland a lively location for the promotion of fair housing. This activism helped the Cleveland Urban League secure grants for Operation Equality (OE) totaling $405,000 from the Ford Foundation and the Cleveland Foundation. Cleveland was the first Urban League chapter to be funded to implement the national organization's fair housing initiative. Its purpose was to promote open housing in the metropolitan area. They started by targeting "economically able Negroes."[12]

The three-year start-up funding was announced in November 1966, and OE opened its doors early in 1967, two years after the Fair Housing Council was launched to help African Americans secure their legal right to housing without discrimination.

Rev. Richard Rangoon, a Congregational minister from Long Island who had previously led a nonprofit community action organization there, was chosen to lead the project's staff of nine workers. Operation Equality operated as a joint effort of the Urban League and the Fair Housing Council, and in its first year, it helped 113 African-American families move throughout the county, often using FHI as the broker.[13]

In 1968, Joe Battle, a black realtor who lived in the Ludlow neighborhood of Shaker Heights, took over as the director and remained in the position until OE closed in June 1976.[14] Battle became the first black member of the Cleveland Area Board of Realtors, and in 1970, was elected the first president of National Neighbors, a coalition of fair housing organizations operating in integrated communities across the country. Battle believed that the only way to change realtor behavior was to make realtors deal with a steady supply of black buyers. He was a regular advisor and active partner with HCHR and subsequent Cleveland Heights organizations that focused on suburban integration.

Outreach to potential black buyers was an ongoing part of promoting suburban integration. Before partnering with Operation Equality, HCHR recruited blacks to look for housing in Cleveland Heights by speaking at community events in Cleveland. Bernice Lott, a black member of HCHR, arranged for Mary Boenke to market the suburb to members of a black sorority. Similarly, Operation Equality organized monthly outings, referred to as Operation House Shop, for black city residents to inspect housing in the suburbs. That initiative relied on black churches and civic groups to recruit interested black buyers who were matched with white suburban volunteers who marketed their neighborhoods.

On December 3, 1967, OE matched more than 50 HCHR volunteers with members of Mt. Zion Congregational Church, an elite black congregation in University Circle in Cleveland. Each pair inspected three houses in Cleveland Heights or University Heights: one listing known to be available on an open basis; another, an open house sponsored by a realtor where access was unclear; and finally, in order to ensure exposure to at least three properties, the home of the escort. Participants ended the afternoon at the home of Sam and Roz Wolpert "to have coffee and to share experiences."[15]

White volunteers also helped advance equal treatment by serving as escorts and checkers. HCHR's Sara Hunter explained the escorting and checking roles to FHC volunteers this way:

> Escorting involves accompanying individual Negroes and members of other minorities seeking housing. Its purposes are to help ensure that the Negro applicant gets an opportunity to view the housing and to supply corroborating evidence of the manner in which Negro applicants are received. The escort helps the consumer gain access by setting up the appointment and getting there early so the owner can't give the usual excuse for exclusion: 'already rented.' If a renter is turned away, a volunteer white checker visits the same unit or house to test if they experience the same reception. Their treatment is evidence of discrimination.[16]

In 1967, HCHR participated in a new OE project. Volunteers agreed to work with a black family until they found housing. A pitch in the February 1968 HCHR Newsletter to recruit volunteers described their role:

> They go to opens together. The escort calls brokers for the Negro family and tries to fend off any unpleasant situations which so often arise when a Negro tries to work on his own. In addition there is a very important educational process derived from this work when white sellers and realtors are confronted with escort and clients.[17]

A March 1968 newspaper account of the escort and checking activities credits the fair housing groups and liberal homeowners with the movement of 10,000 Negroes to the suburbs in the previous year. It also describes the effect on white volunteers who "have moments when they know what it is like to be a Negro" as they witnessed discrimination.[18]

After the federal government passed fair housing legislation, there was a surge in black households looking for rental property. As a result, the FHC turned to HCHR to scout for rental units that blacks could view. HCHR created the Survey Committee to search for available rental property in Cleveland Heights and University Heights while the FHC shared the listings with black clients. Volunteers working for OE and the Fair Housing Council talked to realtors and homeowners, escorted blacks into the all-white housing market, collected information, checked for discrimination, and changed attitudes. These were the critical activities to open doors that had until then been closed.

Experiencing racism firsthand was powerful for many volunteers. It hardened their resolve, but it also had an adverse effect. For fair housing leader Gerda Freedheim, one of the most engaged in the daily work of helping blacks access housing on white streets, the constant contact with white racism made her a self-described "white hater." She "looked at a white person and saw racist." Sadly, this response prompted her to withdraw from fair housing activism in 1972.[19]

In addition to working with individuals as they navigated an unwelcoming housing market, the regional groups pressured local government and realtors to cooperate. Operation Equality lobbied 57 communities in Cuyahoga County to adopt open housing ordinances. It also encouraged the real estate industry to explicitly embrace and enforce the law regulating their behavior and urged large management companies not to discriminate. In addition, they supported real estate firms, like Haggins Realty, that wanted to operate as open housing businesses. By 1969, they advocated for the construction of affordable housing in order to increase housing options for low-income blacks.

HCHR gained a well-deserved reputation for its activism and its supportive alliances with those groups. Together they transformed Cleveland Heights and University Heights and became leaders and foot soldiers in activities to open the entire suburban housing market.

**Violence Spurs City Government Action**

While the Cleveland Heights-University Heights Board of Education turned out to be a positive and enthusiastic partner in supporting HCHR's early integration goals, city government was a different matter. An entrenched, conservative white male establishment had governed Cleveland Heights for three decades. Citizen involvement was discouraged, and government activity was minimal. In the mid-60s, the proposed freeway that would cut through the middle of Cleveland Heights along with the conversion of aging mansions into condominiums presented new challenges to elected leaders. Housing discrimination was not on the agenda of the local decision-makers. They certainly weren't about to throw open the doors of their white enclave and invite all to move in.

HCHR interceded by taking a leadership role in creating change. Unlike reluctant elected officials, citizens were free to pursue unpopular goals. While HCHR was skeptical about City involvement, they knew it was important to their cause. As early as May 1964, HCHR's Fact Finding Committee identified city government as a critical resource for fair housing. They believed a local fair housing ordinance and a welcoming human relations policy would make the city attractive to more blacks and could help establish a positive community response to change. Also, local laws would increase enforcement options and local interventions.

However, Cleveland Heights Mayor Kenneth Nash was hostile to the group. After two racially motivated bombings rocked the community in October 1966, Walter Page, HCHR's Government and Business Committee chair, offered to assist Mayor Nash. When Page asked Nash how HCHR could help, Nash replied, "You can disband."[20]

In 1966, the Real Estate Committee observed that the state's 1965 fair housing law was "widely ignored and disobeyed." Having already been rebuffed by city leaders, HCHR abandoned any hope that city council would appoint a committee to study and enforce the law. Barbara Roderick concluded, "Our Council will act after a crisis or a serious problem arises and not with advanced planning."[21]

HCHR had hoped that integration would be met with "dignity and understanding." By pouring energy into building community acceptance for racial change they sought to make integration positive and prevent intimidation and violence – ugly tools used to discourage black and white participation in integration. For the most part, change proceeded without such violence, and when it did occur, it actually backfired. Attacks on the homes of new black homeowners or sympathetic whites stimulated greater resolve to integrate along with widespread expressions of public support for black rights. In addition, violence forced a resistant city council to grapple with its role in integration. As Roderick had predicted, crisis led to greater city government investment in integration.

Reports of harassment dated back to the graffiti and threatening calls that followed the Madison family when they moved to North Park in 1960. In May 1964, the Cooley family moved to Monticello Boulevard, buying their home at a sheriff's sale. Teenaged vandals harassed them and broke windows several times before being apprehended.

Rev. Jack Sersig, pastor of Bethlehem Lutheran Church on Mayfield Road, commented on the incident in a letter to friends:

> Just a week ago, we had the good fortune of having a Negro couple move into our white ghetto. Their advent into the area has been marred on two occasions already by having rocks hurled through their living room window. This is probably the work of outsiders, since a series of neighborhood meetings before their coming gave every indication that the families most directly involved would react intelligently and cordially.[22]

This was just the beginning. On October 19, 1965, two weeks before Ohio's fair housing law took effect, two bombs detonated ten minutes apart, damaging the homes of Roger Saffold, a black accountant living on Euclid Heights Boulevard, and a white couple who were entertaining blacks in their home on Edwards Court. City council, at its very next meeting, increased the penalties for damaging property and trespassing.

Councilman Stashower noted, "We hope that in adopting these amendments we will communicate to the residents of our city that the private and personal property rights of all of our citizens are going to be protected and we are not going to tolerate such incidents as occurred this week."[23] But council neither embraced open housing nor condemned discrimination. Part of the legislation included this statement that acknowledged that race was relevant to the incident:

> As our American society advances, we find today that peoples of different races seek the advantages of a home in our city. Undoubtedly more of these people will follow as the American dream that 'all men are created equal' continues to emerge into reality.

> The City Council enacts this legislation to strengthen the protection of each citizen's home and reaffirms its historic policy that enforcement of the law will be vigorously executed to the end, that each citizen, his family and his home may be secured from violence and protected from assault.

We appeal to our citizens each to do his part to preserve our community as a good place to live for all respectable people.[24]

The fourth racially motivated bombing took place on June 28, 1966, a few weeks before the Hough Riot in nearby Cleveland. The home of Mr. and Mrs. Charles Gard at 2604 E. Overlook Road was listed for sale with Fair Housing Inc. when an explosion knocked out most of the windows and damaged the living room. HCHR used the incident to mobilize community support for integration.

"I thought it was going to be a quiet summer!" HCHR president Mary Boenke wrote in the July *HCHR Newsletter*. At 7:30 a.m., she learned of the bombing. She stated, "By noon we decided to hold a rally." That evening more than 300 concerned residents gathered at St. Paul's Church to condemn the violence. They raised $365 for the victims and voted to attend the next meeting of the Cleveland Heights City Council.

The *Cleveland Plain Dealer* coverage of the event observed, "At a Cleveland Heights meeting notable for the absence of Mayor Kenneth Nash, all councilmen and city officials, 300 citizens called for fair housing action by councils of both Cleveland Heights and University Heights."[25]

In the same article, HCHR's president Boenke expressed hope that the bombing had made discrimination more visible: "Perhaps our community has become more aware of the problems of segregation and discrimination existing 'in our own backyard.' Perhaps we have taken another step forward in the long process toward the solution." At the same time, she noted Mayor Nash's response to her overtures: "Perhaps if people like you weren't engaged in this sort of activity, these incidents would not occur."

The following week, 280 HCHR supporters attended the Cleveland Heights City Council meeting. Boenke spoke for the group and urged the City to support integration by: 1) adopting a policy statement welcoming all persons as residents, regardless of race or creed; 2) employing a professional human relations staff person; and 3) adopting a local fair housing ordinance. These recommendations would give city government an active role in encouraging integration and taking action in cases of discrimination.

After the meeting, HCHR supporters marched two blocks east on Mayfield Road to the Heights Temple and planned their next move. They were eager to do more to rally and educate the community about the value of integration. They divided up responsibility for reaching out to religious and civic groups and collected funds for a full-page newspaper ad promoting their commitment to integration and human rights. More than 250 HCHR supporters signed the ad and paid for it to be published in the September 20, 1966, *Sun Press*. The banner headline read, "Is Your Door Open?" The ad stated:

> An open heart and an open mind are not enough. Democracy requires an open door as well. Our neighborhoods, schools, and businesses must all reflect our basic belief in the rights and dignity of each person. The Heights Citizens for Human Rights, Inc. is a fast-growing voluntary group, serving Cleveland Heights and University Heights concerned with the full achievement of those human rights which have been largely denied through racial prejudice and segregation. Our community, like many others, is integrating. We believe this can be a healthy and encouraging experience.

On November 21, 1966, Cleveland Heights City Council issued a policy statement in response to HCHR's three-point plan for city action. The statement reiterated city commitment to enforcing the law to protect property, but it rejected adopting a fair housing ordinance. Council did pledge to meet new Negro residents, to prohibit discrimination in hiring, and to study human relations problems affecting the community.

The policy conclusion, penned by council member Oliver Schroeder, included a passing endorsement of integration. HCHR used the statement on its brochures:

> The Council believes that our Cleveland Heights Community has a bright future as a place of residence for any respectable citizen who desires a safe and orderly city, excellent education and religious facilities, fine recreational and cultural opportunities, close proximity to professional and business employment, government responsive to the citizens' needs, and above all, a citizenry rich in their diversities of religion, ethnic origin, and race.[26]

On May 13, 1967 for the second time in less than two years, the house at 2604 E. Overlook Road was rocked by explosives. This time, a dozen sticks of dynamite created extensive damage to the house now owned by J. Newton Hill, the newly hired African-American director of Karamu House. A day later, an anonymous caller threatened HCHR activist Barbara Roderick: "You are next."[27] This incident moved the city one step closer to playing an active role in creating a climate for diversity, holding realtors accountable, and preventing white flight.

The morning after the bombing, 40 HCHR members met to organize yet another rally at St. Paul's Church. That evening, more than 700 residents and civic and religious leaders attended the meeting. They raised reward money and signed petitions saying that they "would not be intimidated by terrorist activities and that they support open housing."[28] The bombing also stimulated an outpouring of support for the Hill family from individuals and organizations, including the Lincoln Boulevard street club.

Rather than discourage integration, violence shined a light on a real problem and stimulated many new voices to publicly support housing choice. The Heights Chamber of Commerce issued this statement: "We shall not be intimidated by a maniacal fringe that would revert to violence."[29] A week later, more than 50 ministers and rabbis called for the community to support HCHR efforts in open housing.[30] The *Sun Press* editorialized against violence and supported integration: "The repeated Heights bombings do not slow the lawful right of a man to buy a home or rent a home he can afford. In fact, it acts as a spur to renew efforts toward peaceful integration."[31]

On June 5, 1967, less than a year after HCHR first asked the City to act, Ralph Brody, HCHR's new president, addressed city council. He observed that the response to the latest bombing incident demonstrated that "while there are extremists whose strong prejudicial feelings lead them to violence, there is an ever-increasing number of people who are willing to come forth and positively accept Negro and other minority families in the Heights community." Brody argued, "The broad community is ready – now more than ever before – to accept enlightened leadership on race relations." He pushed for the council to issue a clear, public statement welcoming persons of all races and religions; hire a full-time human relations professional; and adopt local fair housing legislation. He called attention to the significance of the issue by stating, "Cleveland Heights has the opportunity to meet *the* challenge of the 20th century. We look to

City Council to fulfill its leadership role by taking a more vigorous stand in integrating our suburb."[32]

Once again, city leaders rejected the request. However, they did assign assistant city manager Charles Mauger responsibility for meeting with residents on integrating streets to reduce tension and anxiety and prevent panic selling. Mauger soon became a valuable partner in the integration work.

In 1967, the City adopted a ban on for-sale signs as a way to prevent panic selling. HCHR opposed the ban as ineffective and pressed for what they thought got to the point: a local fair housing law.

As racial change continued, council members became concerned about the future stability of the community. They wrote a letter to the community on racial integration, a topic they defined as "rarely discussed frankly and dispassionately." In their April 30, 1968 correspondence, council expressed concern for "the preservation of the fine residential character of our city" and urged residents: "don't let yourself be frightened by rumors of excessive changes." They outlined city activities to work with realtors and to recruit new residents through outreach to area universities and major employers. They also pledged to prosecute any party guilty of blockbusting. They invited residents to report any unscrupulous activity to city hall. The letter ended with this upbeat message.

> By working together, we have an opportunity to make of Cleveland Heights a community of meaningful purpose and of enduring values. No city is more advantageously located. No city provides better municipal services. No city offers finer police and fire protection. No city is more concerned with the recreation, welfare, and education of the community. No city could have a brighter future. We hope you want to share that future with us.[33]

Nevertheless, it remained unclear how far they would go to support integration.

As part of Operation Equality's push to support integration and end the dual housing market, black real estate broker Isaac Haggins opened an office at 2221 N. Taylor Road in Cleveland Heights. His goal was to serve all clients, regardless of race. The staff included two white women with established track records in fair housing as volunteers with HCHR, Barbara Roderick and Cathie Wherley.

The February 1969 *HCHR Newsletter* noted in welcoming Haggins: "Integration has been severely hampered in the past because white brokers held the listings and Negro brokers had the customers and the two seldom met."[34]

Despite high hopes, on February 14, 1969, the open housing real estate firm's office was rocked by another racially motivated bombing. HCHR once again took action. Joined by CHALLENGE, the religious branch of OE, they invited people to meet at Hope Lutheran Church – directly across the street from the Haggins office – on February 23 to sign a statement supporting the realtor and condemning violence. More than 2,500 people signed the statement:

> We abhor this act of violence and admire Mr. Haggins' refusal to be intimidated. We call upon all men of good will to affirm the right of reputable businessmen to operate in the community without regard to color or creed. In the American tradition of free enterprise, fair play, and equal opportunity, we welcome Mr. Haggins to our community.[35]

The Heights Area Chamber of Commerce, League of Women Voters, Fair Housing Council, Council of Churches, Jewish Community Federation, and the Catholic Commission were among the civic, religious, and neighborhood groups that expressed support for the realtor. Mr. Haggins appreciated the support calling it a "display of true democracy."[36]

The *Sun Press* editorialized about the incident and condemned the violence:

> Until the bombing, integration in Cleveland Heights had proceeded quietly, in an orderly and socially acceptable fashion. It was perhaps the best example of how integration is accomplished with a minimum of community disruption. It will continue to work this way despite the outrageous bombing that has aroused and angered decent people everywhere.[37]

Even if violence was only occasional, it was evidence that racial change continued to cast a shadow over the "bright future" that city leaders had proclaimed lay ahead. Pressure to integrate Cleveland Heights was not going to end; neither was realtor resistance.

Finally, in November 1970, Cleveland Heights stepped up its role in integration. It hired Barbara Roderick as its first housing program director, a significant new city investment in integration. HCHR was delighted. HCHR president Gerda Freeheim praised the choice:

> Although only one person, her background and knowledge and dedication to open housing make her equivalent to ten. Her orientation has been through HCHR, her own street association and as a colleague of Isaac Haggins when he opened his Cleveland Heights Office. She comes well qualified, we think, to address herself and the city to some of the problems in housing we are facing today. We congratulate City Council on its fine choice and hope we can be of great support and service to them in this positive and responsive step.[38]

HCHR did not let up. Freedheim and other housing committee members issued a position paper outlining how the City should support fair housing. In a letter for members, Freedheim reiterated the board's opinion that the City should make sure realtors comply with fair housing laws, and that the City not discriminate in housing services it provides.[39] The position paper recommended the following: that the City involve a black real estate broker in shaping housing policy; that it work only with realtors who sign an agreement to comply with fair housing laws; that it advertise it will investigate and refer complaints about discrimination; that it develop educational programs for street associations about how to use the law; that it educate realtors about the benefits of Cleveland Heights; and that it promote the Heights to major employers.[40] Fearing some form of racial steering to achieve racial balance, they cautioned against "manipulating" the housing market.

In July 1971, the City announced its official housing program. It would promote stability in three ways: by preventing white flight, maintaining white demand, and recruiting realtors as allies. It would focus on developing street organizations to resist panic selling and work with realtors to sell Cleveland Heights as a "preferred residential community."[41]

A few months later, Gerda Freedheim gave a supportive review of the city effort and outlined the significant issues faced by the city six years into the process of racial change. Hard-won integration was still threatened by blockbusting, racial steering, and an aging and deteriorating housing stock. These challenges would need sustained, vigilant engagement.[42]

ON MAY 14, 1963, DURING A FUNDRAISING VISIT TO CLEVELAND, DR. MARTIN LUTHER KING, JR. AND LOCAL LEADERS URGED PEOPLE TO LOBBY FOR A FAIR HOUSING LAW FOR OHIO. HE IS PICTURED WITH (FROM LEFT TO RIGHT) DR. KENNETH CLEMENT, A UNIVERSITY HEIGHTS RESIDENT AND CO-FOUNDER OF FAIR HOUSING INC., CLARENCE CLEMONS, REV. RALPH ABERNATHY, AND CHARLES LUCAS. (CLEVELAND PUBLIC LIBRARY)

JOE BATTLE DIRECTED OPERATION EQUALITY, WAS A VALUED PARTNER AND TRUSTED ADVISOR TO CLEVELAND HEIGHTS HOUSING ACTIVISTS, AND A NATIONAL FAIR HOUSING LEADER. HE BECAME THE FIRST AFRICAN-AMERICAN MEMBER OF THE CLEVELAND AREA BOARD OF REALTORS. (CLEVELAND PUBLIC LIBRARY)

WHITE FAIR HOUSING VOLUNTEERS WORKING THROUGH REGIONAL ORGANIZATIONS ESCORTED AFRICAN AMERICANS AS THEY SHOPPED FOR HOUSING IN WHITE SUBURBS. THEY ALSO TESTED FOR FAIR TREATMENT, AND IN CASES OF SUSPECTED DISCRIMINATION, HELPED FILE COMPLAINTS WITH THE OHIO CIVIL RIGHTS COMMISSION. (CLEVELAND STATE UNIVERSITY, CLEVELAND PRESS COLLECTION)

HCHR USED THE DISPLAY CASE AT THE LEE ROAD LIBRARY TO PROMOTE ITS FAIR HOUSING GOALS AND TO RECRUIT MEMBERS. (GERDA FREEDHEIM)

# BLACK HERITAGE SERIES

## 1 SUNDAY APRIL 13 7 - 10 p.m.

### AFRICA

PROGRAM

American's Black heritage begins with African roots. Program One will present—via the mixed media of lecture, slides, drums and dance — an overview of the vast and colorful African continent south of the Sahara.

PARTICIPANTS

J. Newton Hill — Executive Director, Karamu House.
William Wingfield — Dance Department, Karamu House.
African and American students from local universities.

## 2 SUNDAY APRIL 20 7 - 10 p.m.

### SLAVERY

PROGRAM

Two hundred years of slavery were crucial in shaping our nation's Black heritage. Program Two is concerned with the impact and nature of slavery as an institution as seen through music and literature.

PARTICIPANTS

Thornton Webster — Director, Project Bridge.
The Clevelanders — Vocal Ensemble.
Annetta Jefferson — WVIZ.

## 3 SUNDAY APRIL 27 7 - 10 p.m.

### SOUL

PROGRAM

A common quality of deep feeling links Black men the world over. Program Three presents several expressions of this feeling which we call Soul.

PARTICIPANTS

Hugh Thompson — Faculty Cleveland Music School Settlement.
Regina McConnell — Soprano.
Delores White — Pianist.
Drama Students from local universities.

## 4 SUNDAY MAY 4 7 - 10 p.m.

### PROTEST

PROGRAM

Protest about the condition of Black people in American society has taken many forms. This protest is a vital part of America's past and present and will surely shape the future. Program Four deals with the historic and current aspects of this protest.

PARTICIPANTS

William Pickard — Executive Director, NAACP.
Panel representing current points of view and programs for protest in the Black community.

PRESENTED BY HEIGHTS CITIZENS FOR HUMAN RIGHTS, INC.

This series is presented as a community service. All programs will be held at Forest Hills Presbyterian Church, Lee and Monticello Boulevard, Cleveland Heights, Ohio.

Subscription is limited. Make your reservations and order tickets now!

Series Price $3.00 per person for series of 4 programs.
$1.00 per person for single program.
Students half price.

RESERVATIONS - BLACK HERITAGE SERIES

No. of Tickets for Series ............ @ $3.00
Name ...........................
No. of Tickets for Single Session
Address ................... (please specify) ............ @ $1.00
Phone ................... Amount Enclosed $ .............
Please make checks payable to: Heights Citizens for Human Rights
Mail with stamped self-addressed envelope to:
Mrs. John Moffett, 3336 East Berkshire, Cleveland Heights, Ohio 44118 Telephone 932-3678

MORE THAN 2,000 PEOPLE PARTICIPATED IN HCHR'S FOUR-PART SERIES CELEBRATING BLACK HERITAGE HELD AT FOREST HILL CHURCH. (PHYLLIS BRODY)

IN 1969 HCHR PRESIDENT DUDLEY MCCONNELL ACCEPTED THE AMERICAN JEWISH COMMITTEE'S ISAIAH AWARD THAT RECOGNIZED THE CONTRIBUTION THAT THE BLACK HERITAGE SERIES MADE TO RACIAL UNDERSTANDING. (CLEVELAND STATE UNIVERSITY, CLEVELAND PRESS COLLECTION)

# ACTIVISTS' HOMES SUBJECTED TO VIOLENCE

IN 1960 LEATRICE AND ROBERT MADISON MOVED INTO THE HOME HE DESIGNED AT 2339 NORTH PARK. THIS PIONEERING FAMILY WAS NOT STOPPED BY GRAFFITI AND A WHITE NEIGHBOR WHO ATTEMPTED TO PREVENT THEM FROM MOVING TO CLEVELAND HEIGHTS BY BUYING THE UNDEVELOPED PROPERTY. (SUSAN KAESER)

KEN COOLEY AND HIS FAMILY CIRCUMVENTED REALTORS IN 1964 BY PURCHASING THEIR HOME AT 3670 MONTICELLO BOULEVARD AT A PUBLIC AUCTION OF FORECLOSED PROPERTY. THE NEW RESIDENTS WERE REPEATEDLY HARASSED BY VANDALS. (SUSAN KAESER)

ON OCTOBER 9, 1965 A BOMB DAMAGED ROGER SAFFOLD'S HOME AT 2624 EUCLID HEIGHTS BOULEVARD. TEN MINUTES LATER, A SECOND RACIALLY MOTIVATED EXPLOSION OCCURRED AT THE DIRENFELD'S HOME AT 2352 EDWARDS COURT. (SUSAN KAESER)

ON JUNE 28, 1966, AFTER CHARLES GARD LISTED THIS HOUSE AT 2604 OVERLOOK ROAD WITH FAIR HOUSING INC. IT WAS BOMBED. NEWTON HILL PURCHASED THE HOUSE, AND LESS THAN A YEAR LATER, ON MAY 13, 1967, IT WAS SERIOUSLY DAMAGED BY DYNAMITE. (CLEVELAND STATE UNIVERSITY, CLEVELAND PRESS COLLECTION)

ISAAC HAGGINS OPENED HIS FAIR HOUSING REAL ESTATE FIRM AT 2221 N. TAYLOR ROAD IN FEBRUARY 1969.
ON FEBRUARY 14 THE BUILDING WAS BOMBED, PROMPTING AN OUTPOURING OF SUPPORT FOR THE NEW BLACK-OWNED BUSINESS.
(CLEVELAND PUBLIC LIBRARY)

A FIREBOMB DAMAGED THE APPLING FAMILY HOME AT 3656 BRINKMORE ROAD IN SEPTEMBER 1972.
MAYOR SCHROEDER CONDEMNED THE VIOLENCE AND SUPPORTED THE FAMILY. FAIR HOUSING ADVOCATES
WELCOMED THE NEW CITY LEADERSHIP. (SUSAN KAESER)

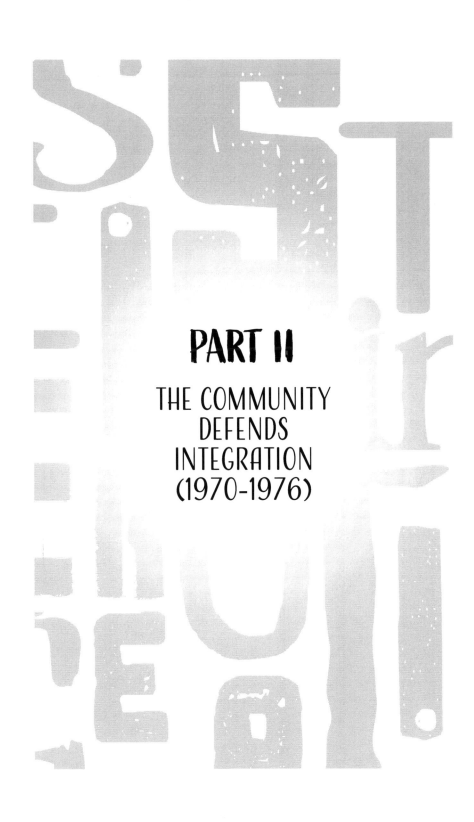

# PART II

## THE COMMUNITY
## DEFENDS
## INTEGRATION
## (1970-1976)

# CIVIL RIGHTS DEVELOPMENTS AT THE NATIONAL AND LOCAL LEVELS 1970-1976

**L** LOCAL          **N** NATIONAL

**70**

**N** JANUARY 1, 1970 – THE FEDERAL FAIR HOUSING ACT OF 1968 TAKES EFFECT.

**L** 1970 – THE FAIR HOUSING COUNCIL CLOSES.

**L** 1970 – THE JEWISH COMMUNITY FEDERATION FORMS THE HEIGHTS AREA PROJECT.

**L** MAY 23-25, 1970 – NATIONAL NEIGHBORS ATTRACTS 33 COMMUNITIES TO ITS FIRST MEETING. BARBARA RODERICK ATTENDS FOR THE HCHR.

**L** SUMMER, 1970 – AFTER WHITE YOUTH ATTACK BLACK YOUTH AT THE HEIGHTS YMCA, BLACK PARENTS FOUND COMMITTEE TO IMPROVE COMMUNITY RELATIONS (CICR).

**L** SEPTEMBER 27, 1970 – REV. NED EDWARDS INSTALLED AS SENIOR PASTOR AT FOREST HILL CHURCH.

**L** NOVEMBER 1, 1970 – THE CITY OF CLEVELAND HEIGHTS HIRES BARBARA RODERICK TO LEAD ITS HOUSING PROGRAMS.

**71**

**L** FEBRUARY 14, 1971 – CICR MEMBERS ELECT OFFICERS.

**L** FEBRUARY 24, 1971 – THE CATHOLIC COMMISSION LAUNCHES "ACTION FOR A CHANGE."

**L** JUNE 8, 1971 – THE CICR REGISTERS COMPLAINT WITH POLICE CHIEF ABOUT HARASSMENT OF BLACK RESIDENTS.

**L** JUNE 28, 1971 – THE FOREST HILL CHURCH SESSION AGREES TO SPONSOR THE FOREST HILL CHURCH HOUSING CORPORATION.

**L** JULY, 1971 – BARBARA RODERICK ANNOUNCES CITY HOUSING STRATEGY.

**L** AUGUST, 1971 – THE HEIGHTS AREA PROJECT LAUNCHES ITS DOWN PAYMENT ASSISTANCE PROGRAM.

**L** FALL, 1971 – FOREST HILL CHURCH HOUSING CORPORATION RENOVATES A HOUSE THROUGH THE HUD 235 PROGRAM.

**L** SEPTEMBER, 1971 – FOUNDERS DISSOLVE FAIR HOUSING INC.

**72**

**L** JANUARY 28, 1972 – A FIGHT AT HEIGHTS HIGH SCHOOL REVEALS RACIAL TENSIONS.

**L** JANUARY 29, 1972 – DORIS ALLEN CALLS COMMUNITY MEETING TO DISCUSS THE CONFLICT. SCHOOL LEADERS ASK FOR HELP TO ADDRESS RACISM.

**L** FEBRUARY 22, 1972 – FR. BONNELL AND HOWARD BERGER CONVENE THE HEIGHTS ACTION COMMITTEE (HAC) AT THE CARMELITE MONASTERY.

**L** MARCH 8, 1972 – THE HAC PROPOSES ITS MISSION "TO PROMOTE AN OPEN INTEGRATED COMMUNITY."

MARCH 15, 1972 – THE HAC'S CATHOLIC MEMBERS ASK THE DIOCESE TO ASSIGN HARRY FAGAN TO WORK ON THE COMMITTEE.

MARCH 22, 1972 – THE ST. ANN HOUSING ACTION COMMITTEE MEETS WITH JULIETTE SALTMAN TO LEARN ABOUT HOUSING AUDITS.

MARCH 27, 1972 – FOREST HILL CHURCH ADOPTS A NEW MISSION STATEMENT THAT COMMITS TO COMMUNITY INVOLVEMENT.

MAY 19 TO JULY 14, 1972 – THE ST. ANN SOCIAL ACTION HOUSING COMMITTEE CONDUCTS AN AUDIT OF REAL ESTATE PRACTICES.

JUNE 6, 1972 – HARRY FAGAN OFFERS THE "200% SOLUTION."

AUGUST 10, 1972 – THE HAC PROPOSES TO COMMUNITY LEADERS A NEW ORGANIZATION, THE HEIGHTS COMMUNITY CONGRESS (HCC).

SEPTEMBER 6, 1972 – SUE NIGRO AND TOM REIM REPORT FINDINGS OF THE ST. ANN AUDIT TO CLEVELAND HEIGHTS CITY COUNCIL.

SEPTEMBER 14, 1972 – ROBERT APPLING HOME AT 3656 BRINKMORE IS FIRE BOMBED. MAYOR SCHROEDER STEPS IN.

SEPTEMBER 21, 1972 – A STEERING COMMITTEE IS ELECTED TO GOVERN THE HCC.

73

JANUARY 1, 1973 – FR. BONNELL FILES INCORPORATION PAPERS FOR THE HCC.

JANUARY 22, 1973 – FOREST HILL CHURCH SPONSORS ECUMENICAL FILM FESTIVAL AS A MARTIN LUTHER KING, JR. CELEBRATION.

FEBRUARY, 1973 – THE HCC STARTS THE HOUSING TASK FORCE.

FEBRUARY 20, 1973 – THE CLEVELAND FOUNDATION AWARDS THE HCC A $48,000 GRANT.

MARCH 13, 1973 – THE CUYAHOGA PLAN IS FOUNDED.

JULY 28, 1973 – THE CICR FILES FOR INCORPORATION.

SEPTEMBER 24, 1973 – FOREST HILL CHURCH MAKES A $500 DONATION TO BEGIN THE CHALLENGE FUND.

NOVEMBER, 1973 – HARRY FAGAN BECOMES EXECUTIVE DIRECTOR OF THE HCC.

74

MARCH, 1974 – CLEVELAND HEIGHTS CITY COUNCIL APPROVES CONTRACT WITH THE HCC FOR A HOUSING SERVICE.

MARCH, 1974 – CH-UH SUPERINTENDENT MOBERLY MEETS WITH BLACK STUDENTS TO ADDRESS THEIR GRIEVANCES.

JUNE 6, 1974 – CICR DEMONSTRATES AT A SCHOOL BOARD MEETING TO SUPPORT STUDENT DEMANDS.

JUNE 17, 1974 – THE CH-UH BOARD OF EDUCATION HOLDS A SPECIAL MEETING TO DISCUSS BLACK STUDENT DEMANDS.

SEPTEMBER 1974 – THE SCHOOL DISTRICT BEGINS
HUMAN RELATIONS TRAINING.

OCTOBER, 1974 – THE CICR FILES A COMPLAINT WITH THE U.S.
DEPARTMENT OF JUSTICE, COMMUNITY RELATIONS DIVISION.

NOVEMBER 19, 1974 – THE HCC BOARD OF TRUSTEES
FILES SUIT UNDER THE 1968 FAIR HOUSING ACT AGAINST
ROSENBLATT REALTY.

NOVEMBER, 1974 – THE CH-UH BOARD OF EDUCATION
APPOINTS BERNICE LOTT TO FILL A VACANCY.

**75**

JANUARY 14, 1975 – THE FIRST MEETING OF THE CICR,
BOARD OF EDUCATION, AND MEDIATOR FOR THE JUSTICE
DEPARTMENT TAKES PLACE.

MARCH 11, 1975 – JUDGE FRANK BATTISTI RULES THAT THE HCC
HAS STANDING TO FILE THE ROSENBLATT COMPLAINT.

APRIL 1, 1975 – THE CICR AND CH-UH BOARD OF
EDUCATION AGREE TO A CONSENT DECREE.

**76**

JANUARY, 1976 – REV. NED EDWARDS IS ELECTED PRESIDENT OF THE HCC.

JANUARY 12, 1976 – THE FIRST SCHOOL DISTRICT-SPONSORED
HOLIDAY HONORING DR. MARTIN LUTHER KING, JR. TAKES PLACE.

1976 – OPERATION EQUALITY CLOSES.

MARCH 15, 1976 – CLEVELAND HEIGHTS CITY
COUNCIL ADOPTS ITS NINE-POINT PLAN.

APRIL 10, 1976 – THE CICR HOLDS A SCHOLARSHIP BALL
AT THE CLEVELAND MUSEUM OF NATURAL HISTORY.

APRIL 1976 – CLEVELAND HEIGHTS NAMED AN ALL-AMERICAN CITY.

JUNE 1976 – CITY COUNCIL ENDS ITS HOUSING SERVICE
CONTRACT WITH THE HCC.

JULY 4, 1976 – THE CICR SPONSORS A FOOD
AND HISTORY BOOTH AT CAIN PARK.

AUGUST 1, 1976 - SUSANNA NIERMANN O'NEIL BECOMES
DIRECTOR OF THE CITY-RUN HOUSING SERVICE.

SEPTEMBER, 1976 – THE AMERICAN JEWISH
COMMITTEE AWARDS THE ISAIAH AWARD TO THE HCC.

# CHAPTER 5

# FOREST HILL CHURCH GRAPPLES WITH RACE

The fervor of the civil rights movement, the Cleveland school segregation fight, and mandates from the Presbyterian Church USA and its progressive clergy and members pushed the all-white Forest Hill Church Presbyterian congregation to confront racism. Located in a neighborhood developed during the era of restrictive covenants, the church and its members were transformed by the imperative of racial equality. After several years of tension, conflict, pain, and loss, Forest Hill Church, as an institution, emerged committed to integration. By 1971, the church had an energetic senior pastor, Rev. Ned Edwards, who had helped build that commitment. It also had many dedicated young leaders, a governing structure that made social concerns a church priority, and a housing initiative – the Forest Hill Church Housing Corporation (FHCHC).

FHCHC founders disagreed with the long-standing narrative that segregation was needed to preserve property values. For them, the threat was not who owned property but how able they were to maintain it. The congregation put its faith into action by sponsoring a new nonprofit to keep the community's aging housing stock in good repair in support of stable integration.

The idea "came from the members who were challenged by the church's theology," remembers Diana Woodbridge, one of four church members who incorporated FHCHC and for more than 35 years served as its founding director. It was part of the church's social justice mission and, according to Woodbridge, a reason people continue to join the church.[1] The Housing Corporation united the congregation, and it solidified a new direction and identity for the church as a place that worked in earnest to reduce prejudice and embrace diversity and racial equality. This identity has persisted throughout changes in leadership and membership over the last five decades.

## History of the Forest Hill Church Congregation

Forest Hill Church Presbyterian is as old as Cleveland Heights itself. The first meeting of about 40 Cleveland Heights Presbyterians took place in a house on Radnor Road in 1903, as a "mission" church of Beckwith Church on East 107th street in Cleveland, which later became Church of the Covenant. In 1946, the growing congregation known as Cleveland Heights Presbyterian called World War II veteran Rev. Yoder Leith as its pastor during the post-war baby boom. When construction began on a new church at the corner of Monticello and Lee Boulevards in 1950, they renamed the congregation Forest Hill Church in honor of its new location in the Forest Hill neighborhood. This was their fourth home and fourth name in 50 years.[2]

Forest Hill was developed as a "model community" by the Abeyton Realty Company, owned by John D. Rockefeller, Jr. on land that had been part of his father's estate. Construction of 81 carefully designed homes began in 1929. The Forest Hill Development straddles two suburbs. It is bounded by North Taylor Road, Lee Boulevard, and Mayfield Road in Cleveland Heights, and Glynn Road in East Cleveland. By September of 1930, the first 15 houses, all found in the East Cleveland portion of the development, were complete and the development was announced to the public. After multiple interruptions, most of the remaining development took place after World War II.[3]

As was typical at the time, the developer attached deed restrictions to the property that defined acceptable architectural features, landscaping, and placement of driveways and garages. The Forest Hill regulations stipulated that for ten years, potential buyers had to be approved by the developer or ten neighbors. While the exclusion of blacks and Jews was not directly stated, none lived there. The result was a self-perpetuating, homogeneous, white, Protestant neighborhood.[4]

In 1950, after the 1948 Supreme Court decision that made deed restrictions unenforceable, the developer turned over governance of the Forest Hill neighborhood to the Forest Hill Homeowners Association (FHHA). All residents were entitled to be members. Its purpose: "to promote, safeguard, and improve the property values and the general welfare of the community known as Forest Hill."[5]

Forest Hill Church drew many of its members from its immediate neighborhood. When the population of Cleveland Heights peaked in 1960, the church had also reached an all-time high with 2,000 members. To accommodate the large congregation, the church hired Rev. George Mace to assist Rev. Leith and held three Sunday services. By 1963, they broke ground for an addition and hired a third minister to care for the 400 children who participated in its church school. On May 5, 1963, the congregation installed Rev. Ned Edwards, a 28-year-old graduate of Yale Divinity School, as the pastor for Christian Education and Youth Programs.[6]

**The Transformation of Forest Hill Church and its Clergy (1963-1971)**

When Rev. Edwards joined the Forest Hill staff, he found a congregation of successful young families, governed by all-white male elders content with the status quo. He described the congregation and its impressive facility as being "at the height of white, post-war success."[7]

Racial equality was not on the agenda of Forest Hill Church. Its location within a neighborhood that had been segregated by design made commitment to open housing unlikely. Edwards recalls, "I had no idea of the racial tensions that were brewing. It was an amazing journey through the next 29 years."

On May 14, 1963, a week after Rev. Edwards was installed, Dr. King spoke at St. Paul's Episcopal Church in Cleveland Heights and challenged churches to change and to lead, saying, "The church must remove the yoke of segregation from its body."[8]

Less than two months later, in his famous letter from the Birmingham jail, Dr. King beseeched religious leaders to work for racial justice:

So here we are, moving toward the exit of the 20th century with a religious community largely adjusted to the status quo, standing as a tail light behind other agencies, rather than a headlight leading men to higher levels of justice.

Now is the time to make justice a reality for all God's children.[9]

This was also the period when activists pressed the Cleveland Board of Education to stop segregating the Glenville students it bused to white schools. Two Presbyterian ministers, Rev. Bruce Klunder, who directed the campus ministry at Church of the Covenant, and Rev. David Zuverink, Glenville Presbyterian church pastor, were in the forefront of grassroots activities to pressure the district to integrate its students.[10] Revs. Edwards and Klunder, both residents of Cleveland Heights, had been classmates at Yale.

Rev. Edwards' first involvement with the school issue came in January 1964 when the senior pastor, Rev. Yoder Leith, invited him to observe a UFM-sponsored protest in Little Italy in the wake of the breakdown in negotiations to integrate students. An armed white mob attacked the protestors that day, one of the worst incidents in the protracted challenge to segregation. Edwards recalls Rev. Leith saying, "We've got to try to understand this movement and help work it out."[11]

In April, construction began on new schools in Cleveland which were designed specifically to segregate students. Zuverink and Klunder recruited Rev. Edwards and other clergy to demonstrate at the Stephen Howe Elementary School construction site. Edwards was not able to attend the April 7 protest, but a week later, he marched to protest the death of his friend, Rev. Bruce Klunder. The death galvanized activists' determination and inspired Rev. Edwards to lead the congregation as it responded to a request from the Presbyterian Church USA (PCUSA) to examine racism.

As a denomination, the PCUSA first addressed segregation in 1946 when it called for a "non-segregated church in a non-segregated society." It was the first national religious body to endorse the Supreme Court's 1954 *Brown v. Board of Education* decision with this statement: "enforced segregation of the races is discrimination which is out of harmony with Christian theology and ethics."[12]

In 1963, the 175th General Assembly of PCUSA formed the Commission on Religion and Race to design and coordinate race relations activities that would reach into all of its congregations. Dr. Eugene Carson

Blake chaired the Commission that had as its goal: "to purge its own house of the unclean practice of color prejudice." The Commission invited all congregations to "study prayerfully all Pronouncements" that called for a non-segregated society.[13]

At Forest Hill Church, the Board of Christian Education, moderated by Rev. Edwards, led the process to examine race prejudice. This process included an open meeting for the congregation to discuss the position on race. Rev. Rawlings, from the Presbytery of the Western Reserve's Committee on Religion and Race, facilitated the discussion.

Presbyterian congregations are governed by the Session, a lay committee elected by its members. On June 15, 1964, the Session of Forest Hill Church approved a seven-point statement of beliefs about race – the outcome of the congregation's "prayerful" consideration of the need for a non-segregated society. It stated as follows:

As Christians we hold

1. That men are created equal in the sight of God and are meant to live together in a love that means equality of opportunity and privilege.
2. That racial discrimination and segregation are denials of human worth and are contrary to the will of God.
3. That we welcome all peoples who accept Christ in their hearts in the life and work of Forest Hill Church.
4. That Forest Hill Church accepts the responsibility to minister to its immediate total community without distinction as to origin or worldly conditions.
5. That we condemn the actions of any individuals who willfully and knowingly incite others to a disrespect for law.
6. That we condemn any failure, deliberate or otherwise, of legally constituted authorities to safeguard all persons within their jurisdiction against mob violence.
7. That because God makes no distinctions as to race or origin, all citizens of our country shall have equal access to the rights, responsibilities, and privileges, of citizenship, and that they be allowed to find full participation in the work and worship of Christ's Church.[14]

Shortly after that meeting, a Forest Hill Church elder encountered Rev. Edwards in the church parking lot, grabbed him by the collar, shoved him against the church building, and demanded to know, "Are you going to bring niggers to Forest Hill?" According to Edwards, this was the turning point that led to his "conversion and activism for the civil rights movement."[15]

In 1967, the Presbyterian Church USA revised its 300-year-old *Book of Confessions*, the official doctrinal standard of beliefs. A new section identified ending racial discrimination as a central tenet of their faith:

God has created the people of the earth to be one universal family. In his reconciling love he overcomes the barriers between brothers and breaks down every form of discrimination based on racial or ethnic difference, real or imaginary. Therefore, the church labors for the abolition of all racial discrimination and ministers to those injured by it. Congregations, individuals, or groups of Christians who exclude, dominate or patronize their fellow men, however subtly, resist the Spirit of God and bring contempt on the faith which they profess.[16]

According to Rev. Edwards, "To have that statement on the same official plane as 'Jesus was the Son of God' and 'The Bible is the Word of God,' was revolutionary. It gave authority to everything Forest Hill Church was about."[17]

Unstable integration was a reality that concerned church members. It had already affected East Cleveland, the suburb that included part of the Forest Hill neighborhood. As Rev. Edwards remembers, "This change was a major source of fear to the people living in Forest Hill. I don't think we were prepared for it, but the challenges forced church and community to take sides and become educated."[18]

On April 4, 1968, at the time the congregation was examining how to act on the mandate of the *Book of Confessions*, Dr. King was assassinated. His death prompted Rev. Edwards to speak about the civil rights leader a few days later in his Palm Sunday sermon. He described Dr. King as a modern Jesus, "dying for our sins."[19]

A month later, the church's governing board approved a position statement on open housing. The position stated:

We believe that:

1. In a free and open society, the right of all individuals must be recognized and protected.

2. The denial of housing opportunities to any person on the basis of race, color, religion or national origin by express agreement, by custom or by silence is morally wrong.

3. Members of Forest Hill Church as Christians witnessing to Christ's love for people should welcome any responsible person or family to live in our respective neighborhoods.[20]

The policy was controversial. According to Rev. Edwards, "the exodus from the church by members fearing the devaluation of their homes was huge. I think we lost about 400 members in a month."[21]

In June, the Session added a sixth committee to its governing structure: the Board of Church and Society. The decision institutionalized the congregation's role in the community and elevated its importance. This took effect in 1969. The Board of Church and Society became the vehicle for the congregation to address issues affecting the community and to provide resources to affect them.

In March 1972, the Session approved a new mission statement making involvement in the community a way to realize the expectations of the *The Book of Confession* of 1967. To fulfill its responsibility "to work for every form of human being," Forest Hill Church "affirms its commitment to be a positive force, an active participant directly involved in the life of the community, striving for the benefit of all its residents."[22]

The church used education programs, discussion, and worship to engage members in thinking about significant social concerns – from abortion and poverty to the Vietnam War and housing. During worship services, adult education activities, and special events, members of this white congregation took up the denomination's call to examine their own racism and prejudices, and to reshape their attitudes.

Interracial experiences were essential to developing new attitudes. In 1967, Rev. Terry Schoener became the pastor at Glenville Presbyterian, a mostly black Cleveland congregation that had been deeply involved in the Cleveland school crisis. The governing boards of Forest Hill and Glenville Presbyterian met to plan events together including joint worship and choir exchanges. In 1969, the Forest Hill Church and Society committee discussed forming a "yoke relationship" with the congregation, which led to financial support for Glenville's needy families, a family adoption program, and nursery school scholarships.

Rev. Edwards and the adult education committee designed an education series that focused on racial discrimination: "Operation Open Mind – A Festival of Change." During four Sundays in October 1968, the congregation immersed itself in activities devoted to racial awareness. The activities addressed the denomination's desire to "purge its own house of the unclean practice of color prejudice." The series brochure explained the goal:

> That the entire congregation of Forest Hill Church become totally immersed in an effort to accept change and to become individually motivated toward making an attitude adjustment concerning our black citizens through education and sensory means.[23]

Guest preachers experienced in urban issues offered sermons. They included African-American leaders Rev. Lenton Gunn, pastor of St. Mark's Presbyterian, the oldest black congregation in the Presbytery of the Western Reserve, and elder Steve Minter from Glenville Presbyterian, the Assistant Director of County Welfare. One worship service included a choir exchange with Glenville Presbyterian that ruffled some feathers when members of the ensemble raised their fists, a declaration of black power.[24] The series exemplified the congregation's willingness to move outside of its comfort zone and try unconventional approaches to the Sunday service.

Operation Open Mind also included a seven-week adult education course that explored "The Racial and Urban Crisis in America," using the *Kerner Commission Report on Civil Disorder* as its text. Two evening programs featured candidates for Congress. Additional evening events focused on black arts with music, dance and drama programs, and an exhibit featuring 15 black artists. These events exposed white church members to black people and black culture.

A year later, during October 1969, the congregation once again dove into racial awareness and urban issues during worship and in adult education activities. Each week, the adult education hour featured a speaker who focused on "The Dynamics of Community Change." The four-part series examined community change, and in three of the meetings focused on responses to change by government, the community, and individuals.[25]

These educational events set the stage for a final activity in which church members in living room conversations focused on race with the goal of identifying the barriers to integrating their congregation. The primary resource for these conversations was the *Human Rights Guide*, the 1968 revised version of the *HomeSellers Project Work Sheet* developed by Gerda Freedheim and Martin Bloom, and used by Heights Citizens for Human Rights to challenge the six myths used to justify segregation.

The series took place in the midst of a change in pastoral leadership. At the end of 1968, Rev. Leith had announced his intention to retire by May 31, 1970. Presbyterian protocol requires that if a senior pastor resigns, so does the assistant pastor, freeing the congregation to define what it wants in its next leaders. At its September 22, 1969, meeting, the Session accepted Rev. Edwards' resignation effective on the same day as Rev. Leith in 1970, and appointed a Pulpit Committee to search for a new pastor.[26]

Rev. Edwards delivered the first sermon in the month-long focus on social change on October 5, 1969, two weeks after the Session accepted his resignation. He was certain that he was too controversial to succeed the retiring pastor, so he felt free to fully express his beliefs. In the sermon, "The Sacrament of Mind Opening," Edwards challenged the congregation to confront the fear that leads to discrimination.

> I'm convinced what stands between the white and black community is fear. I wish there were some way in which we as a congregation could express those fears; get them out of ourselves; some way in which we could even bring those fears and offer them to God. I think the basic ones are the fears of losing our own identity as superior people. We face the fear of accepting change. We face the fear of losing our power.
>
> Perhaps one of these simple questions might strike a fear in your heart: 1) Would you sell your house to a black family? 2) Would you let your daughter date or marry a black person? 3) Would you marry a black person yourself? 4) Would you bus your children to an all-black school? 5) Would you be offended if you saw a black person touch a white person on a TV show? 6) Would you vote for a black man as mayor of your city? 7) Would you call a black

man as a pastor of your church? 8) Would you go to see a black dentist? What are the fears ... How can we as a congregation deal with them?[27]

The following week, Rev. Robert Hare, pastor of the Church of Reconciliation – an experimental integrated Presbyterian church located in University Circle – preached on the Black Manifesto. When an African-American man in African dress stood to recite it, according to Rev. Edwards, he "scared everyone out of their minds. Trustees were ready to close the church, feeling no one would ever support it again."[28]

Racial tension and awakening continued a week later when the Session held a previously scheduled joint meeting with ten elders from Glenville Presbyterian Church to discuss an upcoming joint communion service. A Forest Hill elder proposed withholding publicity for the integrated event until after the church's fundraising campaign. According to Edwards, "all hell broke loose right there in the meeting." The ensuing conversation resulted in maintaining the service as scheduled.[29]

For the final sermon in the "Change" series, Rev. Edwards told the story of this emotional meeting of the two Sessions and invited the congregation to role-play how they would have handled the situation. It ended in a creative discussion in the sanctuary that inspired Edwards to rethink his future: "I'm almost tempted to stay here."[30]

Rev. Edwards' resignation took effect at the end of May 1970. The Pulpit Committee surprised the skeptical pastor and recommended him for the senior position. The congregation met on June 7, 1970, to vote on the recommendation. Many inactive members participated, and the divided membership voted 436 in favor and 288 against. Because the vote was not unanimous, the Presbytery intervened to investigate the division. Six weeks later, the Presbytery voted to hire Rev. Edwards. Two members of the Session and 100 church members resigned in protest.

As assistant pastor, Edwards had pressed the congregation to grapple with racism and housing integration. Obviously, not everyone fully embraced this agenda. While the vote was about hiring Rev. Edwards, he interpreted it as "a referendum on the position of the church on fair housing."[31]

The leadership transition had not been a smooth one, and it was hard on the congregation. In remarks given at the 63rd annual meeting on January 18, 1971, elder Edward Macke, Jr., chairman of the Board of Worship, commented on the contentious transition that had dominated the previous year, observing, "We came into 1970 with anxiety, fear, and trepidation and now, happily, we put it behind us with a sense of tremendous confidence and optimistic anticipation for the future."[32] His comment amounted to an endorsement of the new senior pastor, Rev. Edwards.

### Founding the Forest Hill Church Housing Corporation

The Board of Church and Society planned a third education series for spring 1971. It featured mayors from East Cleveland, Cleveland Heights, and South Euclid who talked about housing and racial change.

Like many of her colleagues who had been affected by the church's educational activities to promote support for racial justice, program planner Diana Woodbridge observed, "We were tired of educating people, and ready to take action." This series was designed to end with an action plan. It worked. By June, the housing subcommittee of the Board of Church and Society had a plan.

At the June 28, 1971 Session meeting, elder Charles Ault, speaking on behalf of the housing subgroup, proposed that the church sponsor a new nonprofit organization to address housing rehabilitation needs in the community. Church leaders agreed. Ault returned on September 27 with specific plans for the Forest Hill Church Housing Corporation and requested a $5,000 loan to "carry out the purposes" of the organization. The idea again won support. Within days, Margery Phillips, Diana Woodbridge, James Murphy, and Charles Ault filed the papers to incorporate the new housing resource. The full board, that included Don Head, Dr. Dan Phillips, David Hunter, Nancy Shrader, and Julie Clement, met for the first time on September 30, 1971.[33]

Fear of deteriorating neighborhoods and housing values was frequently expressed in informal discussions of racial change. For Diana Woodbridge, a conversation with an elderly neighbor on Cambridge Road clarified the importance of addressing home maintenance. The neighbor was not concerned about racial change as long as the new owners maintained their property. This concern for housing maintenance was well placed since most of the housing stock in Cleveland Heights was 40 to 60 years old, well-worn, and likely in need of repair.

A stable community depended on maintaining these aging properties.

This could be especially challenging for inexperienced, first-time homebuyers who could not spot problems and did not budget for repairs. Discrimination amplified this challenge because many African Americans were denied credit and bought their homes with cash, limiting funds to make repairs.

New homeowners in Cleveland Heights were especially vulnerable. The City's lack of inspection requirements meant sellers could cover up repair problems and pass them on to unsuspecting buyers, many of whom did not plan for those expenses. For example, Diana Woodbridge inspected a home where holes in the walls had been covered with wall paper and old plumbing was made to look new with silver paint.

The four activists who launched the Housing Corporation to address these challenges were an interesting combination of youthful idealistic energy and experienced church leaders. Both qualities were needed to make the effort a success.

Passion for change came from two young women, Margery Phillips and Diana Woodbridge. Phillips was an advocate for integration and low-income housing, two issues that would disrupt the community's identity as an elite white suburb. She was active with Heights Citizens for Human Rights and led a committee that pushed for a controversial proposal to permit public housing in Cleveland Heights. In 1972, Phillips was elected to the Session. The next year Woodbridge joined the governing board.

Woodbridge had joined the church in 1968 looking for a good home for her faith-driven idealism. A young parent and former teacher, Woodbridge served as a checker with Suburban Citizens for Open Housing and witnessed discrimination up close as a young black woman was denied access to the same apartment offered to Woodbridge. The experience inspired her fair housing activism. She was also deeply affected by the presenters in the change series, especially the minister who talked about the role of individuals. It made her believe she could make a difference. Phillips and Woodbridge, who were among a handful of women to serve as elders, became close friends and effective collaborators in moving the church's housing strategy forward.

Essential expertise and experience came from two highly respected congregation leaders, Charles Ault and Jim Murphy. Ault, a mentor to Woodbridge, was elected elder in 1971 and chaired the Board of Church and Society. He was the church's attorney and treasurer, a resident of

Brewster Road in East Cleveland, a member of the Forest Hill Homeowners Association, a conservative Republican, and a committed social activist. He understood the threat to housing values and the reality of unstable integration. He had standing in the congregation and the community, as well as substantial legal expertise.

Jim Murphy was an accountant and a resident of the Oxford neighborhood, one of the last parts of the city to integrate. A committed and active church member, he brought standing in the congregation and essential financial expertise to the project. His wife Chichi was the activist in the family and a member of the Board of Church and Society that proposed the housing project. She convinced Murphy to help.

To get started, the Housing Corporation participated in HUD's 235 program which gave qualified buyers (those a bank had certified as having adequate financial means to purchase a home) ownership of an affordable and desirable rehabilitated house. FHCHC planned to renovate and sell ten homes. They had $5,000 to invest in purchasing and upgrading their first property, a duplex on North Taylor Road that they returned to single-family use. Working from her living room as a volunteer, Woodbridge led the project.

The team was not experienced at housing renovation and set a high bar for the quality of repairs. They paid too much for the property and seriously underestimated the renovation costs. "We lost our shirts," remembers Woodbridge.[34] To close the gap between available funds and the repair needs, crews of church members volunteered their time. The hands-on involvement gave them concrete ways to support the community and turned an otherwise difficult first venture into a success. The volunteers took pride in providing the new owners with quality housing in a community with a high quality of life.

After this initial sale, some members of the Forest Hill Homeowners Association expressed concern about who might move into their neighborhood. Woodbridge remembers a meeting convened by Ault to explain the program to his doubtful neighbors. "I was terrified. Racism was alive," she remembers as Ault patiently explained to attendees that FHCHC would only sell to qualified buyers.

In 1973, the federal government ended the program, and the Housing Corporation then embarked on its signature strategy – providing mortgage guarantees so people who had difficulty obtaining credit could finance essential home repairs. Forest Hill Church contributed $500 to a new revolving loan fund to be used by the Housing Corporation to support homeowners, and challenged 30 other Cleveland Heights congregations and organizations to match their gift. The Housing Corporation reached the goal within a year and made the first loan in 1974. The fund was named the Challenge Fund, and subsequent contributions from the Cleveland Foundation and other donors created a $180,000 fund that is still in use today.[35]

Charles Ault, who as the church's treasurer knew the vice president of Cleveland Trust, negotiated with the Cleveland Heights branch manager to be the Housing Corporation's partner.[36] As a result, the local branch agreed to administer the loan program. FHCHC volunteers then worked closely with homeowners to define essential repairs and establish an affordable budget. The fund was used to guarantee 40% of the loan amount needed to complete the repairs. If the owner defaulted, the fund would pay back the bank. By guaranteeing the loan and reducing the risk to lenders, this program helped homeowners overcome disqualifying restrictions such as no credit history, limited equity, or unstable income. It gave new owners access to funds and made them responsible for repaying the loans.

Inauspiciously, the first loan ended in default, and the Corporation paid off the debt. However, after that, defaults were unusual because loans were carefully crafted to be affordable, and the homeowners were anxious to follow through in good faith because of the faith that was extended to them.

Once Cleveland Heights adopted its home inspection program in 1976 and started to enforce housing code violations, it created a steady supply of homeowners needing help. The Challenge Fund became an essential resource to help homeowners comply with court-ordered home repairs that also added value to their neighborhoods and stability to the community.

The Forest Hill Church Housing Corporation was independent of the church that founded it. In 1976, it opened an office in the Heights Rockefeller Building, and in 1977, hired Diana Woodbridge as the first paid staff member. Its impact grew in 1978 with the award of its first Community Development Block Grant allocation from the City of Cleveland Heights. In 2000, it was rebranded as the Home Repair Resource Center. In 2012, this enduring community resource celebrated 40 years of "keeping Cleveland Heights in good repair."

**Forest Hill Church Engages with the Community**

As the challenges of stable integration became more obvious, Forest Hill Church reached out to other religious congregations based in Cleveland Heights to create joint initiatives to address racial change. Rev. Edwards was instrumental in founding the Heights Interfaith Council. The church hosted a film festival and musical celebration on January 22, 1973, to celebrate Dr. King. In September and October 1974, they co-sponsored with First Baptist Church, Park and Taylor Road synagogues, and St. Louis and St. Ann Catholic churches a four-part series on human relations. Experts employed by the school district led the training. The event was promoted as an opportunity for ecumenical action and a "unique opportunity for communication across traditional religious boundaries."[37]

The Forest Hill Church congregation continued to aggressively address difficult issues including low-income housing and equal opportunity employment within the church and the businesses it patronized. The 1976 education series focused on "What Does It Mean to Be Moral." Members examined the meaning of church teachings in relation to school desegregation, open housing, and other issues. That year the congregation made a commitment to support peaceful school desegregation in Cleveland.

For Rev. Edwards, the civil rights era at Forest Hill Church was a challenging highpoint of his career:

> We had a righteous cause in civil rights and fair housing, and we had a team in the church that was committed to sticking with these issues. The challenge was always to deal with controversy over these things by listening to and understanding those who disagreed with these progressive steps.[38]

As Cleveland Heights was transformed by racial change, so was Forest Hill Church. Through its intensive exploration of its role in racial justice between 1964 and 1976, it helped defeat the narrative that integration could not be sustained. It emerged as a community resource for human needs and stable integration; a proactive agent for reconciliation, individual growth, and ecumenical action; and a magnet for those seeking a religious community where social issues were paramount.

# DIANA WOODBRIDGE

AS A MEMBER OF FOREST HILL
CHURCH, DIANA WOODBRIDGE
LOBBIED FOR THE CONGREGATION
TO SUPPORT THE FOREST HILL
CHURCH HOUSING CORPORATION,
AND THEN SERVED AS ITS
EXECUTIVE DIRECTOR FOR 35 YEARS.
(HOME REPAIR RESOURCE CENTER)

*In 1966, Shaker Heights native Diana Woodbridge and her young family moved to the Oxford neighborhood of Cleveland Heights from Painesville. In 1968 she volunteered as a checker for Suburban Citizens for Open Housing and witnessed discrimination firsthand. This transformative experience made fair housing her passion.*

*In 1968 she took another formative step: she joined Forest Hill Church. The congregation provided a long-term home for her faith, a religious doctrine that supports social justice, a community with which to develop her understanding of race and discrimination, and a platform for creating change. Both Forest Hill Church and fair housing remain her focus.*

*As a new church member, Diana was deeply affected by the adult education activities designed to transform members' thinking about race. She was among a small group within the congregation who designed and garnered church support for creating the Forest Hill Church Housing Corporation. She then joined six other church members to incorporate the new nonprofit organization. Her leadership continued as a board member and board chair, and then for 35 years, she implemented its programs as its first executive director. She retired in 2006.*

*Now operating as the Home Repair Resource Center, the organization has never strayed from its initial mission: to help keep Cleveland Heights in good repair in support of its diversity. It is one of the oldest nonprofits in the community and an essential resource for community stability.*

*In addition to the social activism centered at Forest Hill, Diana became an important church leader. She was among the first women to serve on the Session, the governing body for the congregation, and then as the Clerk of Session.*

*Woodbridge recognized that the community would always be vulnerable to resegregation, and that constant vigilance was required. She remained vigilant by serving on the Cleveland Heights Planning Commission and the housing advisory committee. As a member of Greater Cleveland Congregations she and a team of other citizen housing experts, including Kermit Lind, have pushed lenders to invest in properties in the Noble Neighborhood, a part of Cleveland Heights that the 2008 foreclosure crisis hit especially hard.*

THE WOODBRIDGE FAMILY MOVED TO 917 CAMBRIDGE ROAD IN 1966. (SUSAN KAESER)

# REV. NED EDWARDS

REV. NEW EDWARDS JOINED THE FOREST HILL CHURCH STAFF IN 1963 AND BECAME THE SENIOR PASTOR IN 1970. HE WAS A DRIVING FORCE IN BUILDING THE CONGREGATION'S RACIAL AWARENESS AND COMMITMENT TO INTEGRATION AND SOCIAL JUSTICE. (FOREST HILL CHURCH)

*Rev. Ned Edwards and Rev. Bruce Klunder were classmates at Yale Divinity School, became Presbyterian ministers, and moved to Cleveland Heights. These close friends were part of a generation of young idealists who challenged the status quo and helped their own denomination become more relevant in relation to social injustices.*

*As the staff person for the Center for Christian Life for college students at University Circle, Rev. Klunder helped students explore ethical questions and find ways to create change. He also held a leadership position in the Congress of Racial Equality (CORE) and was active in the forefront of the Cleveland school crisis. He became a martyr to the cause when killed at age 27 while trying to stop the construction of a school during a protest.*

*Deeply affected by Klunder's death, Edwards developed a new resolve to confront racial injustice. He encouraged change by challenging the members of his congregation.*

*As the minister in charge of Christian Education at Forest Hill Church, Presbyterian, and later as senior pastor, he introduced fresh ideas which produced some discomfort in many members of this traditional, upper middle-class congregation. In pressuring his congregation to grapple with racism and inequality, he and other young members of the church created a microcosm of the situation facing Cleveland Heights as a whole. This caused some members to leave the church, but most stayed, and embraced their responsibility for social justice and, ultimately, served as resources for their community.*

*By engaging members in this learning process in the safe confines of a religious community, Edwards found an untapped reservoir of good will and helped the congregation members redirect their religious commitment toward social justice and a strong, integrated community.*

*In making social justice a centerpiece of the congregation's mission, the members recognized the difficulty some citizens faced in maintaining the aging housing stock. As a result, they designed a new organization to address this issue and gained church support to launch it – the Forest Hill Church Housing Corporation. Today, this nonprofit organization is one of the oldest and most effective community-based organizations in Cleveland Heights. It has had a powerful effect on the city's stability by making it possible for more residents to keep their homes in good condition.*

*In its first 40 years, FHCHC renovated nine homes, made more than 1,200 repair loans, educated residents through more than 1,400 repair workshops, held 161 home buyer education workshops, and counseled more than 600 people facing foreclosure. Thousands of homeowners have made repairs costing millions of dollars through the assistance of this organization. Its work continues to be beneficial to the community today.*

*Edwards arrived in Cleveland Heights in 1963, unaware of the racial tension bubbling in the community as a result of integration. He forcefully addressed this tension, riding the wave of conflict, and for over 29 years led the congregation in its role as a community resource. In 1992, Edwards retired and returned to his home state of Michigan. He was succeeded by Rev. Dr. John Lentz who, like Edwards, has been a long-time leader and innovator as the church has worked to maintain its principles.*

*Race remains a central concern for the church. Recently, Forest Hill has become not just a congregation that values integration, but an integrated congregation itself. It now has a black caucus and engages in ongoing education related to race. In 2019, the congregation took another step toward racial equality, and hired an African-American woman, Rev. Dr. Veronica Goines, to share the senior pastor position with Dr. Lentz.*

REV. EDWARDS AND HIS FAMILY MOVED TO 3904 ORCHARD ROAD IN 1963. (SUSAN KAESER)

CLEVELAND HEIGHTS PRESBYTERIAN CHURCH CHANGED ITS NAME TO FOREST HILL CHURCH, PRESBYTERIAN IN 1950 WHEN IT BROKE GROUND FOR ITS NEW HOME AT 3031 MONTICELLO BOULEVARD IN THE FOREST HILL NEIGHBORHOOD. (SUSAN KAESER)

JOHN D. ROCKEFELLER, JR. USED DEED RESTRICTIONS TO CONTROL WHO COULD OWN A HOME IN THE FOREST HILL DEVELOPMENT, HIS NEW PLANNED COMMUNITY. CONSTRUCTION OF THE FIRST 81 HOMES BEGAN IN 1929. (SUSAN KAESER)

CLEVELAND TRUST BANK MANAGER ED PAUL (LEFT) ADMINISTERED THE CHALLENGE FUND. HE IS PICTURED WITH FOREST HILL CHURCH HOUSING CORPORATION ACTIVISTS BETSY ANDREWS AND RICHARD OBERMANNS. (HOME REPAIR RESOURCE CENTER)

FHCHC USED THIS MODEL HOUSE TO PROMOTE THE CHALLENGE FUND, A SIGNATURE PROGRAM THAT SINCE ITS INCEPTION HAS HELPED HOMEOWNERS FINANCE CRITICAL HOME REPAIRS. (HOME REPAIR RESOURCE CENTER)

THE HOUSING CORPORATION'S PROGRAMS EMPOWER HOMEOWNERS TO MAINTAIN THEIR PROPERTY.
(HOME REPAIR RESOURCE CENTER ARCHIVES)

THESE FHCHC BOARD PRESIDENTS GATHERED IN 2001 TO CELEBRATE THE ORGANIZATION'S 30TH ANNIVERSARY.
FROM LEFT, JONATHAN BUCHTER, TOM BIER, DIANA WOODBRIDGE, RICHARD OBERMANNS, DEAN SIECK, AND CHARLES AULT.
THE ORGANIZATION'S MISSION HAS NEVER CHANGED. (DIANA WOODBRIDGE)

FOREST HILL CHURCH ELDER CHARLES AULT LIVED AT 15681 BREWSTER ROAD IN THIS EAST CLEVELAND HOME BUILT AS PART OF ROCKEFELLER'S FOREST HILL DEVELOPMENT. HIS STATURE IN THE FOREST HILL CONGREGATION WAS IMPORTANT TO ADVANCING THE HOUSING CORPORATION. (SUSAN KAESER)

# CHAPTER 6

# AFRICAN AMERICANS LEAD THE WAY

Integration would not have existed in Cleveland Heights without African-American pioneers who were willing to take personal risks to settle in a white community that was not always welcoming. And Cleveland Heights would have fallen short as an inclusive community without the activism and leadership of its new black residents.

African Americans did not move to the suburbs to be treated as second-class citizens. They were ready to advocate for their own interests, and they played a crucial role in transforming this white community into a place that made meaningful progress toward racial inclusion. Their leadership helped make integration beneficial to the diverse residents of Cleveland Heights – both black and white.

Even if white residents accepted racial change as a good idea, the reality of integration was rarely comfortable or natural for people accustomed to one-race living. All-white city government and public schools were inexperienced in serving a diverse population. Racial conflict and tension were common and often exposed new black residents to insensitivity and prejudice. Stereotypes thwarted acceptance. Black residents often found themselves in the awkward position of educating whites and challenging their perceptions.

Not only did neighbors and classmates have to learn how to share their community and its opportunities, so did the police and the public schools. Individual and institutional responses were clouded by stereotypes and revealed ignorance, insensitivity, and hurtful racism.

To address these issues, African-American residents of Cleveland Heights joined together in 1970 to create the Committee to Improve Community Relations (CICR), and through this organization made a significant impact on City and school district practices. CICR existed to confront mistreatment and build acceptance as community members. In so doing, they earned respect as concerned and capable citizens.

Involvement and activism were essential to achieving the goals of the CICR: these goals were not something sympathetic white activists could secure for them. They advocated for themselves with skill, diplomacy, persistence, and effect. As Betty Nelson, a CICR member who moved to Cleveland Heights in 1971 put it, "The way to get respect is to demand it."[1] They did.

In an article reminding CICR members of the need to be involved, Carl Campbell, long-time editor of the organization's newsletter, reminded other African-American community members that involvement was essential.

Since the presumption is that most of us moved here to improve our 'quality of life, quality of education and all the good things,' because it was an improvement over what we left – the logic then is how does a community retain these qualities if those moving in are not going to participate in its welfare? If our attitude is to 'leave it to the white folks' and everything will be hunky dory. Right? – Wrong![2]

## CICR Confronts Mistreatment

Racial change was disruptive. Racial prejudice drove segregation, and as the community integrated, it prompted harassment of African-American transplants. In addition to the highly visible and soundly rebuked acts of violence directed against African-American homeowners, they were subjected to passers-by littering on their lawns, cross burnings, petty vandalism, and social snubs.

Black youth were frequent targets of harassment and physical threats from peers and police. For example, in 1971 a carload of menacing white youths chased a child walking to Roxboro school, and a garbage worker wielding a screw driver and shouting profanities attacked the daughter of CICR founders Doris and Wendell Allen as she walked home with two white friends. Carl and Maryann Campbell's children were harassed by police while walking on the street where they lived. White neighbors were quick to call the police if they had a complaint rather than talk directly to the adults or children whose presence bothered them. On one occasion, police were called about a black eight-year-old carrying a comb.[3]

In summer 1970, white teens carrying baseball bats and metal pipes harassed black youths at the Heights YMCA/YWCA on Lee Road. The police sent the perpetrators home with only a mild reprimand. Staff member Doris Allen, who witnessed the event, found the police response unacceptable. That evening, three black couples who were neighbors on Lee Road met at the home of Bernice and Lacy Lott to formulate a response. They agreed to create a new organization to hold public institutions accountable. This was the origin of the Committee to Improve Community Relations.

It is ironic that six years earlier, at the founding meeting of HCHR's Neighborhood Committee, Ralph Brody expressed concern about the possibility of a "ghettoized" neighborhood forming on Lee Road between Mayfield and Somerton Road because of a "concentration of Negro families." He was referring to Bernice and Lacy Lott, Doris and Wendell Allen, and Delores and Cornelius Edwards, the founders of CICR and the nucleus of black civic leadership in Cleveland Heights.

These three couples participated both in HCHR and its integration-oriented activities, and CICR, the organization they created to advance the concerns of black parents. They understood that it would take more than a Cleveland Heights address to provide the full benefits of suburban living. They, therefore, focused on securing the quality of life that motivated their move to the suburbs.

Doris and Wendell Allen bought their home at 1724 Lee Road in 1964. He was a postal worker and she directed youth programs at the Heights YMCA/YWCA where her mentor, Bernice Lott, chaired the board. Doris grew up in the Glenville neighborhood of Cleveland when it was integrated, and enjoyed the ease of connections across racial and religious distinctions. She was attracted to Cleveland Heights for the chance to repeat this. Wendell served as HCHR's treasurer from 1966 through 1970 and was the vice president for membership in 1972. He was a mentor to white HCHR activists like Margery Phillips. This activist couple frequently hosted soirees and other HCHR events.

The Allen family moved to Lee Road to take advantage of the Cleveland Heights amenities: good schools, recreation facilities, and community safety that were the hallmarks of suburban living. Doris Allen expected, "to be comfortable, accepted and involved."[4]

Bernice and Lacy Lott, owners of Lott Construction, moved to 1692 Lee Road in 1962. By 1965, Bernice was an officer in Heights Citizens for Human Rights, and over the years, she filled nearly every leadership role in the open housing organization from newsletter editor to community education chair to vice president. She was also active in the PTA of each school the Lott children attended, along with the Urban League. In addition, she was among the community leaders who in 1973 helped shape the Heights Community Congress (see Chapter 8). She was appointed to a position on the Board of Education in 1974, becoming Cleveland Heights' first African-American public official. She then won an election for the board in 1975 and in 1977 was elected president.[5]

Cornelius Edwards, another postal worker, and his wife Delores and family lived at 1687 Lee Road. He was CICR's president for most of its first decade and penned many of the organization's gracious letters to the police and school district outlining concerns and asking for assurances of proper treatment and fair solutions. He recruited another postal worker, Carl Campbell and his wife Mary Anne, to the CICR cause. In 1973, Edwards became a founding trustee of the Heights Community Congress.

On February 14, 1971, the founders of the Committee to Improve Community Relations adopted a structure and elected officers. The leadership came from the three founding couples, and two other neighbors on Whitethorn Road, John Maddox and Jean Pattillo. They also recruited Matt Smith, William Robinson, and Madelyn Blunt. Al Cunningham, who at the time was president of Heights Citizens for Human Rights, was appointed the public relations chair and spokesperson for the organization.

They named the group the Committee to Improve Community Relations and while focused on the concerns of black parents, chose not to use those terms in the organization's name because, "although we find it necessary to be a black group initially, at some point we may wish to open membership to others."[6]

The group's promotional brochure explained why it needed to be a purely black organization: "not as a separatist organization to exclude whites, but specifically formed to speak directly to Black people's concerns." It offered this philosophical rationale: "Historically, Black people have been dysfunctional as a united group of people. We of CICR believe that this disunity and fragmentation can no longer be tolerated if we expect to be a force that is to be reckoned with in this community."[7]

Working together was critical to making the greater community work for them. They reached out to other black families and invited them to join if they wanted to eliminate racism, identify and address racial injustice, and create a climate that "assures that all children are treated with equality and dignity." They planned to bring together other concerned citizens and "enlighten, educate, and inform on current situations, so we may move effectively in the total community."[8] They met monthly on Sunday evenings at Heights Presbyterian Church on Washington Boulevard and hoped to form a junior group for high school students.

CICR bylaws established standing committees to address their concerns and advocate for their interests as citizens of Cleveland Heights. The Safety and Council Committee scrutinized safety forces and attended city council meetings. The Education Committee monitored the board of education and organized educational programs for members about schools, government, and the political process. The Scholarship Committee granted financial aid to high school graduates. The Social and Program group planned social events which were important for fundraising and community building.

Cornelius Edwards filed incorporation papers for the two-year-old group on July 28, 1973. The other incorporators were John Maddox, Doris Allen, Charles Matthews, Bernice Lott, and Eleanor Barrett. The organization was granted nonprofit status the next month. Within a year, they had 300 members. The 1975 recruiting flyer captured their agenda: "If you feel concerned about the quality of life, the quality of education, quality of civic involvement, quality of Black pride, Black awareness, Black respect, friendship, and fellowship, if you feel a commitment to this kind of effort... we welcome you to CICR."[9]

**Involvement is Essential to Inclusion**

Carl Campbell and his wife Mary Ann and their five children moved to Antisdale Road in 1969 from Cleveland, looking for what he described as the "good things" available in Cleveland Heights. Carl embraced involvement: "To get what you want you must be involved day in and day out." He worked nights so he could be available at all times to advocate for his children. He and his wife "wanted to make sure our children had every advantage every other child had."[10]

Campbell took his first step as an activist during the family's first week in the community. When they enrolled their gifted daughter in elementary school, she was not assigned to the gifted class. Campbell noted that the school wrongly assumed that "if you come from Cleveland you must be a low performer. We had to fix that right away."[11]

As CICR's long-time newsletter editor, Campbell frequently opined on the need to be involved. After low voter turnout resulted in the defeat of a school levy, he wrote:

What are we going to do to keep this community our kind of community? We are going to register – vote – and we are going to be involved in every facet pertaining to Cleveland Heights-University Heights, and its whole school district . . . Don't let Rosa (Parks) down.[12]

In 1977 he reiterated the need for blacks to take action:

Something that Black folk and white . . . but especially Blacks must constantly be aware of is that we cannot afford to take white people for granted. That is, to assume that if everything is left up to them, they'll take care of us Black people. Staying on their backs keeps them on their toes and causes them to do a better job.[13]

Since it was easy to discount and ignore those who were not visible, showing up was a very important part of black citizen activism. By being visible and present, they could witness how the system was treating people, advocate for their concerns, and demonstrate that they were citizens too. "We were fighting so many stereotypes," recalls CICR founder Doris Allen, "and that required a strategic approach."[14]

Their strategy included an emergency phone network that could turn out ten black men in ten minutes. Their presence could not only quell a conflict, but it fought stereotypes of the uninvolved black father, the idea that all black families were single-parent households, and the assumption that if you were black, you were poor and disengaged.

To fight black male stereotypes, they made a point of electing black men as leaders. Cornelius Edwards led the organization for at least six years and was followed by Hilton Smith, William Smith, Century Prince, and Rev. William Dockens. Mary Ann Campbell and Beverly Harrison – the last president and the second generation in her family to serve in that role – were among a handful of women who served as president.

CICR members were particularly concerned about how the police treated their children. Prompted by frequent incidents of police harassment of black youth and negative treatment when called for help, Cornelius Edwards sent a letter to the Cleveland Heights chief of police in June 1971. The letter described a series of incidents "with racial overtones" when the police response was unsatisfactory. One example was the discourteous response of an annoyed police officer when the principal of Roosevelt Junior High called for help to diffuse a tense situation. After detailing the infractions, the letter concludes: "It had been assumed that any call for assistance was worthy and completely within reasonable expectations. We would like to receive from you the assurance that if the Police are called, they will respond in a responsible manner."[15]

Letters were followed with calls and meetings. Doris Allen recalls multiple meetings with the police at city hall and in her living room. Detective Martin Lentz, who later became chief of police, regularly met with the group as they pushed for fair treatment, made the case for better police training, and encouraged the hiring of non-white police officers. Black parents also tried to protect their children by teaching them how to react when stopped by the police: note the badge number and the time. CICR worked through channels to create change. Their language was diplomatic and respectful. The group prided itself in identifying concerns and bringing them to the attention of the appropriate authorities, and then always offering solutions. Matt Smith, chair of the education committee, summed up their approach this way:

As responsible black citizens in this community we have from time to time spoken out regarding what we felt to be inequalities.

We have not criticized without offering an alternative plan, nor have we made ourselves unavailable. While CICR has been most militant in some respects, we nevertheless are cooperative in every respect when it comes to community involvement.[16]

The organization was vocal, constructive, and persistent. Because members were engaged, they formed relationships with elected officials and the staff of the schools and city government. This earned them respect and access, and produced solutions.

## Advocacy Creates Institutional Changes at Heights High

Racial tension, a predicted outcome of racial integration, existed in the schools, and on occasion, erupted in fights. A serious incident took place at Heights High School on January 28, 1972, when a number of violent skirmishes took place after school. Initial news coverage called it a race riot. One account reported seven black and white students had injuries that required treatment. Among them was William Allen, who was attacked by boys carrying chains and metal bars. His mother, CICR leader Doris Allen, called a meeting for parents and administrators the following day at the Heights YMCA/YWCA.[17] The incident provided an opportunity for CICR and the community to address racism, discomfort with racial change, and ways to make the public schools equitable for all participants. It was a catalyst for the founding of the Heights Community Congress.

In 1974, black students at Heights High School started a crusade to transform their educational experience. They believed the high school was Eurocentric in its curriculum and often unfair in its treatment of African-American students. On March 11, 1974, the Cleveland Public Schools closed for Black Achievement Day. This caught the interest of black Heights students, a growing presence in the mostly Jewish high school.

Heights High had traditionally closed for two Jewish holidays and Christmas. Over the next few weeks, the students called for a Black Achievement Day and formulated a longer list of concerns that they presented to the Board of Education: the small number of minority teachers, the absence of a black point of view in the curriculum, a discriminatory suspension policy, a lack of counseling support, and the unchecked racist behavior and derogatory language of white staffers.[18]

CICR supported the high school students and urged them to work through the system. After identifying their concerns, 35 students accompanied by Cornelius Edwards and other adult observers met with Superintendent David Moberly who agreed to talk with his staff and follow up with representatives of the group. He thought in-service training, which was scheduled to begin that fall, would address some of their concerns.[19] Carl Campbell noted in a newspaper interview that Superintendent Moberly had been sympathetic but failed to take action. On June 10, about 65 CICR members demonstrated outside the Board of Education office before expressing their demands at the Board meeting. In response, the Board called a special meeting for June 17 and invited a representative group of youth and adults to attend. In other business that night, they approved the school district calendar for the next year but did not include the request for a Martin Luther King, Jr. holiday.[20]

Heights High student Terri Gilliam charged that resistance to creating a day to honor Dr. King was part of institutional racism at the school. Another student, Lincoln Scott, said, "black students were being denied their personhood."[21] As a follow-up, the Board of Education sent CICR a letter notifying them that it would provide a written response to their concerns by July 15. The July CICR newsletter noted, "We think this is positive, and we look forward to hearing from them."

The Board of Education kept its commitment, but CICR leaders were not satisfied with the report and sent a four-page letter to Board President Nelson Weiss expressing their disappointment. The letter, dated July 26, 1974, and signed by Chairman Cornelius Edwards, asked for an executive session with members of the Board because, as he stated, "our purpose is not to inflame or encourage public opinion, but to convey to you our honest reactions." The letter continues:

> We know we have some strong statements to make, but we do not wish to make them in a circus atmosphere. It is not our purpose to make headlines. We wish to make progress.

> Our original demonstration was held because black youngsters, whom we had advised to go through channels and use accepted forms of request had been so terribly dejected by the reception they had received from the Administration.

As adults and parents, we can relate to their feelings of frustration and rejection. As adults and parents, we also feel conscience-bound to relate to you our feelings of impending hostilities. We do not wish to see another violent confrontation at the high school. Unfortunately, piecemeal answers from the Board have left the black community in the position of either seeking clarification or going elsewhere for justice.

Doris Allen recalls that their threat to go elsewhere was a bluff. But in October 1974, CICR filed a complaint with the U.S. Department of Justice charging discrimination due to unmet needs of black students. Much to their surprise, they prevailed. The Department of Justice appointed Jesse Taylor from the Community Relations Service as the mediator to work with representatives of the Board of Education and CICR to resolve the complaint. The first of three meetings was held January 14, 1975. On April 1, Harvey Feinberg, President of the CH-UH Board of Education and Cornelius Edwards, Chairman of CICR, signed a consent decree that resolved all seven demands.[22]

After nearly a decade of racial change, the agreement provided the school district with a focused and comprehensive plan for becoming more inclusive. The seven provisions of the agreement validated student demands and CICR's concerns, and set the district on a path that made it more responsive to a racially diverse student body.

The agreement guaranteed community input on an updated guidance program and the rewriting of the high school American History course to include the historical and cultural contributions of African Americans. The district agreed to add a Martin Luther King, Jr. commemorative holiday to the school calendar beginning in the 1975-76 school year. They also agreed to a process for the administration to investigate allegations of racist behavior and a commitment to follow the District's newly adopted discipline procedures.[23]

One of the most enduring achievements was the requirement to hire minority teachers and administrators with a specific goal that by 1980, minorities would account for 15% of certificated staff. A letter to the editor from two community members, Barry and Eva Sands, that appeared in the April 10, 1975 *Sun Press* demonstrates that not everyone welcomed this affirmative hiring goal:

We don't know who comprises the Committee to Improve Community Relations, but we are shocked at their demands; and even more shocked at the Cleveland Heights-University Heights School Board to give in to them!

So 15 per cent of the teachers and administrators of the school system must be black to combat racism! That's strange! To us it sounds like the purest racism that dictates what color a person must be to teach.

The *Call and Post* offered a different view in their April 12 edition. In a column titled "Step in the Right Direction," they commended the school district for helping fashion a positive agreement and gave credit to black parents for pushing for change:

Results can be achieved when concerned parents subscribe to meaningful and realistic goals, and bring the full strength of organization into the fight. Another lesson, however obscure it may be to school officials in other suburban areas, is that sooner or later they are going to have to deal with determined black parents who will settle for nothing less than the best in education for their children.

Starting in the fall 1975, two CICR representatives, Mary Ann Campbell and Cornelius Edwards, began to meet monthly with the superintendent and his staff to "stay appraised of all the communications and information that the community should be aware of."[24] These meetings were referred to as Neighbors and Educators Together, and Carl Campbell felt that they were in some ways welcomed by district personnel. Neighbors and Educators Together gave school leaders an identifiable group of black parents to work with as they addressed real issues. Campbell described some meetings as "getting a little hot," but felt school leaders embraced the chance for dialogue.[25]

At the time of the consent decree, 8.8% of the district's certificated staff members were minority. At the start of the 1980-81 school year, it was 12.9%, still short of the 15% goal. CICR and the Board returned to the negotiating table and the decree was revised, raising the goal to 20% and extending the deadline to 1985. The agreement signed by CICR chair Mary Ann Campbell and Board of Education president Ava Hastert added another powerful provision: starting in March 1982, the Board of Education and CICR would meet annually to "review the status of the provisions of this agreement."[26] The school district was now accountable to parents. This relationship continued at least through 1990.

In addition to advocating for fair treatment by City and school personnel, CICR provided direct support to youth and to each other. Members organized a number of social events and fundraisers including a gala at the Natural History Museum, a bowling tournament, and the sale of Bar-B-Q at the Cain Park Arts Festival to raise funds for college scholarships for African-American high school seniors. The scholarships, eventually named for Bernice and Lacy Lott, continued through 2007. Betty Nelson, CICR secretary, administered the scholarship program for more than 20 years.

In 1973, after the founding of a new integration advocacy organization, the Heights Community Congress, CICR and the Congress collaborated on several initiatives. The two organizations co-sponsored events to improve race relations and facilitate a black communication network to enhance black involvement and power in the community. CICR was also the source of volunteers for the HCC's fair housing programs. Several CICR members, including Cornelius Edwards and Lacy and Bernice Lott, served on the Congress board representing black community organizations.

The founding members of CICR remained involved for more than two decades. Unfortunately, they had difficulty recruiting new leadership and while the scholarship program continued until 2007, their activism ended in the 1990s. Black leaders who came to the fore through this organization, like so many of the activists who shaped the community during the civil rights era, were in it for the long haul and continued to find ways to contribute to making Cleveland Heights a viable, integrated community.

# BERNICE LOTT

IN 1974 BERNICE LOTT WAS APPOINTED TO THE CLEVELAND HEIGHTS-UNIVERSITY HEIGHTS BOARD OF EDUCATION AND BECAME THE FIRST AFRICAN AMERICAN TO HOLD PUBLIC OFFICE IN CLEVELAND HEIGHTS. (CLEVELAND STATE UNIVERSITY, CLEVELAND PRESS COLLECTION)

*Nearly everyone involved in the history of civil rights activities in Cleveland Heights knew Bernice Lott, respected her, and valued her leadership. She fervently embraced and promoted integration by connecting black and white activists and generously mentoring young leaders.*

*Early black integration pioneers Bernice Lott and her husband Lacy Lott moved from Glenville in 1962 to 1692 Lee Road in Cleveland Heights. They owned the Lott Construction Company and quickly became well connected with their neighbors and the community as a whole.*

*Bernice, a gracious and outgoing business woman, was an officer in Heights Citizens for Human Rights, co-founded the Committee to Improve Community Relations, and was a founding trustee of the Heights Community Congress. She served as the president of the board of the Cuyahoga Plan, the Heights YWCA, and several units of the local PTA.*

*She was also active with the League of Women Voters and the Urban League. According to her obituary, more than 25 civic groups in Cleveland Heights and in Cleveland benefitted from Lott's energy and involvement.*

*Lott was appointed to the Cleveland Heights – University Heights Board of Education in 1974, making her the first African-American public official to serve Cleveland Heights. Given her extensive civic engagement, she was an obvious choice. Lott was elected to a second term and served as board president, and finished her service in 1979. She died of cancer in October of 1983.*

*During Bernice Lott's service on the governing boards of the Heights Community Congree and the Cuyahoga Plan, Kermit Lind served as executive director. He described her as "a real hero who knew how to lead." He appreciated that she challenged opponents of integration "on the grounds that it was anti-black."*

*According to St. Ann Audit leader Sue Nigro, "everyone looked up to her." Joan Dowling described her as "dynamic." For Doris Allen, cofounder of CICR, her childhood friend and mentor was like family. Inspired by her civic leadership, the Heights Community Congress created the Bernice Lott Award to recognize the contributions of community leaders.*

BERNICE AND LACY LOTT MOVED TO 1692 LEE ROAD IN 1962. (SUSAN KAESER)

# DORIS ALLEN

WHEN WENDELL AND DORIS ALLEN MOVED TO CLEVELAND HEIGHTS IN 1964 THEY EXPECTED TO BE INVOLVED. THEIR FAMILY WAS A FREQUENT TARGET OF RACIST BEHAVIOR. (DORIS ALLEN)

*Doris Allen grew up in the Glenville neighborhood of Cleveland when it was still integrated. She recalls fond memories of walking in the street arm-in-arm with her white, Jewish, and black friends. The sound of morning prayers coming through the open doors of homes of Jewish families always moved her. So as a young married woman with two children, she wanted that same sort of childhood experience for her family.*

*In January of 1965, she and her husband Wendell, a postal worker, moved to Cleveland Heights from Shaker Heights, drawn to its religious and growing racial diversity. The young family's home, at 1724 Lee Road, was a few doors away from Bernice Lott, her childhood neighbor. Lott mentored and encouraged Allen as a youth in Cleveland and as an adult activist in Cleveland Heights.*

*Many groups invited Doris and Wendell Allen to*

*participate in their work. This pioneering black couple seized every opportunity to make integration work for themselves and for their community. As fearless advocates, they were frequent targets of white resistance and institutional racism. The police, white youths, and strangers harassed their children and threatened them. Hostile neighbors littered their yard and tossed stink bombs at their home. In one incident, a young man from the Murray Hill neighborhood threatened their daughter with a screw driver, ordering her to "go home and tell your parents to keep their mouths shut."*

*Undeterred, the Allens pressed for blacks to be able to use the community swimming pool, walk the streets freely, participate in various school activities, associate with white friends spontaneously, and experience the fair treatment that was their right. Whenever impeded from these activities, they took action.*

*As a high school student, Allen was a "Y Teen," and soon after moving to Cleveland Heights, Bernice Lott, president of the board of the Heights YWCA, encouraged her to volunteer at the local branch. In 1966, the YMCA hired her to be the organization's Youth Program Director, and she held the position until 1975. She attended the national meeting of the YWCA held in Houston in 1970. It was during this meeting that the group adopted its guiding imperative – to "eliminate racism."*

DORIS ALLEN WAS IN
CHARGE OF YOUTH
PROGRAMS AT THE
HEIGHTS YMCA.
(DORIS ALLEN)

*The "Y" put Allen in touch with other Clevelan*
*leaders who served on its board: Leslie Brooks W*
*became a federal judge; Mary Boyle, who becam*
*legislator; Joan Dowling, who helped create ..c.ynis*
*Citizens for Human Rights; and Sara Hunter, who became a*
*municipal court judge.*

*In 1970, Allen witnessed a group of white boys*
*assaulting African-American youths at the YMCA. She*
*was disturbed by what she thought was a tepid police*
*response to the violent encounter. Outraged, that evening*
*she and Bernice Lott called a meeting of their friends that*
*launched the Committee to Improve Community Relations.*
*She participated in the organization for the next 20 years,*
*and continued to confront the power structure when black*
*residents, and children in particular, were not well-served.*
*After the 1972 racial conflict at the high school, Allen called*
*the parent meeting to press for solutions.*

*Both Doris and Wendell were involved with other civil*
*rights groups. He served as treasurer for HCHR for seven*
*years and the couple hosted many meetings and parties for*
*the organization. During a period when the Allen family*
*was being harassed, HCHR members held an all-night*
*vigil in their home. In 1972, they were paired with Jeanne*
*Martin and her husband as checkers for the St. Ann Audit.*
*The couple continued to monitor housing discrimination as*
*checkers for the Heights Community Congress.*

*Doris was also active in Democratic party politics, and*
*in many other civic groups. She is especially enthusiastic*
*about the League of Women Voters because, as she states, it*
*"gave me so much energy. It gave me the knowledge to act."*

*In 1975 she worked on the judicial campaign of Sara*
*Hunter. Hunter, a civil rights activist with the Fair Housing*
*Council, HCHR, and the YWCA, had challenged former*
*mayor and sitting Cleveland Heights Municipal Court*
*judge Kenneth Nash. She recruited Allen to work on her*
*campaign, and in a political upset, Hunter was elected and*
*hired Doris Allen as her bailiff. They became the first all-*

*female court, and Allen, the first African-American bailiff in the country.*

*In 1983, Allen took a six-week sabbatical from her court job to care for her mentor, neighbor, and friend Bernice Lott, who passed away later that year. Allen retired from the court in 1986 when Wendell was diagnosed with Parkinson's disease. She was succeeded by Lincoln Scott, one of the leaders of the high school students whose concerns about lack of support for black students led to the complaint CICR filed with the Justice Department in 1974.*

*During her retirement, Allen has remained a community activist with much of her attention focused on Forest Hill Church. Attracted by its progressive values and proximity to home, she joined the church in 2004. She initiated a black history program at the church, helped found its Black Caucus, and initiated a college scholarship for black graduates of Heights High in honor of another black church member and long-time school board member, Ron Register.*

DORIS AND WENDELL ALLEN BOUGHT THEIR HOME AT 1724 LEE ROAD FROM A WILLING WHITE SELLER. THEY LIVED ON THE SAME BLOCK AS HER CHILDHOOD MENTOR AND FRIEND, BERNICE LOTT. (SUSAN KAESER)

IN 1970 DORIS ALLEN
WITNESSED WHITE TEENAGERS
MENACING BLACK YOUTH
AT THE HEIGHTS YMCA AND
CALLED THE POLICE. THE
RESPONSE WAS DISAPPOINTING.
THAT NIGHT SHE MET WITH
HER NEIGHBORS, THE LOTTS
AND THE EDWARDS, TO START
THE COMMITTEE TO IMPROVE
COMMUNITY RELATIONS.
(SUSAN KAESER)

THE INCREASED DIVERSITY OF SCHOOL DISTRICT STUDENTS PROMPTED THE CLEVELAND HEIGHTS-UNIVERSITY HEIGHTS
SCHOOL DISTRICT TO OFFER THEIR STAFF HUMAN RELATIONS TRAINING. A LARGE NUMBER OF DISTRICT PERSONNEL
SERVED AS FACILITATORS. (CLEVELAND HEIGHTS-UNIVERSITY HEIGHTS CITY SCHOOL DISTRICT ARCHIVES)

HEIGHTS HIGH ENGLISH TEACHER WILLIAM TARTER DIRECTED THE 20-MEMBER HEIGHTS HIGH GOSPEL CHOIR.
THE NEW EXTRACURRICULAR ACTIVITY SERVED THE MUSICAL INTERESTS OF THE NEWLY INTEGRATED STUDENT BODY.
(1976 CALDRON, CLEVELAND HEIGHTS HIGH SCHOOL YEARBOOK)

HARVEY FEINBERG (SEATED NEXT TO BERNICE LOTT), PRESIDENT OF THE CLEVELAND HEIGHTS-UNIVERSITY HEIGHTS BOARD OF
EDUCATION, SIGNED A CONSENT DECREE WITH CICR ON APRIL 1, 1975. IT MADE SCHOOL DISTRICT PRACTICES MORE INCLUSIVE OF
ITS AFRICAN-AMERICAN STUDENTS. (1976 CALDRON, CLEVELAND HEIGHTS HIGH SCHOOL YEARBOOK)

Report on Minority Staffing
April, 1990
Total Certificated

| School Year | Minority | Total | Percent |
| --- | --- | --- | --- |
| 1975-76 | 57.0 | 645.0 | 8.83 |
| 1976-77 | 54.5 | 588.6 | 9.25 |
| 1977-78 | 65.0 | 593.0 | 10.96 |
| 1978-79 | 80.0 | 590.0 | 13.50 |
| 1979-80 | 83.6 | 586.0 | 14.26 |
| 1980-81 | 63.1 | 487.3 | 12.90 |
| 1981-82 | 85.0 | 546.72 | 15.54 |
| 1982-83 | 94.0 | 552.0 | 17.02 |
| 1983-84 | 101.0 | 560.0 | 18.03 |
| 1984-85 | 111.0 | 554.0 | 20.04 |
| 1985-86 | 119.0 | 592.0 | 20.10 |
| 1986-87 | 119.0 | 593.0 | 20.06 |
| 1987-88 | 112.0 | 570.0 | 19.65 |
| 1988-89 | 105.0 | 582.0 | 18.04 |
| 1989-90 | 109.0 | 579.0 | 18.83 |

AS PART OF THE 1975 CONSENT DECREE, THE BOARD OF EDUCATION AGREED TO INCREASE HIRING OF
MINORITY STAFF TO 15% BY 1980. THE BOARD WAS REQUIRED TO REPORT ANNUALLY TO CICR ON PROGRESS
ON ALL SEVEN ASPECTS OF THE CONSENT DECREE. (CH-UH BOARD OF EDUCATION, REPORT, 1980)

# CHAPTER 7

# HOUSING AUDIT DOCUMENTS DISCRIMINATION

In 1971 five women formed the St. Ann Social Action Housing Committee to gauge realtor compliance with fair housing laws. Between May 19 and July 14, 1972, the team, led by Suzanne Nigro, supervised volunteers who gave more than 1,500 hours to check for equal treatment. The report they issued, "Housing Audit I: Assessment of Real Estate Practices in the Eastern Suburbs of Cleveland, Ohio," was damning in its findings and ground-breaking in its use.[1] The audit uncovered widespread though subtle forms of racial discrimination. Racial steering was common as realtors discouraged white clients from looking for homes in Cleveland Heights and Shaker Heights, two integrated communities, and directed black buyers to those communities.

"We uncovered the reality of the situation. You can't operate on innuendo," explained Nigro.[2] The evidence showed that all ten firms that handled property in Cleveland Heights systematically violated state and federal fair housing laws, a violation of African-American civil rights and a threat to stable integration. It also made clear to hopeful housing activists that fair housing legislation had not settled the matter and they needed to stay in the fight.

Nigro's committee operated under the auspices of the Social Action Committee of the Parish Council at St. Ann Catholic Church, and was an outgrowth of the Cleveland Catholic Diocese project, "Action for A Change." Tom Reim chaired the parish council. On September 7, 1972, Nigro and Reim delivered the audit report and its findings to the Cleveland Heights City Council.

The St. Ann Audit was a short-term project with a long-term effect. The report findings revealed the limits of fair housing laws and the need for local vigilance and continued activism. The report gave the audit team and other fair housing advocates what they needed to put the real estate industry on notice, and to educate the community and public officials about threats to open housing. It established auditing as an important tool to prevent discrimination.

The report was shared widely, reaching Ohio governor John Gilligan and Cleveland-area civil rights groups. On the national level, it was shared at a national real estate meeting sponsored by the Assistant Director of the U.S. Department of Housing and Urban Development (HUD), and it was sent by HUD to all of its regional offices.[3] The audit had a direct impact on public policy in Cleveland Heights. The report pushed city council to become more proactive on fair housing, and when the council finally adopted its Nine-Point Plan in 1976, it included many recommendations offered by the audit committee.

### Audit Roots: The Social Mission of the Catholic Church

In 1962, Pope John XXIII convened Vatican II, the historic gathering of more than 2,000 bishops from across the globe, to "open the windows of the church and let in some fresh air."[4] This rare review of the status and work of the Catholic church opened on October 11, 1962, and concluded on December 8, 1965. Among its many recommendations was greater pursuit of a social mission which provided an impetus for Catholics to get involved in civil rights.[5]

Four years after Vatican II, two local social justice-focused clergy, Auxiliary Bishop William Cosgrove and Father Dan Reidy, convinced Bishop Clarence Issenmann to approve a new vehicle to engage Cleveland Catholics in the church's social mission. In 1969, they founded the Commission on Catholic Community Action (CCCA). While Presbyterian congregations had the autonomy to set a social agenda and pursue it, Catholics did not. In the top-down governance of the Catholic

Church, a Diocese-wide structure like the Commission was essential for parish participation in social action.

The Commission gave lay leaders new opportunities to participate. They served on task forces and provided direction for action in parishes located in the eight counties of the Cleveland Diocese. Bishop Cosgrove and African-American journalist George Moore, founder of the Catholic Interracial Council, were the first co-chairs of the Commission. Richard M. Kelley was the first executive director and Fr. Neil Conway, secretary to Bishop Cosgrove, was the program director.

Fr. Reidy, the architect of the Commission, was impatient with the "half-hearted effort to show our love to our brothers in need." He argued that human problems "must be approached with immediacy, an urgency that means TOTAL RESPONSE."[6]

The Commission needed a way to promote Fr. Reidy's aspiration for a "total response." So Kelley and Conway designed a program that combined education and action. It would help people in every parish to "prepare themselves to take responsibility for solving some of the problems which we face in society." This detailed approach was outlined in a concept paper dated October 23, 1970: "The Social Mission of the Church Through Action for A Change."[7]

The social justice initiative focused on housing, education, employment, poverty, and health. Catholics from parishes in Summit and Cuyahoga counties were invited to participate in the two-phase project: six weekly learning sessions followed by a long-term commitment to action. Each parish was expected to create an action committee to oversee the follow-up work.

Harry Fagan, a Cleveland Heights resident and progressive lay leader of the Diocese, left his job as advertising manager for the *Cleveland Plain Dealer* to implement "Action for A Change." Fagan and his wife Sheila developed the interactive lessons that were the core of the education phase of the plan. Described by contemporaries as a people person, Fagan was an energetic, charismatic, and effective organizer.

The Social Mission Task force of the Commission began "Action for A Change" during the first week of Lent in 1971. More than 300 trained facilitators led the series of educational meetings. More than 3,500 individuals from 89 Cleveland Diocese parishes participated in 240 small study groups.[8]

Participants received the Church's publication, *Reflections on the Social Mission of the Church*, which provided the religious basis for the action program. They also received an *Action Directory*, an exhaustive list of agencies working in the Cleveland area to improve lives. The *Directory* stated, "At this moment we are either unconsciously destroying or consciously building the future. It is our future. Let us shape it together."[9] Participants used the directory to design their action plans.

The pilot phase of "Action for A Change" began on February 24, 1971, and continued with weekly living room meetings for the next five weeks. The curriculum included mid-week field trips and activities, many of which focused on fair housing. Fagan, the salesman for the project, told reporters that in addition to facilitator-led conversations, participants made more than 2,500 visits to social action agencies. The series was repeated, using revised materials, starting in October of that year, with an additional 1,000 participants joining the education-to-action series.

## St. Ann Social Action Housing Committee

Members of the three parishes that serve residents of Cleveland Heights and University Heights participated in the February 1971 launch of "Action for A Change." There were six groups at St. Ann, five at St. Louis, and nine at Gesu.[10]

For the next three years, Tom Reim, parish council president at St. Ann, wrote a newsletter updating the parish on parishioner-led activities. According to the May 1971 edition of the *St. Ann Action for A Change Newsletter*, "Most of us finished the 'Action for A Change' study program feeling that the 71 people in St. Ann's who participated represented a substantial force for action."[11] The newsletter lists steps that members had already taken: lobbying for welfare legislation, attending city council meetings, and joining forces with Heights Citizens for Human Rights. It also noted that Reim, Cathy Heintz, Bernie Doherty, and Lana Cowell gathered more than 425 signatures on a petition to support fair housing.

The "Action for A Change" curriculum included visits with leaders of five fair housing organizations: the Ludlow Community Association, Fair Housing Inc., the Ohio Civil Rights Commission, Suburban Citizens for Open Housing (SCOH), and Operation Equality. After a field trip to the Operation Equality office and meeting its director, Joe Battle, Nigro and Jeanne Martin chose fair housing as their issue. They learned about "checking" as the method fair housing organizations used to gather evidence of discrimination to support individual complaints filed with the Ohio Civil Rights Commission. Unfortunately, complaints had not yet stopped realtors from discriminating.

In March 1972, St. Ann members Nigro, Cowell, Linda Johnston, and Lynn Gordon met with local experts including Barbara Roderick from city hall. They learned that discriminatory housing practices, though subtle, were affecting Cleveland Heights as a whole, and racial steering was affecting some streets and neighborhoods. The nascent group's first action step was to draft a letter to Vincent Aveni, President of the Cleveland Board of Realtors, expressing support for fair housing legislation and opposition to discrimination. The letter concludes, "Hoping you share our views, and will convey this message to area realtors."[12]

By May, the housing committee added Jeanne Martin and Nancy Cappelletti to its ranks, but lost Lynn Gordon. Nigro, Martin, and Johnston were all trained nurses, which won the group the informal title of the "nurses' group." While raising their young children, these volunteers spearheaded a systematic audit of real estate practices to test compliance with the law. It was, as Nigro observed, "the issue of our time."[13]

The St. Ann Housing Action Committee turned to local expert Joe Battle of Operation Equality, and Dr. Juliet Saltman of the Fair Housing Contact Service in Akron to help them design research to detect overt and subtle forms of discrimination by realtors serving Cleveland Heights. They employed checking, first used in New York in 1957, to determine if realtors treated clients equally. Their design borrowed from large-scale audits of rental housing in St. Louis, Missouri; Palo Alto, California; and Akron, Ohio. Rather than focus on individual complaints, they used checking to test patterns of behavior employed by a real estate firm. They monitored all ten firms that did business in Cleveland Heights. As one of the first large-scale audits of housing sales, the St. Ann team's efforts helped establish this strategy to "bring about fundamental reforms in institutional systems that control the housing market."[14]

To detect discrimination, two "checkers" of different races who have the same financial ability, housing needs, and family characteristics, ask to inspect the same housing unit. They record how they are treated by the realtor and whether they have been offered the unit. The experiences are compared in order to identify any differences in treatment.

The committee recruited and trained 17 volunteer checkers, some of whom had already done this work with Operation Equality. Each committee member coordinated a team. The process began with a matched pair calling the same real estate firm about the same house offered for sale in the newspaper. In order to gauge racial steering toward already integrated communities, they looked for properties located outside of Cleveland Heights and Shaker Heights. Each participant kept detailed records of their encounters. They monitored 13 variables that documented what was said and the kind of attention they received. After an encounter with a realtor, the checker detailed a written record of what transpired and then recounted the experience to their supervisor who compared how both checkers were treated.[15]

Collecting exact details exposed 41 examples of discrimination spread across all ten firms. Nigro observed, "As we learned by our experience, the federal law may have stopped open, blatant discrimination, but it hasn't ended the subtle kind."[16] They discovered,

1.  It was harder for black volunteers to set up an appointment with the realtor than a white one. Blacks had to make 88% more calls to receive attention.
2.  On their first appointment, black volunteers saw fewer homes than their white counterparts.
3.  After initial contact with realtors, black volunteers rarely had the chance to see more homes while most whites did. Realtors made follow-up calls to 82% of white checkers but only 27% of blacks.[17]

The most insidious finding from Nigro's perspective was pervasive racial steering that damaged Cleveland Heights:

Nearly half of the black and white volunteers were steered into or away from specific areas. Whites were never brought into already integrated areas. Some blacks on the other hand were directed into Cleveland Heights after specifically requesting suburbs farther east . . . which are virtually all-white suburbs.[18]

The St. Ann Housing Committee hoped the audit findings would prod a resistant city council to use its authority to counter negative realtor behavior. The report included eight recommendations to attack discrimination from both an enforcement and cooperation stance. It called for local legislation to prohibit racial steering, for the formation of a citizens housing commission, and for citizens to report instances of discrimination to the City for legal action. It also proposed that the City offer realtors "a human relations educational program to counter 'myths, fears, and hostile attitudes' relating to integrating the community," and to "work with the real estate companies and educational institutions to develop an ongoing human relations program for all persons involved in the sale or rental of homes in Cleveland Heights or Shaker Heights." Another recommendation called for the City to use its force and ingenuity "to enlist the active and positive support of all the eastern suburbs for truly open housing in their communities."[19]

The final recommendation tackled a fundamental source of unequal treatment: the listing services that kept white realtors in control of housing listings. The committee wanted them to be replaced by a "central computerized real estate listing service" and wanted to "abolish the existing multiplicity of individual listing services."[20]

The committee determined that follow-up was essential. They had a carefully considered and crafted plan to deliver their findings to the right audiences so they would have a maximum impact on realtor behavior, on city leaders' responses, and on public understanding of the threat.

The auditors operated under the auspices of the St. Ann Parish Council, so as a courtesy, they reported their findings to the council before going public. However, they chose not to ask the parish council for approval since they did not need it and quite likely would not receive it.[21] In another strategic move, both Nigro and Reim reported the findings to the city councils of Cleveland Heights and Shaker Heights, the two communities most impacted by racial steering. Reim had not conducted the audits, but the all-women committee felt a male voice would help. "We were young. They didn't want to listen to women. We needed Tom," explained Nigro.[22]

The St. Ann Housing Committee used its findings to educate realtors, not take them to court. The fair housing law was new and untested, so it was unclear what kind of legal evidence would suffice and what outcome it would produce. Also, a lawsuit would be costly and time consuming. Nigro explained this critical strategic decision: "We were not sure we had enough good evidence for successful litigation, but plenty for education."

Martin further explained their hesitation: "They would have chewed us up if we went to court."[23]

The St. Ann team kept the names of offending realtors and firms confidential. This enabled them to work with all firms, not just the ten they audited. It also made it easier to take a cooperative stance, inviting realtors to learn more about the audit, fair housing, agent training, and compliance with the law. Despite the committee's resolve not to litigate, both the Cleveland Heights law director and a representative of the federal Department of Justice requested the names of firms that violated the law so they could prosecute them. The committee refused the request and stuck to the education strategy.

Not all realtors were receptive to their recommendations. Nigro describes a meeting with a broker who "became so enraged during my presentation that he threw his briefcase across the table at me and said, 'It is a waste of time meeting with a housewife.'"[24]

The project challenged realtors and the status quo, and it was not fully welcomed by the members of St. Ann parish. In a January 1973 newspaper article, "A Congregation Divided," Tom Reim stated that he had been warned "not to rock the boat, you don't want to split the parish do you?" Another parishioner told the reporter they "wished the whole thing would go away." Msgr. Walsh, the parish priest, never delivered a sermon on the issue and noted, "I was doubtful about laying blame on the real estate firms because I felt they were just representing the wishes of their customers."[25]

The public response, however, was positive. On September 7, the day they reported on the audit findings, the *Sun Press* editorialized on the subject. They found the findings credible and challenged realtors to follow the law: "It is up to white-owned real estate companies . . . to foster integration. The audit reported in this issue indicates that this does not seem to be the case."[26] A subsequent editorial called for people to change: "What is needed is not more reports, not finger waving, not table pounding, but a change in people's attitudes."[27] Nigro received hundreds of supportive phone calls, letters, and requests to speak from across the country.

The report had an impact. Tom Reim observed that while white suburbs like Lyndhurst, Mayfield, and South Euclid had not yet become integrated, "It has put the fear of God in the real estate people."[28]

The Housing Action Committee shared its findings with interested groups from around the nation. As a result of the audit, the members of the St. Ann Social Action Housing Committee became recognized experts in the fair housing field. Checkers and committee members appeared on television to share their story. Nigro traveled to communities across the country and presented at the annual meeting of National Neighbors, the network of fair housing organizations working in more than 40 integrated communities nationwide.

In an April 1973 report to Harry Fagan evaluating the impact of the "Action for A Change" program, Tom Reim acknowledged the important work of the Audit Committee by claiming, "Our open housing study was probably the best thing we've done, thanks to five dedicated gals."[29] Nigro stated, "'Action for A Change' was a seminar that altered my life and inspired me and others to help alter life in Cleveland Heights and surrounding communities."[30]

On September 21, 1972, just two weeks after the St. Ann group went public with its findings, the Heights Action Committee, a small group of Jewish and Catholic leaders, convened a large community meeting to launch the Heights Community Congress. Its purpose was to make Cleveland Heights a stable, integrated community. Nigro described the timing as "a miracle of sorts."[31] The audit provided hard evidence that housing discrimination was damaging the community, and demonstrated the need for an effective organized response. By February 1973, the Heights Community Congress was in place and formed a housing task force that carried forward the work started by the nurses group. All five women joined the task force and Sue Nigro became the chair.

# SUZANNE NIGRO

IN 1974 THE CITY FUNDED THE HEIGHTS HOUSING SERVICE TO MARKET CLEVELAND HEIGHTS TO PROSPECTIVE HOME BUYERS. SUZANNE NIGRO (FAR RIGHT), WHO DIRECTED THE PROGRAM, IS PICTURED WITH PAT BOYD AND LINDA JOHNSTON. THEY LED TOURS OF ALL HOUSING AVAILABLE IN EACH CLIENT'S PRICE RANGE. (SUZANNE NIGRO)

*When they moved to Cleveland Heights in 1965 from Navy housing in Connecticut, Suzanne Nigro and her husband Sam experienced racial steering – but they didn't know what to call it. Realtors discouraged the young family of four from looking in Cleveland Heights, encouraging them to look farther east. They ignored the realtors and found the right house in Cleveland Heights, close to Sam's new position as a resident in child psychiatry at University Hospitals. Five years later, the growing family moved to another larger Cleveland Heights home without the help of a realtor. They joined St. Ann Church on Coventry Road.*

*Although a trained nurse, in the 1970s, Nigro worked as a stay-at-home mom. She readily participated in "Action for A Change," the social action awareness project launched by the newly formed Catholic Commission on Community Action during Lent in 1971. During the six-week education process, she found a strong cadre of women who shared her interest in fair housing, an issue of growing concern in Cleveland Heights. She became the chair of the St. Ann Social Action Housing Committee.*

*Starting in May of 1972, the committee conducted the groundbreaking audit of realtor behavior that documented widespread racial steering, a violation of fair housing law. The finding, released on September 7, 1972, became one rationale for founding the Heights Community Congress. It was also essential to awakening city council interest in addressing this challenge to the city's future stability.*

*Nigro was soon inundated with inquiries about housing discrimination. The audit propelled Nigro into public view as a spokesperson for the group. She became an expert in the emerging field of fair housing.*

*When the Heights Community Congress became an official organization in January of 1973, Nigro and her four audit colleagues were among the members of the new organization's Fair Housing Task Force. In 1974, the Congress won a contract with the City of Cleveland Heights to run the Heights Housing Service and hired Nigro as the director. This collaboration between the City and the Congress contributed to Cleveland Heights earning the designation as an "All-American City" in 1975-76.*

*In 1976, the City abruptly ended the contract. While Nigro lost her job, she remained committed to fair housing, an issue that centers her activism to this day.*

*After the birth of her fifth child, Nigro enrolled at Cleveland Marshall College of Law and in the 1980s launched a legal career that focused both on housing and employment discrimination. Nigro remains a member of St. Ann Church, and her relationship with the HCC came full circle in the mid-1990s when she joined the board of this now-mature community organization. Between her professional life and volunteer activities, Cleveland Heights, fair housing, and social justice remain her focus and her life's work.*

AFTER REALTORS STEERED THEM AWAY FROM HOUSES IN CLEVELAND HEIGHTS, IN 1970
THE NIGROS FOUND THEIR PERFECT HOME AT 2517 GUILDFORD ROAD. (SUSAN KAESER)

FIVE "ACTION FOR A CHANGE" PARTICIPANTS FROM ST. ANN PARISH DOCUMENTED DISCRIMINATORY PRACTICES
BY REALTORS IN EASTERN SUBURBS IN VIOLATION OF FEDERAL LAW. THE PARISH PRIEST NEVER PREACHED ON THE CONCERNS
RAISED BY THEIR GROUND-BREAKING RESEARCH. (SUSAN KAESER)

# CHAPTER 8

# INSTITUTIONS UNITE TO SUPPORT INTEGRATION

Open housing activists had always wanted African-American buyers, not realtors, to decide where they would live. Despite laws prohibiting discrimination, many realtors continued to impose their preference for segregation, especially in neighborhoods experiencing racial change. The common assumption was that once a community reached a certain tipping point, it had five years before becoming all-black. Gerda Freedheim had long warned that in the name of protecting property values, realtors could "destroy a community."[1] She had seen it happen.

By 1972, Cleveland Heights' African-American population was growing at an accelerated pace. As more blacks moved to the suburb, the community became increasingly vulnerable to realtor pressures to reimpose segregation. Blockbusting and racial steering became prevalent.

City government neither embraced diversity nor invested in its success. According to Jack Boyle, who served on city council at the time and later as mayor, officials "tip toed" around the issue. Even after hiring Barbara Roderick in 1970 to focus on housing, in his view the council "kept her at arm's length."[2]

A stable, integrated community depended on a more complete response than merely helping African Americans move to white neighborhoods, the dominant strategy of the 1960s. It required an active role for city government and every institution in town to resist resegregation.

In February 1972, a dozen Jewish and Catholic leaders and the Heights High School principal gathered in the Carmelite Monastery in Cleveland Heights to strategize how to defend integration and protect their substantial institutional investments. Jewish leaders feared that the Cleveland Heights Jewish community might flee the suburb as they had left Cleveland neighborhoods when integration began there 20 years earlier. White flight would also be costly to the Catholic institutions.

The planning group called itself the Heights Action Committee (HAC) since it drew many of its members from the Catholic social action project, "Action for A Change." By September, the members launched a new community organization to support integration – the Heights Community Congress (HCC). It united the community's organizations and public institutions to build and sustain a vibrant, integrated community with strong resident ownership. It became a long-lasting fair housing organization.

Mary Boyle, a participant in the Carmelite meetings, expressed the core concern driving their solution: "If we don't do this together, we won't win it." She also articulated HAC's frustration with the City's lack of attention to the challenge: "If leadership is not leading, what can we do? How do we drag the institutions along in this?"[3]

During its formative years, the Heights Congress put the brakes on destructive real estate practices that would rip apart integrated communities, and it facilitated an active citizen role in formulating local solutions to important community concerns. Community organizing provided a powerful counter-force to flight. Public pressure orchestrated by the HCC finally forced city government to take a more proactive role in maintaining integration.

HCC's local initiatives had national impact. Two ground-breaking lawsuits filed by the HCC in 1973 and 1979 that challenged the Cleveland real estate industry offered early tests of the federal fair housing law. The cases raised national awareness of the law and helped establish legal precedents for admissible evidence, standing, and consequences of violating the law.

Research on lending practices conducted by the Heights Congress in conjunction with the Cleveland Heights chapter of the League of Women Voters documented a pattern of racial discrimination. Senator William

Proxmire used the findings to justify new federal legislation, the Home Mortgage Disclosure Act of 1975, which guarantees public scrutiny of lending institutions.

HCC's strategies and its ability to move city government to become proactive in relation to housing integration made a difference. This new resource helped secure integration and was instrumental in making Cleveland Heights a recognized national example of long-lasting integration.

## The Jewish Roots of the Heights Action Committee

In 1920, about ten percent of Cleveland's population was Jewish. Glenville and Mt. Pleasant, two Eastside city neighborhoods, were home to 28% and 14%, respectively, of Cleveland's Jews. Cleveland Heights also had a small Jewish population.

The first Jewish institution, the Oakwood Country Club, opened in the Heights in 1905. The second, Temple on the Heights, opened in 1926. By 1940, as blacks moved into Jewish neighborhoods in the city, Jewish movement to the suburbs accelerated. Twenty years later, Cleveland Heights was home to 35% of the Jewish residents of greater Cleveland. Many came from the Glenville neighborhood, less than two miles away. Over a short period, this integrated city neighborhood became all black.[4]

Jewish-owned businesses and religious, cultural, and human service agencies were soon found along Taylor Road, the center of Jewish life in Cleveland Heights. By 1960, there were 16 Jewish institutions located in the suburb, including multiple conservative, reformed, and orthodox synagogues, Jewish Family Services, Montefiore Home, Council Gardens apartments, Hebrew Academy, and the newly opened Jewish Community Center.

Despite significant investment in Cleveland Heights, by 1969, Jewish outmigration to suburbs farther east had already started. That year, Temple on the Heights voted to move to Pepper Pike. This signaled that prospects for the future of the Jewish community in Cleveland Heights were in doubt. That year, fearing a repeat of the Jewish exodus from Cleveland, the Jewish institutions banded together as the Cleveland Heights Assembly. Their goal: to keep the 16,000 Jewish residents of Cleveland Heights from moving and abandoning the institutions that served them.

In 1970, the Jewish Community Federation voted to support the work of the Cleveland Heights Assembly. The Federation's Community Relations division hired David Sarnat, an idealistic young social worker, to staff the Assembly and its new initiative, the Heights Stabilization Program. It soon became the Heights Area Project.

Flight was fueled, in part, by blockbusting, and according to one news report, the fear mongering was not welcomed by Jewish residents. The report stated, "The reaction of residents to what they feel is harassment by some real estate dealers indicates an attitude not of panic but of concern and even anger that speculators would interfere in the life of pleasant neighborhoods in which Jews and non-Jews, white and black people live together harmoniously."[5]

In his January 29, 1971, editorial, "Cleveland Heights, Can It Remain Jewish?," Jerry Barch praised the Assembly's work to curb Jewish flight from this integrating older suburb.

> It's an American Jewish tragedy. Why a tragedy? Because each time a neighborhood is abandoned, a little bit of the way of life of that neighborhood is never revived. There are human attachments that never seem to be quite the same.
>
> And then there is the staggering cost of rebuilding all of the Jewish institutions that graced the old neighborhood.
>
> Then there is the nagging thought. Even when a new community center or grand new synagogue is erected 'farther out' how long will it be before the pattern repeats itself.
>
> Is there a solution? Yes, if soon enough.
>
> The solution is the Cleveland Heights Assembly whose task is to examine what lies ahead for Cleveland Heights and what can be done to retain its Jewish character.[6]

In August 1971, the Heights Area Project launched a down payment assistance program that provided Jewish families interest-free loans to buy homes in Cleveland Heights. Rabbi Marvin Spiegelman was the director. A $20,000 grant from the Jewish Community Federation's endowment provided start-up funds. The goal was not to "prevent Negroes from moving into the area but to maintain Jewish demand as houses became available for purchase."[7]

Rabbi Spiegelman was adamant that Jews needed to get over their "refugee" mentality and stop moving. He stated, "People tend to forget that there's a tremendous moral issue involved. They forget that by deliberately abandoning a neighborhood they are causing damage to the general as well as the Jewish community."[8]

By 1975, 150 families had used the grants and many more had moved in with encouragement from Rabbi Spiegelman's program. Marketing the community had clearly proved effective.

## High School Fights Spark Meeting

During the 1971-72 school year, Cleveland Heights High School enrolled 3,200 students, of whom 65% were Jewish and 5% were African-American. Black enrollment had increased from about 50 students three years before to 165. Mounting racial tension among students erupted on January 28, 1972, with after-school skirmishes that led to a dozen injuries. The incident had initially been reported as black gang violence, a misrepresentation of the fight.[9]

William Allen was one of the injured students. His mother, Doris Allen, a leader of the black parent organization Committee to Improve Community Relations, called a community meeting for the following day at the Heights YMCA/YWCA. More than 100 parents showed up to air their concerns and hear a report from Superintendent David Moberly. When school opened on the following Monday, six white parents and six black parents were there to help keep the day calm and safe.[10]

The incident was a crisis for the school and a wake-up call for the community. Moberly was candid, defining the problem as racism. A week later, 800 people attended a follow-up meeting. The superintendent asked for help. "Schools can't fight racism alone," he said, and called for families, churches, and community organizations to get involved. Heights High Principal James O'Toole reinforced the need for a broader solution claiming, "If we should be satisfied by the expulsions, we wouldn't really understand our problems and our responsibilities in solving them."[11]

George Moore's February 4 column in *The Cleveland Press* called the incident "a warning of growing symptoms of racial problems besetting that community, and further, indication that some very positive steps need to be taken to improve human relations that will embrace all residents, white and black." *Call and Post* reporter Cindy Cooper wrote, "In the final analysis Heights is on the brink of becoming an integrated or confrontation school." She quoted a Heights athlete who observed,

"Most white kids are prejudiced. If kids don't learn to respect each other things will just blow up."[12]

The oldest justification for racial segregation is that people of different races can't get along; the fight not only revealed the ugly nature and reality of racial hostility, but it added to the existing anxiety about the possibility of stable integration. Race relations had to improve for integration to succeed.

In response to the principal's plea for a community response, Fr. Robert Bonnell, chaplain of the Carmelite Monastery on Fairmount Boulevard, and Cleveland Heights resident Howard Berger, director of community relations for the Jewish Community Federation, met with Principal O'Toole. On February 22, less than a month after the disheartening high school fight, Fr. Bonnell welcomed O'Toole, Berger, and ten Jewish and Catholic representatives to a meeting in the basement of the Carmelite Monastery to forge a community-led, organized, and effective way to challenge racism.

Fr. Bonnell reached out to the principal of Beaumont High School and three local Catholic parish priests to recruit participants from the "Action for A Change" program to represent their institutions at the meeting. In addition to Bonnell, the Catholic participants were Tom Reim, Tom Hanrahan, Mary Boyle, Frank McGowan, Sr. Sheila Marie, and Tony Satullo. Berger recruited the contingent representing Jewish institutions. He was joined by Bob Silverman, David Sarnat, Ken Merkel, and Sid Vincent.[13]

These participants were motivated by idealism and a practical concern for the continued viability of Jewish and Catholic institutions. If too many of the city's residents pulled out, integration would be fleeting, their institutions would not survive, and the massive investment they represented would be lost. As a result, the entire community would suffer.

In a few weeks, Boyle, Sarnat, and O'Toole proposed a statement of purpose and areas of action to the full group for feedback. The statement became the guiding purpose from that point forward. It read:

> Heights Action Committee is a coalition of Cleveland Heights religious and public institutions with a common goal of promoting an open, integrated community. We will act to foster an environment which accepts religious, racial, and

cultural diversity and which nurtures a variety of institutions and life-styles.[14]

They proposed three core activities: change realtor and banker practices, increase the attractiveness of the community as a place to live, and facilitate communication among the stakeholders in the city.

In mid-March, the Catholic members of the group sent a letter to the co-chairs of the Commission on Catholic Community Action requesting that they assign Harry Fagan to work with them. They explained that he "is experienced in and familiar with the kinds of community action we envision."[15] Because the education phase of "Action for A Change" was over and Fagan's role in the follow-up phase was minimal, he was available and eager to participate.

By the next meeting, Fagan was on board, and in June, he unveiled the "200% Solution," a two-pronged approach to integration. The first 100% focused on stabilizing the community by ending white flight; the other 100% focused on marketing the community to new residents. A coalition of organizations would implement the plan which, according to Fagan, "must be orchestrated to ensure every facet of the problem is being dealt with."[16]

Fagan offered a variety of tactics to promote stability. He proposed working with neighborhood groups, censuring negative behavior of realtors (with lawsuits if necessary), marketing housing, and helping elderly homeowners maintain their homes. The plan called for a comprehensive public relations scheme, outreach to relocation offices of major employers, resident and City housing service cooperation with realtors, financial incentives for new buyers, and a progressive plan for the city's future.

The active participation of city government was essential for success. As Fagan articulated in the 200% solution proposal:

Cleveland Heights government would use imagination and efficiency in securing better city services to make our community more than a competitive housing market. Advancing progressive legislation and solidify [sic] new building projects would also be main parts of their task. A very important vehicle would be the establishing of a quarterly newsletter as a vehicle to communicate regularly with their constituency.[17]

Once the purpose, vision, analysis, and strategies took form, the HAC invited community leaders to join the discussion. Mayor Oliver Schroeder agreed to sign letters inviting community leaders to two public meetings to learn about the 200% Solution. He also suggested the name for the new organization: Cleveland Heights Community Congress.[18]

More than 65 people attended one or both of the public meetings held on August 10 and September 21, 1972. Mayor Schroeder was joined by Councilwoman Marjory Wright and Housing Coordinator Barbara Roderick. Assistant Superintendent Al Abramowitz and O'Toole represented the school district.[19] Pippa Kiraly, president of Heights Citizens for Human Rights also attended, and she presented this report to HCHR members:

> I was at first afraid that the principles of HCHR wouldn't have adequate recognition here, being only one group among so many. But after a couple of meetings I realized that a good half of the people present, no matter what groups they were representing, were also members of HCHR and I was reassured.
>
> The potential for the Heights Community Congress is enormous. It remains to be seen whether we can all work together without undue friction.[20]

Designers of the congress wanted the new organization to unite all of the community's business, civic, religious, and neighborhood organizations, along with city government and the school district, to mount a non-partisan, coordinated attack on community problems. The structure called for the community to be divided into classes reflecting the many interest groups of the city. Each class would elect a representative to serve on the policymaking board of trustees. Citizen-led task forces would research and define solutions to critical problems and propose them to the trustees for approval and action by the staff.[21]

The second public meeting, held on September 11, 1972, marked an important turning point. It was the end of the Action Committee's planning process and the beginning of a new organization. HAC leaders Bonnell, Reim, Boyle, Fagan and Sarnat introduced the idea of the Heights Community Congress and its governing structure. After voting to approve the concept, participants divided into eight different interest groups that represented the "classes" of members that would be represented on the governing board. Each class elected a representative to serve on the steering committee that served as the governing board. They also identified nine task forces and individuals to serve on each of them.[22]

The new governing board and the "classes" they represented were: Rev. Charles Mayer, for the Protestant community; Fr. Hailiko, for the Catholic community; and Julian Kolby, for the Jewish community. The schools and city government were represented by Assistant Superintendent Al Abramowitz and Barbara Roderick, respectively. Chuck Matthews was chosen to represent neighborhoods and Cornelius Edwards, civic organizations. At a subsequent meeting they elected Herbert Greenwald to represent businesses. They also elected Fr. Bonnell as an ex-officio member. This committee had the task of bringing to fruition the vision established by the Heights Action Committee.

The meeting marked the formal end of the HAC. The future of the Heights Community Congress (HCC) was now in the hands of a new, elected leadership team. At the close of the meeting, Reim encouraged the group to pay attention to three issues of immediate importance: the school district bond issue, the September 12 fire-bombing of the Appling home, and the St. Ann Housing Study.

The steering committee set to work on September 27, 1972. It confirmed the purposes of the Cleveland Heights Community Congress and then agreed to "start the development of a program of action geared to creating an on-going structure and permanent organization with adequate financing, lay leadership, and manpower to deal with our common concerns."[23] The committee recognized that cooperation from local government was essential moving forward, so the resolution acknowledged Mayor Schroeder's support.

Sarnat and Fagan provided temporary staff as extensions of their responsibilities with the Jewish Community Federation and the Commission on Catholic Community Action. They helped draft grant proposals and kept the process moving.

On January 1, 1973, Fr. Bonnell filed incorporation papers and the Steering Committee members became the founding trustees. Three weeks later, the trustees met at the monastery for the first official meeting of the Heights Community Congress. Not long afterwards, on February 20, 1973, the Cleveland Foundation provided the group a $48,000 start-up grant.

In addition, Marshall Motors gave them free office space on the second floor of its dealership at 2158 Lee Road, at the intersection with Cedar Road.[24] Bob Ketrain, Susanna Niermann O'Neil, and Irene Shapiro served the office as its founding staff. By November, Fagan, assistant director of the Catholic Commission, became part-time director of the HCC. Task forces were fully in place to address housing, neighborhood associations, public relations, community relations, education, and public safety.

In less than a year, a small group of people with a vested interest in the future of the community had identified a need, created a plan, developed an organizational structure, mobilized many segments of the community, and founded a new, long-lasting community resource.

A year later, the *Sun Press* reported on the new organization's progress. The article noted, "It's Fagan, as director of HCC, who has the sticky job of keeping the wheels greased, the human energy flowing instead of clashing, and of walking the tight rope between the HCC and city hall." He's "a skilled operator."[25] The nine paid staff members attended an average of 30 meetings a week working with the 13 classes, the 15 task forces, and a growing number of neighborhood groups.

Director Fagan was good at his job. He was an effective strategist, and people listened and responded to him. He was like the pied piper. People who worked with him like Sue Nigro, Chip Bromley, Kermit Lind, Susanna Niermann O'Neil, and Jack and Mary Boyle all responded to his energy, respected his ideas, and even quoted his philosophy.

The Congress organized more than 150 block clubs and supported active community organizations in all ten elementary school neighborhoods. Citizen-led task forces addressed a wide range of community problems, including housing. It was an intense effort to mobilize and engage the community in solving problems and deepening their investment in the community.

Jack Boyle attended many of the meetings that he says saved the community. Worried neighbors had an opportunity to meet each other, vent, and talk about their concerns. According to Boyle, white neighbors frequently expressed their concern about instability and loss of property values because of integration. Fagan's response was, "The problem isn't blacks moving in; it's whites moving out." He would advise people to stay put so it wouldn't be a problem.[26]

By the end of 1974, the HCC had eclipsed Heights Citizens for Human Rights as the community organization that promoted and defended integration. In fact, many HCHR members continued their activism through the HCC. An energetic staff, the 200% Solution, and a broad coalition of community organizations provided the firepower needed to confront the escalating threats to stable integration.

## Housing Agenda

By February 1973, many pioneer fair housing activists found their way to the HCC's Housing Task Force and participated in one of three subcommittees. Dick Weigand, who later was elected to city council, led the work on housing codes. Suzanne Nigro of the St. Ann Audit led the open housing work and realtor Dave O'Konski, chaired the realtor education subcommittee. Other St. Ann's housing activists Lynn Gordon, Jeanne Martin, Linda Johnston, Lana Cowell, and Nancy Cappiletti also joined the housing task force. Forest Hill Church housing activists Diana Woodbridge and Margery Phillips also signed on, as did Barbara Roderick. Other committee members included Art Brooks, Nancy Hall, Paul Martin, and Diane Weiner.[27]

Well-maintained property was essential to a stable and healthy community, so the Housing Task Force developed a proposal for the City to implement systematic interior inspections of housing. On August 22, 1974, task force member Diana Woodbridge, representing the Housing Corporation, and Pat Solomon, representing the League of Women Voters, brought the plan to council. It would take two more years for the City to agree to implement it.[28]

The City of Cleveland Heights and the HCC justifiably remained concerned about real estate practices that would undermine integration. In October 1972, the City entered into a three-year voluntary agreement with realtors who pledged to stop racial steering and blockbusting; but despite this agreement, the HCC repeatedly uncovered discrimination.[29]

On November 19, 1974, a year after the task force began to meet, the HCC Board of Trustees took a bold step and filed a lawsuit in the federal district court under the 1968 Fair Housing Act. Based on evidence collected by checking, they charged that the Rosenblatt Realty Company engaged in racial steering and asked for $1 million in damages. Attorneys Alan Bellman and Avery Friedman represented the Congress.

HCC Board President Rev. Charles Mayer expressed regret that the HCC needed to litigate, but the realty firm was unwilling to cooperate. He explained the group's stance in this way:

> As a sincerely concerned community organization dedicated to promote and maintain an open integrated community, we are incensed by these illegal steering practices and simply cannot stand by and condone illegal and manipulative real estate methods that work against the maintenance of integrated communities.[30]

At the time, the federal fair housing law was largely untested. It was unclear what kind of evidence was required and how the courts would respond. *Heights Community Congress v. Rosenblatt Realty* proved to be a significant test of the law and had national implications since it established that checking was a legitimate source of evidence, and subsequently established that violating the law had substantial consequences.

On March 11, 1975, Federal District Court chief judge Frank Battisti ruled that the HCC had standing to file the complaint. It qualified as a class action suit that affected all residents of Cleveland Heights who wanted – and were deprived of – the opportunity to live in an integrated community. The trial date was set for August 18 but was delayed. Meanwhile, the HCC mailed notices to 21,000 Cleveland Heights households informing them that they were party to a class action suit. Since neither side wanted the expense of the trial, the parties ultimately settled the case on May 26, 1976. Rosenblatt agreed to pay the HCC $15,000, the largest settlement made to date in a racial steering case. The firm also stopped working in Cleveland Heights.[31]

## Lending Practices

Realtors frequently referred to African-American prospects as "cash buyers." This thinly veiled insult described the reality that lenders seldomly provided mortgages to blacks. New Deal housing policy made mortgages affordable, but hadn't guaranteed equal access. This remained true despite the Fair Housing Act of 1968.

In 1973 and 1974, the HCC's Housing Task Force staffed by Chip Bromley, along with the Cleveland Heights League of Women Voters (LWV) led by Donalene Poduska, teamed up to examine how lenders were treating their entire community.[32] They spent days at the County Auditor's office comparing who made loans in Lakewood and Cleveland Heights, suburbs which had developed at the same time with comparable housing stock but different demographics. They found glaring differences in access to conventional loans. Compared with homeowners in Lakewood, Cleveland Heights buyers had to rely more on FHA loans than mortgages by private lenders.

These findings played an important role in shaping the federal Home Lending Disclosure Act. Cleveland Heights Mayor Jack Boyle shared the hard evidence with U.S. Senate Banking Committee member William Proxmire, Democrat from Wisconsin, who championed the law that took effect on December 31, 1975. The legislation, still in effect, facilitates public scrutiny of lending practices, which provides a check on fairness.

**Heights Housing Service**

By 1970, Heights Citizens for Human Rights, the League of Women Voters, and the City housing staff started to strategize ways to promote a positive image of Cleveland Heights in order to maintain a healthy demand for its housing. Given the long-standing realtor view of integration as undesirable, it was important to promote a different perspective. Residents could tell their own stories of their favorable experiences. Mayor Schroeder invited the members of the emerging HCC and many other community leaders to share their ideas for selling integration and Cleveland Heights to realtors. In February 1973, Barbara Roderick organized the first of many meetings with realtors to sell them on the benefits of living in Cleveland Heights, and she also shared ideas she collected from community members.

City government also expanded its investment in marketing in 1974. Councilman Richard Weigand, who had served on the HCC's Housing Task Force, introduced a plan designed to "ensure that prospective buyers are shown the benefits of living in Cleveland Heights."[33] It won approval on a 4 to 3 vote. The ideas came from the St. Ann Audit report. The City contracted with an advertising firm to develop a promotional campaign to sell Cleveland Heights and contracted with the HCC to operate the Heights Housing Service. The $20,000 City contract with HCC supported a coordinator and four part-time staffers who escorted prospective residents on tours of all of the housing available in Cleveland Heights in their price range, and who also promoted the advantages of living in the community.

The close council vote for this plan reflected the relatively weak position of the liberal majority that was elected in 1973. Though Mayor Schroeder, a member of the old guard, had been supportive of the HCC and espoused fair housing, he did not support the marketing ordinance. The City's 12-member Real Estate Advisory Board, which included six realtors, also objected, saying it violated the terms of the voluntary agreement with realtors who pledged not to discriminate. Another complaint was that "the city was making the Congress an unofficial arm of the government."[34]

An additional impediment was the Cleveland Area Board of Realtors (CABOR), who saw the housing service as competition and tried to block the program. They rejected Fagan's assurances that the role of the housing service was to sell the community and to create more business for realtors. CABOR insisted that the staff would be practicing real estate without a license. CABOR filed a complaint in Common Pleas Court and asked the Ohio Real Estate Commission to investigate the housing offices in Shaker Heights and Cleveland Heights.[35]

Despite these obstacles, the Heights Housing Service opened in the Congress office on Lee Road in May 1974. Housing activists staffed the service, and Suzanne Nigro accepted the job of coordinator. Her team included Jeanne Martin, Linda Johnston, and Nancy Hall. Susanna Niermann O'Neil, who had worked on tenant rights as a member of Coventry Neighbors, became the rental coordinator and Irene Shapiro, who had worked for the Heights Area Project, was the secretary.

Their job was to create drive-by routes for prospects to view houses in their price range, and in cases where the home was for sale by owner, to arrange visits. These Cleveland Heights boosters sold the community, and as Martin explained, "helped get sales to happen."[36] They received nominal pay, but according to Nigro, they were willing to do the work because "everyone was committed to fair housing and to the concept that potential buyers should see everything that was available in their price range."[37]

Much like HCHR's system for recruiting white homeowners to sell on the "open" basis, Nigro and her staff recruited a volunteer for every street and coordinators for the ten elementary school areas. Volunteers reported to their coordinator any houses for sale and responded to calls from interested prospects who wanted to know more about a street. Widespread concern about the discriminatory practices found by the St. Ann Audit made it easy to recruit help for the project.

"We had no shortage of clients," recalls Nigro.[38] Word of mouth and advertising by the City directed prospective buyers to the Housing Service. Each month, Nigro would report to city hall on their activities with prospects. At the November 17, 1975 council meeting, Fagan reported on the total impact of the Housing Service during its first 16 months. By this point, the staff had worked with 473 families, of whom 398 or 89% were white. Of those served, 169 white clients and 17 black clients bought houses in Cleveland Heights. Realtors were involved in 126 of the 186 sales, with the remainder conducted by the owner. The program was working, and realtors were benefiting.[39]

Despite the success of the Housing Service, it still faced opposition in council. Council member Alfred Connors had opposed the housing service when he ran for office, and in spite of Nigro's positive report, he continued his opposition. He and Marjory Wright objected to the request for additional funds for the Housing Office, and they expressed their opposition by challenging the reliability of the report. This foreshadowed trouble ahead for the Housing Service.

Nevertheless, this opposition did not discourage Sue Nigro, who described the contribution of the housing service in her memoir:

> For the two and a half years that the HHS was a program of the HCC the idea took off – whites and blacks continued to buy all over Cleveland Heights. Panic selling diminished and neighborhoods began to feel they had some control over how their area was shown to prospective buyers. Of course, the HHS success was also dependent upon all the other efforts occurring: enforcement of the anti-solicitation laws, housing being brought up to code, and the public relations efforts begun by city government.[40]

Unfortunately, the 1975 election had negative consequences for the HCC. Allies Jack Boyle and Lucille Huston were defeated, and Libby Resnik and Dick Weigand were now outnumbered. In addition, the City faced a revenue short fall. Consequently, in June 1976, the City prematurely ended the housing service contract and began administering the program in-house. Many community activists who thought the program's identity as a community-based resource was important to its success resented the City takeover. Nigro feared that the focus on open housing might be lost.

City manager Bob Edwards invited Susanna Niermann O'Neil to move inside city hall and take charge of the program. When she learned that other members of the Housing Service team were not invited, she turned down the offer. Fagan intervened and convinced her to accept the position, confident that she could make a difference.[41] Her career at city hall began on August 1, 1976, and since that time she has served as the principal actor within city government in promoting Cleveland Heights as a great place to live.

"I started fighting city hall, then became part of it," recalls Niermann O'Neil, who brought with her a passion for integration and for Cleveland Heights.[42] Barbara Roderick was her mentor, and together they successfully spearheaded the City's work to support integration. Niermann O'Neil embraced the guiding vision for working with realtors: you sell the houses, we'll sell the community. As the author of the promotional materials that described Cleveland Heights for the next five decades, she was able to follow her heartfelt belief that you don't let others tell your story.

At the same time that Niermann O'Neil moved into city hall, Fagan became the full-time Executive Director of the Commission on Catholic Community Action. Kermit Lind who joined the staff in 1974, stepped in as executive director. Rev. Ned Edwards replaced Rev. Charles Mayer as board president. The nascent organization was faced with the loss of the City contract and the end of start-up funding by the Cleveland Foundation. It was an important transition. Nevertheless, the HCC survived both challenges, and, indeed, thrived.

It didn't take long for the HCC's organizing efforts to gain recognition. In September 1976, the Cleveland Chapter of the American Jewish Committee awarded the Heights Community Congress the Isaiah Award for Human Relations. Tom Reim and Kermit Lind accepted the award. It was the second Cleveland Heights organization to earn attention for its efforts to promote racial understanding and respect. The first was given to Heights Citizens for Human Rights in 1969. The award continues to be given to local nonprofits that promote a more just society.[43]

The HCC became a national model for thwarting the realtor's hold on a community. The approach depended on fully engaging city residents as owners and protectors of their community. The Congress' activities mobilized the residents of Cleveland Heights to solve problems and advance positive race relations. It engaged public institutions as partners in advancing integration and making it a community asset. They never stopped monitoring realtor behavior. Not only had the HCC become a national model, but its work now had national ramifications.

# HARRY FAGAN

HARRY FAGAN WAS AN EFFECTIVE COMMUNITY ORGANIZER. HE IMPLEMENTED "ACTION FOR A CHANGE," HELPED DESIGN AND LEAD THE HEIGHTS COMMUNITY CONGRESS, HELPED SHAPE THE CUYAHOGA PLAN AND THE NINE-POINT PLAN FOR CLEVELAND HEIGHTS, AND DIRECTED THE COMMISSION ON CATHOLIC COMMUNITY ACTION. (CLEVELAND DIOCESE ARCHIVES)

*Harry Fagan's large personality and strategic mind made a lasting impact on Cleveland Heights in a very short period of time. His approach to integration can be summarized by the way he defined the issue, "The problem isn't blacks moving in. It's whites moving out."*

*In 1971, Fagan, a progressive Catholic and resident of Cleveland Heights, left his job selling advertising for the* **Cleveland Plain Dealer** *to implement "Action for A Change," the first large-scale project of the newly formed Commission on Catholic Community Action. This project was a response to Vatican II and its mandate to promote the social justice mission of the Catholic Church. The St. Ann Audit, which took place in 1972, was an outgrowth of the effort.*

*As director of "Action for A Change," Fagan motivated and interacted with Catholics throughout the Cleveland Diocese and developed a reputation as a witty, charismatic leader and effective activist. In 1972, he brought these skills to bear in the struggle for integration in Cleveland Heights.*

*By this time, racial change had accelerated with the African-American population growing to 12% of the residents of Cleveland Heights. The prospect of resegregation loomed in many people's minds. In February of 1972, representatives from Catholic and Jewish institutions began to meet in the Carmelite Monastery to find a way to stabilize racial change and protect their investments in Cleveland Heights. They knew Fagan would be an asset to their organizing. Catholic members of the committee asked the Catholic Commission to assign Fagan to work with them. He joined the group and became the chief architect of the strategy to make integration viable over the long term.*

*For many from this era, Harry Fagan is synonymous with the Heights Community Congress. Sue Janssen, a former checker for the Congress, noted (like many others), "I'm one of Harry's people." By the middle of 1973, he was both the assistant director of the Catholic Commission and the part-time director of Heights Community Congress.*

*Described by Jack Boyle (who worked with the Congress as both a member of council and as mayor) as "a people person with a social conscience," Fagan dedicated his efforts to social justice through grassroot activism. He believed community organizing was the way to get residents to invest in their community and prevent flight. As he once famously said, "if we keep people going to meetings, they won't have time to think about moving out." At the time, most community organizing focused on city neighborhoods. Fagan wanted to be the first person to organize a suburb, something he achieved when he led the HCC.*

*Randy Cunningham, who documented the work of the Catholic Commission, likened Fagan to the pied piper since he had a way of taming critics, energizing allies, and raising funds. He shaped the Congress into an effective, dynamic body and encouraged his staff to be self-directed and energetic. He developed a positive and productive relationship with Cleveland Heights Mayor Oliver Schroeder who helped convene and name the Congress, and who as a council member introduced the Nine-Point Plan that he designed with Fagan, Boyle, and Barbara Roderick.*

*The Congress played an important role in pressing city government, one of the member organizations, to effect change. Jack Boyle noted that Harry was able to gain support from both the old guard and upstart challengers who wanted more from government.*

*Late in 1976, after three years with the Congress, he resigned to devote his full attention to the Catholic Commission as its new executive director. He wrote a book on local organizing in 1980, and in 1983, moved to New York to promote church-based social action as co-founder of the National Pastoral Life Center. He died at age 52 from cancer in December of 1992, a week before the death of the founder of the Commission on Catholic Community Action, Bishop Cosgrove. He left behind a long list of admirers who learned, after working with him, the most effective ways to make change.*

HARRY AND SHEILA FAGAN AND THEIR FAMILY LIVED AT 2303 CANTERBURY ROAD IN CLEVELAND HEIGHTS. (SUSAN KAESER)

# KERMIT LIND

IN 1976 THE AMERICAN JEWISH COMMITTEE RECOGNIZED THE HEIGHTS COMMUNITY CONGRESS FOR ITS WORK ADVANCING HUMAN RELATIONS. IN HIS NEW ROLE AS EXECUTIVE DIRECTOR, KERMIT LIND ACCEPTED THE AWARD. (KERMIT LIND)

*Kermit Lind was raised in a small town in central Kansas by a Mennonite minister, educator, and community leader. He graduated from Goshen College, attended Earlham School of Religion for a year, and pursued a doctorate at the University of Chicago. He moved to Cleveland in 1969 to start a career as a history professor at Cleveland State University. In 1971, after a year "of embarrassing exposure to raw racism in Euclid," he and his wife relocated to an apartment on Euclid Heights Boulevard in Cleveland Heights. He was immediately drawn into Coventry Neighbors, a new grassroots neighborhood group led by Charles Mathews, whose work focused on landlord-tenant issues, parking, and racial justice. So began his career focused on housing integration and neighborhood stability.*

*Coventry Neighbors recruited him to serve as a checker to gather evidence of racial discrimination in rental housing. He worked closely with two other young civil rights activists, Susanna and Dennis Niermann. The* Wethers v. Peters Realty *case filed in 1973, became the first federal fair housing lawsuit in the Northern District Court of Ohio. A newly minted attorney, Avery Friedman, argued the case and won it on appeal in 1976.*

*In 1973, with his dissertation efforts floundering, a forced exodus from his teaching position, and recognition that his future as a history professor was unlikely, he became a volunteer with the newly formed Heights Community Congress and served on its rental housing task force. His willingness to write proposals and otherwise "serve as a scribe" soon earned him a place on the staff as a community organizer for the Coventry area.*

*Lind provided important leadership through a difficult transition period for the fledgling organization when he succeeded founding director Harry Fagan in 1976. That year the Congress lost its charismatic founder, its first board president, and the housing service, an important program and source of funding. It also no longer qualified for start-up funding from local foundations. To close the funding gap, Lind launched the Heights Heritage Tour, an enduring community event that has kept the organization solvent.*

*In 1977, he took over the Cuyahoga Plan of Ohio, the regional fair housing organization incubated by Cleveland Heights leaders. It was an opportunity to apply to the region housing strategies tested in Cleveland Heights. St. Ann Audit team member and HCC staffer Lana Cowell succeeded Lind as director of the Congress and led the organization for 14 years.*

*During Lind's eight years with the Cuyahoga Plan, he earned a law degree, and in 1987, became a staff attorney with the Housing Advocates, a nonprofit fair housing organization.*

*Lind returned to his teaching roots in 1995, as a clinical professor at the Cleveland-Marshall College of Law where he trained future attorneys in the Urban Development Law Clinic until his retirement in 2011. As an active member of Forest Hill Church he continues to focus on housing and racial justice. With the help of Diana Woodbridge, he has challenged banks to be responsible for houses affected by foreclosure due to predatory lending, and city government to use its authority to protect neighborhoods.*

IN DECEMBER 1963 THE CLEVELAND HEIGHTS HIGH SCHOOL CHOIR REHEARSED FOR THE ANNUAL CHANUKAH FESTIVAL AT TEMPLE ON THE HEIGHTS. BY 1971 THE HIGH SCHOOL ENROLLMENT WAS 65% JEWISH AND 5% AFRICAN AMERICAN. JEWISH LEADERS FORMED THE HEIGHTS ASSEMBLY TO PREVENT A JEWISH EXODUS FROM THE COMMUNITY IN REACTION TO INTEGRATION. (CLEVELAND PUBLIC LIBRARY)

AFTER A SKIRMISH AT HEIGHTS HIGH EXPOSED RACIAL TENSION IN THE NEWLY INTEGRATED SCHOOL, PRINCIPAL JAMES O'TOOLE, WHO LIVED AT 2576 EXETER ROAD, JOINED WITH JEWISH AND CATHOLIC LEADERS TO CREATE THE HEIGHTS COMMUNITY CONGRESS. (1972 CALDRON, CLEVELAND HEIGHTS HIGH SCHOOL YEARBOOK)

THE HEIGHTS ACTION COMMITTEE MET IN THE BASEMENT OF THE CARMELITE MONASTERY TO PLAN THE HEIGHTS COMMUNITY CONGRESS. (SUSAN KAESER)

BY THIS DECEMBER 1973 MEETING OF THE HCC BOARD AT THE CLEVELAND HEIGHTS LIBRARY, THE NEW ORGANIZATION HAD ACHIEVED ITS GOAL OF UNITING THE COMMUNITY'S PUBLIC INSTITUTIONS AND DIVERSE INTEREST GROUPS TO SHAPE THE FUTURE. (CLEVELAND HEIGHTS LIBRARY COLLECTION)

THE HEIGHTS COMMUNITY CONGRESS OPENED FOR BUSINESS IN 1974 IN DONATED SPACE ON THE SECOND FLOOR OF THE BUILDING ON THE RIGHT AT THE INTERSECTION OF CEDAR AND LEE ROADS. (CLEVELAND PUBLIC LIBRARY)

# CHAPTER 9

# CITY GOVERNMENT STEPS UP

Cleveland Heights city government had resources and leverage that could complement the citizen voice in demanding equal housing access for African Americans. But historically, city leaders had consistently ignored requests for action and resisted opportunities to support change. Eventually, their initial hostility to integration gradually softened as racial change became a reality and as voters elected new officials.

By the time the 1968 Fair Housing Act took effect in 1970, racial change had begun. Census data for 1970 showed that Cleveland Heights had experienced a net loss of about 1,000 residents over the previous decade but had gained nearly 1,300 black residents. In 1970, there were more than 1,500 African Americans in this elite suburb who accounted for 2.5% of its population. This small but significant change was enough to trigger realtors, who had blocked integration, to try to ignite rapid racial change. City government could no longer afford to be passive if it wanted to preserve the quality of life that the old guard thought they were defending by ignoring the reality of racial change.

Thanks to citizen pressure, the ballot box, and Mayor Oliver Schroeder's evolution as a community leader, city government eventually became a forceful resource for integrated living. In 1976, city council approved its Nine-Point Plan that put into law policies to maintain housing quality, to prevent negative real estate practices, and to market the community and its integration as an asset. These steps established a strong foundation for stable integration.

The Nine-Point Plan included strategies long advocated by housing activists but ignored by city leaders. HCHR leaders Mary Boenke and Ralph Brody first asked for council action in 1965 and 1966. Gerda Freedheim and the Heights Citizens for Human Rights Housing Committee proposed a housing strategy when the City hired Barbara Roderick in 1970. Tom Reim and Sue Nigro offered a blueprint for action in their September 1972 report to council about the findings of the St. Ann's Audit. Harry Fagan and the Heights Community Congress pushed the 200% Solution in 1973.

When these reasonable ideas finally became the law in 1976, it was a decisive victory for citizen activists, and the beginning of an important, new united effort to shape behavior and culture which was needed for stable integration. Many years later when Harry Fagan saw the new Cleveland Heights City Hall, he quipped to Jack Boyle, "If it wasn't for us, they would not have needed this enormous building."[1]

### City Council Elections Pave the Way for a Stronger City Role

For 60 years, city council had been a self-perpetuating body made up of professional white men who were dedicated to low taxes and a limited role for city government. Individuals served for 20 to 30 years and resigned far enough ahead of the next election so a replacement could be appointed and then run as an incumbent. It was a closed shop.[2] In 1969, as civil rights issues became more pressing, as dismay with the self-perpetuating city council grew, and as a new, more independent Cleveland Heights Democratic party emerged, a slate of young outsiders challenged the status quo.

The self-appointed reform group, Citizens Committee for Effective Heights Government, endorsed and campaigned for four Democrats: Anthony Satullo, Robert Chapin, Arthur Brooks, and Robert Sklar. Campaign materials sold the ticket as a way to "Return Representative Government to Cleveland Heights." The platform promised vigorous housing code enforcement, updated building and housing codes, improved police protection, and opposition to new freeways. The candidates promised a responsive city hall.[3] HCHR endorsed the slate.

Nevertheless, the ticket failed to gain even one seat; however, Brooks came within 29 votes of winning and Robert Chapin fell short by 133 votes. The near victories encouraged a second challenge to the old guard in 1971 when Wendell Phillips and HCHR volunteers Jack Boyle and Lucille Huston ran for the three contested seats under the banner PACT – Plan of Action for Citizens Together. This time the two advocacy groups, Committee to Improve Community Relations and HCHR, endorsed the slate.

The November 1971 *HCHR Newsletter* urged members to vote for the trio because "the Community needs them!" The endorsement noted, "The present council has proven by its record its inability to either recognize the needs, or plan for, or solve the needs of the city. Their record IS the issue." Boyle and Huston won, making them the first Democrats to ever serve on the Cleveland Heights City Council.

Jack and his wife, Mary Boyle, were progressive Catholics and part of a national movement of religious lay leaders. Their public service was motivated by faith. Jack Boyle explained, "In our view of Christianity you have to be involved in making the community better, and government service was one of the best ways to do that."[4] In 1964, when the Boyles lived in Cleveland, Jack ran for state representative and lost. After his successful run for Cleveland Heights Council in 1971, he lost a second bid in 1975 but regained a seat in 1977 and served for eight more years. The council elected him mayor for three terms.

Mary Boyle was an active volunteer, participating in "Action for A Change," the Heights Action Committee, and the Heights YWCA. She ran Art Brooks' successful campaign for state representative before being elected Cuyahoga County Commissioner and then state representative.

As a candidate for city council in 1971, Jack Boyle searched for books on how to stabilize integration. There weren't any. Looking back on the 1970s, Boyle concluded, "We wrote the book."

The Cleveland Heights City Council elected Oliver Schroeder as mayor in 1971. The days of the self-perpetuating white elite who had been hostile to integration and resistant to playing a leadership role were over. Among the seven council members were Democratic newcomers Boyle and Huston and two moderate Republicans, Marjory Wright and Schroeder, who joined council in 1965. With a new configuration of council members, Schroeder's leadership, and threats of community destabilization, the City's role and responsibilities became exceedingly influential.

Schroeder was on the faculty of the Case Law School and lived in the Forest Hill neighborhood. In 1965, he penned the City's first public statement supporting racial diversity. In March 1972, Schroeder and mayors of four neighboring communities announced a common ordinance to ban mass telephone solicitation, a key tool for blockbusting.[5] When Councilperson Wright introduced the resolution at the April 3 council meeting, realtors insisted they could police themselves. Two weeks later, council approved a trial 90-day ban on solicitation. Realtors agreed not to call anyone who filled out a card saying they did not want to be contacted about selling their homes.

A few months later, Mayor Schroeder threw his support behind the plan to mobilize the community's institutions to promote integration. He signaled his stance by inviting community leaders to two meetings to introduce and launch the HCC. Schroeder's interest and encouragement were critical to the group's mission and marked the start of closer citizen-city government collaboration.

On September 14, 1972, a week after the public release of the unsettling findings of the St. Ann Audit and a week before the launch of the Heights Community Congress, a firebomb created "havoc and destruction" at Robert Appling's home at 3656 Brinkmore Road. This time, thanks to the mayor's leadership, the City response to racially motivated violence was unequivocal. Mayor Schroeder publicly condemned the action as "not only illegal, vicious and morally reprehensible, it also seeks to destroy the fine integrated community which we have been quietly and effectively building in our city." He also apologized to the Appling family, calling the fire an act of "hate and ignorance."[6]

Barbara Roderick hosted a coffee for Mrs. Appling to meet some of her neighbors, and human relations staff sponsored a street meeting during which more than 50 residents explored forming a neighborhood association. Oxford PTA co-presidents Donalene Poduska and Vickie Browne rallied the school community, and the PTA adopted a resolution supporting equal opportunity in housing and education.

HCHR President Pippa Kiraly praised the City's response and noted that her organization no longer needed to play its traditional role of mobilizing the community to support the victims and oppose the violence. The City was now doing that job.[7]

In October 1972, the City approved a first-of-its-kind agreement with the Cleveland Area Board of Realtors and the Cleveland Association of Real Estate Brokers, who pledged that their members would end soliciting and refrain from racial steering. The City extended the voluntary effort into 1975 but it collapsed in 1974 after the HCC filed suit against Rosenblatt Realty when the firm violated the agreement.

## New Ventures to Advance Integration

Cleveland Heights did not operate in a vacuum; promoting integration throughout the region was essential to the future stability of the suburb and to the overall goal of fair housing. The Fair Housing Council and Fair Housing Inc., regional partners since 1966, had closed. Operation Equality was waning. Suburban Citizens for Open Housing lost its dynamic leader, Gerda Freedheim. So while stable integration and an open housing market necessitated a regional effort, this had become more difficult with the loss of so many important leaders and organizations.

As the City's point person on integration with a broad web of relationships in fair housing, Barbara Roderick convened an ad hoc committee to focus on open housing at the regional level. The committee's first meeting was held in July 1973 and included Cleveland Heights leaders Freedheim and Fagan, Operation Equality staffer Bruce Melville, and Charles Beard and James Huston from Plan of Action for Tomorrow's Housing (PATH). Leslie Weisenberg represented the Cleveland Foundation.[8] At this meeting, the group began to design a regional fair housing resource that would last for the next two decades.

Designated as the Cuyahoga Plan, the organization was incorporated in March 1974 and opened in November with $130,000 in grants from the Cleveland and George Gund foundations. It operated a housing information service and worked with realtors to end segregation. Communities across the county helped fund the organization.

Cleveland Heights not only sought to create regional solutions, but its city government increased its local fair housing activities as well. The 1973 city council election added two more housing activists, Dick Weigand and Libby Resnik, putting a Democratic block of four in the majority. At the council's first meeting in 1974, members elected Jack Boyle as mayor. This new progressive majority promoted the City's role as a resource for housing and a cooperative partner with the Heights

Community Congress. In 1974, the council, on a 4-3 vote, approved a contract with the HCC to carry out an important community marketing program to prospective home buyers. Surprisingly, Schroeder, who had supported founding the HCC, did not endorse the contract.[9]

Fortunately, this split between Schroeder and the HCC did not end their common interest in addressing the city's pressing challenge – stable integration. Jack Boyle remembers going to Schroeder's home with Roderick, Fagan, and David Sarnat to brainstorm how to proceed.[10] During this informal meeting, they sketched out what would, a year later, become known as the Nine-Point Plan. The plan included recommendations made over the years by Cleveland Heights housing activists.

The Nine-Point Plan – and Schroeder's involvement – was pivotal in maintaining stable integration. Jack Boyle and HCC activists Susanna Niermann O'Neil and Kermit Lind credit Schroeder as the key player who united the City and community in addressing stability. His respect for the law, his ability to communicate effectively with everyone, and his knack for uniting all made it possible for the City and nonprofits to collaborate. It also enabled the City to assume a bolder role.

In 1976, Schroeder served as chair of the Cleveland Heights Municipal Service Committee. At the March 15th city council meeting, he introduced two pieces of legislation that firmly committed the City to an active role in fair housing. The first – Resolution 26-1976, known as the Nine-Point Housing Plan – took a positive approach. The legislation summary describes its purpose:

> A resolution committing the City Council to a renewed and expanded comprehensive program to promote the City of Cleveland Heights as a well-maintained, full service residential community, to prevent racial resegregation, and to foster an increased joint effort with Cleveland Heights residents, community organizations, the Board of Education, the business community, and other institutions in the development and implementation of the described program.[11]

Passage of this first piece of legislation did not go smoothly. It took behind-the-scenes pressure by the HCC to force city council action on the legislative measure. The HCC threatened to file suit against realtors doing business in Cleveland Heights to force the council to act.

Lind described the legislation as the "crowning achievement" of a long-term process, led by the community, to make integration work.[12] This led to a point of sale interior house inspection program to protect new owners from unscrupulous sellers.

Resolution 26- 1976 outlined nine activities to promote housing in Cleveland Heights:

1. Educate and train realtors and reward them by naming them preferred agents.
2. Market the community to prospective buyers through the housing service and advertising.
3. Establish a city board to review complaints about violations of the bans on solicitation, steering, and blockbusting.
4. Expand community and public relations activities to promote benefits of living in Cleveland Heights.
5. Promote fair housing throughout the greater Cleveland community by working with the Cuyahoga Plan (the regional fair housing agency).
6. Establish the Financial Institution Advisory Committee to monitor lending practices that affect integration and the success of the community.
7. Improve the use of code enforcement to make sure public lands, commercial properties, and private dwellings are well maintained.
8. Work closely with community organizations and institutions and the business community.
9. Evaluate the effectiveness of these strategies and recommend improvements.

The plan expressed the council's willingness to partner with the community and impact a wide range of issues that affected stability.

Resolution 27-1976, companion legislation adopted at the same meeting, outlawed steering, blockbusting, and unwanted solicitation – realtor tools used to interfere with an open housing market and hasten segregation. While the Nine-Point Plan offered a positive approach to realtors, this legislation made it illegal for them to engage in destructive practices and promised City involvement when discovered. It took ten years to pass the legislation first proposed by Heights Citizens for Human Rights.

These two pieces of legislation marked a new era for Cleveland Heights. Integration was officially an essential community asset worthy of investment by the community and its public agencies.

While Boyle was an architect of the Nine-Point Plan, it was the Republican majority that was responsible for its passage. In the November 1975 election, Boyle and Houston lost their seats. In the same election, civil rights activist Sara Hunter defeated Kenneth Nash, the obstructionist former mayor, for Cleveland Heights municipal court judge.

Coventry Neighbors member David Burwasser noted the irony of the Republican-controlled city council approving this far-reaching legislation. Just the year before, when liberals had four votes, they passed the housing service contract on a 4-3 vote. A year later, the conservative majority passed a much more controversial program on a 7-0 vote. Burwasser stated, "I was reminded of President Nixon's first trip to China – in that this is something that the liberals harmed themselves politically by talking about, and which the conservative finally did."[13]

It was a transformative moment for Cleveland Heights and for the future of racial integration. Citizens working together through many organizations had embraced open housing as legal and right and fought to create and defend it. They established acceptance of, and comfort with, diversity. They challenged disruptive realtors by using and testing legal remedies. They set the stage for a City role, demanded it, and secured it.

The Heights Community Congress, Forest Hill Church Housing Corporation, Community to Improve Community Relations, and the City were well positioned to forge ahead as resources and protectors of integration. Together they built upon the determination of Cleveland Heights residents to create a vibrant community and a national example of integrated living – and all of the opportunities it brought to generations of residents.

The front page headline of the April 15, 1976, *Sun Press* read, "One of the top 10 cities in the U.S." The story announced Cleveland Heights' designation by the American Municipal League as an All-American City. It had earned this recognition because of the combined work of the HCC, the Housing Service, the Heights Area Project, and the FHCHC. The article stated that "Citizens have taken a long look at the community and have tried to come to grips with racial tension, integration of neighborhoods, and the need for commercial and residential improvements."

The efforts honored by the award paid off. Demographic data (see Table 1.4, p.45) indicates that after an initial surge in black access to Cleveland Heights coupled with a comparable loss of white residents, integration held. Changes have continued but at a gradual pace.

As shown in Table 1.4, the decade between 1970 and 1980 was a period of rapid racial change. The number of African Americans increased by 12,500 while the white population dropped by an even larger amount, resulting in a net loss of 4,000 residents. This combination meant that over 10 years the African-American population increased from 2.5% of the population to 24.9%. However, from that point on, the population shift has been gradual. The black population continued to grow between 1980 and peaked at 20,873 in 2000, while the white population gradually declined. Both black and white numbers dropped between 2000 and 2010. During this decade, the African-American population increased from 41.1% of the population to 42.5%, the smallest change in decades.

The expected tipping point for rapid resegregation never took place.

# OLIVER SCHROEDER

AS MAYORS OF CLEVELAND HEIGHTS, OLIVER SCHROEDER AND JACK BOYLE HELPED TRANSFORM THE ROLE OF
CITY GOVERNMENT AS A RESOURCE FOR INTEGRATION. THEY ARE PICTURED WITH OTHER FORMER MAYORS
AT THE 1980 RIBBON CUTTING FOR THE NEW CITY HALL. LEFT TO RIGHT: JACK BOYLE, ALAN RAPAPORT,
MARJORIE WRIGHT, RICHARD WEIGAND, OLIVER SCHROEDER, BOB ARNOLD, AND AL CONNER. (JACK BOYLE)

*In a 1987 tribute to Oliver Schroeder, CWRU law school faculty member Lewis Katz described his colleague and friend in this way: "Although a traditional eastern Republican, Schroeder has always had the personality of a New Dealer," always willing to try something new and embrace it if it were effective. One of his liberal ideas was a commitment to civil rights and the need for racial understanding, ideas he expressed in speeches as a leader of the Cleveland Bar Association in 1964 and as a member of the Cleveland Council of Churches in 1966.*

*He emerged as an important civic leader during the critical moment in Cleveland Heights history when integration stood at a crossroads. Schroeder was born in 1916, raised in East Cleveland, was educated at Case Western Reserve University and Harvard Law School, and* taught in the CWRU law school. After a stint as interim dean of the Case law school, where he is credited with rescuing a faltering institution, in 1965 he was appointed to the Cleveland Heights City Council and elected in 1969 to a four-year term. He brought a new perspective and fresh voice to the long-standing Republican majority that governed the city. In addition, he carried with him a commitment to civil rights.

Noting Schroeder's Republican credentials and liberal beliefs, Jack Boyle, a Democrat who followed him as mayor, considers him the key player who made Cleveland Heights city government an active resource for integration. Throughout his tenure, Schroeder stayed in touch with the community, advocated for a greater city government role, and experimented to find effective ways to strengthen the integrated community.

In August of 1972, when it was time to convene the organizing meeting that launched the Heights Community Congress, Mayor Schroeder signed his name to invitations to the founding meeting and signaled a willingness for the City to be a partner. He proposed the name for the new organization: Cleveland Heights Community Congress. Through this organization, he developed a friendly working relationship with Harry Fagan and fostered City-community collaboration.

Schroeder served as a bridge between generations and between activists and city government. He worked with Boyle, Fagan, and Barbara Roderick to craft the Nine-Point Plan. He introduced the legislation that won support in 1976 and stayed on council through 1977, the first full year of its implementation.

Schroeder lived on Seaton Road in the Forest Hill neighborhood, which set him apart from most council members, who lived in the more elite southwest part of town. Boyle described him as a principled elder statesman who understood the need for the City's role to change if integration was to succeed. He was a people person who, *unlike many of the old guard, used his affability to stay connected with the community.*

*According to Kermit Lind, "he was a great guy. He could talk to everyone." With his personal style, commitment to civil rights, and desire to find solutions, he was able to lead the city's transformation so it was better equipped to govern in the midst of racial change.*

*Oliver Schroeder lived in Cleveland Heights for 50 years. He died on September 25, 2008 at age 92.*

OLIVER SCHROEDER LIVED AT 3375 SEATON ROAD IN THE FOREST HILL NEIGHBORHOOD. AS A MEMBER OF COUNCIL AND AS MAYOR, HE HELPED MAKE STABLE INTEGRATION THE FOCUS OF PUBLIC POLICY.
(SUSAN KAESER)

# SUSANNA NIERMANN O'NEIL

*Susanna Niermann O'Neill started her long career as an advocate for Cleveland Heights and integrated living in 1971 by fighting against city hall. Ironically, she started working for city government in 1976, and since then has used this position to advance the values that inspired her activism.*

*As a volunteer for Coventry Neighbors and then as one of the first members of the Heights Community Congress staff, she became an integral part of the movement to demand a stronger City role in advancing and protecting integration. She was instrumental in implementing the City's long-awaited response, the Nine-Point Plan. To this day, now as interim city manager, she keeps a copy of the plan at her fingertips, and it continues to guide her thinking. She claims responsibility for having written almost every word used to promote Cleveland Heights since 1976.*

*O'Neil grew up in the Collinwood neighborhood of Cleveland and met her husband Dennis Niermann at John Carroll University. The newly married couple, inspired by the idealism of President John F. Kennedy and Dr. Martin Luther King, Jr., were determined to make a difference in their community. They moved to an apartment building in the Coventry neighborhood in 1971, where they were the custodians, and joined Coventry Neighbors, one of the first community organizations in town. It was with this organization that they began their work on issues related to rental housing.*

*At the time, the couple joined Kermit Lind and other volunteers as checkers to monitor racial discrimination in rental housing in their neighborhood. Their work contributed to the Wethers case, the first fair housing court case filed to enforce the new fair housing act. In 1973, the brand-new Heights Community Congress hired Niermann O'Neil to oversee a youth program. The next year, she became the rental housing coordinator for the Heights Housing Service, a City-funded project implemented by the Congress.*

*When the Cleveland Heights City Council made the controversial decision to revoke the Housing Service contract in 1976, she was invited to join the city hall staff and carry out the program from there. The heavy-handed move by city leaders to eliminate this contract discouraged Niermann O'Neil but Harry Fagan convinced her to take the City job. Much to her relief, Barbara Roderick, her new boss, was also like-minded and soon became her mentor. After Roderick left the City in 1979, leadership for marketing the community fell to Niermann O'Neil.*

*She continues to work there today, acting as the guardian of the important history and the critical role played by the city government to maintain successful integration.*

CLEVELAND HEIGHTS EARNED THE STATUS OF ALL-AMERICAN CITY IN 1976. THE AWARD RECOGNIZED COMMUNITY AND CITY GOVERNMENT EFFORTS TO SUPPORT INTEGRATION. (CITY OF CLEVELAND HEIGHTS)

CLEVELAND HEIGHTS ACTIVISTS CHALLENGED SEGREGATION, AND BY 1976 CITY GOVERNMENT CELEBRATED AND MARKETED THE RESULTS. (JOYCE COLLINS)

# CHAPTER 10

# DEMOCRACY IN ACTION

*"Though all neighborhoods are products of their history, integrated neighborhoods are products of a national history that makes them an endangered species. Spawned by a legacy of racism which created black enclaves in each central city, displaced by urban renewal and shunted by denial of free choice to other neighborhoods, there met by small stalwart bands of idealists fired by the wish to welcome and remain side by side with them, such neighborhoods must surely be considered a national treasure. They are the living result of the civil rights movement."*

– Juliet Saltman, The Fragile Movement, 1990.[1]

Cleveland Heights is an enduring outcome of the civil rights movement. It is a national treasure. This previously all-white suburb in a hyper-segregated region was transformed by grassroots energy that challenged the pernicious perception of African Americans as second-class citizens.

Following the lead of black role models, Cleveland Heights residents, working through five local organizations and multiple regional fair housing groups, challenged housing segregation. They resisted two forms of housing segregation: all-white suburbs and the reimposition of segregation on integrated neighborhoods.

Social change is a long and complex process. Social justice activism, originating in living rooms and church basements, often led by young women and parents of young children, proved that organized citizens can be potent engines of change. Black and white activists, working as allies, thwarted segregation, a housing pattern with deep roots and a broad reach, which had been advanced by public policy and built over a long period of time out of fear and the profit motive. They proved that all-white neighborhoods could become integrated, and integrated communities could endure. Because of their activism, change of a magnificent kind took place.

Despite the institutionalization of fairness through laws, in this story, fair housing legislation helped but was insufficient without citizen participation. Gerda Freedheim, the driver of so many of the initiatives to guarantee black inclusion in suburban life during the 1960s, captured the importance of this effort: "We eliminated a blight on our society. We set out to open up Cleveland Heights to anyone who wanted to buy there. It worked!"[2]

Susanna Niermann O'Neil, who went from fighting city hall to becoming the guardian of the City's Nine-Point Plan, described the relevance of this era in these terms: "We built a strong community that shows that white and black can live together. It has been important for generations of children who have grown up with this philosophy."[3]

The Cleveland Heights case provides instructive lessons about citizens as leaders of change and the importance of challenging entrenched issues at the community level. Unlike elected leaders, grassroots activists can more readily take the necessary risks to lead a social revolution. When it comes to historic and seemingly intractable issues like housing segregation, the community level is where change is most possible. This is the scale where citizen voices are the most powerful and problems can be separated into pieces and then solved.

Both the courageous black newcomers who took the risk of seeking housing in white neighborhoods and their white allies who paved the way for them to become neighbors were willing to enter unfamiliar territory, identify their shared goals, and work together to confront the barriers to equality. By looking for housing in white communities, blacks asserted their rights and challenged the status quo. By raising their voices, white residents and black allies ended tacit acceptance of segregation and unleashed the community's untapped willingness to become a different kind of place.

Their actions were heroic yet simple, often tedious, time-consuming, and uncomfortable, and frequently disappointing and painful. But they changed expectations and behavior, produced results, formed lasting friendships, and left behind a legacy of nonprofit organizations that encourage citizen responsibility for the community and its success. They developed homegrown expertise and created a new generation of community leaders. Their work demonstrates what can be achieved by talking with neighbors, attending meetings, learning from others, writing letters, demonstrating, lobbying elected officials – showing up and speaking up.

Their activism was motivated by idealism, concern for social justice, and the practical reality that white flight is devastating to the community and devastating for existing institutions. Idealism and pragmatism motivated participation by a wide swath of individual and institutional players who had the capacity to fight on many fronts and persevere over the long haul.

Black citizens were crucial to achieving integration and establishing its benefits. They took the risk of entering a potentially hostile housing market to demand the right to live wherever they chose. They played a key role in working patiently with well-intentioned, but often unaware, white allies to help shape their community. They provided crucial leadership, insisting that city government and the public schools meet their needs and defend their rights. They effectively used the federal complaint process to advance important equity goals. They played by the rules and followed expected norms to press for legitimate and meaningful change. They earned white respect and validated the idea that integration was beneficial to the community, not something to fear.

Realtors, community members, and market demand for living in Cleveland Heights all determined the viability of integration. Strategies to address each of these factors were essential. Activists and new laws curbed the outsized power of realtors as gatekeepers. Community outreach built resident comfort with racial change and recognition among neighbors that they determined the fate of integration. This helped reduce white flight, nurture community pride, and contribute to making integration a positive experience. Recruitment and marketing fostered demand for housing in Cleveland Heights that was not defined by race.

Advocates for fair housing seized the moment and successfully pushed for laws to prohibit discrimination in housing. They quickly discovered that the existence of a law doesn't in itself produce legal behavior. Realtor and lender discrimination did not end just because it was illegal. Activists had to face the reality that housing laws were necessary but far from sufficient to guarantee equal housing opportunities.

Realtors were a formidable challenge. Weakening their control over who lived in the community demanded an unrelenting and intensive, multifaceted approach. The strength of realtor resistance to the law was heartbreaking to those fighting for desegregated neighborhoods. But those laws defined discrimination as illegal, which gave activists new arguments and new leverage to demand change. And they used them. They were both creative and persistent.

Each organization contributed to the solution. After HCHR put realtors on notice that the community wanted integration and yet, they were still rebuffed, the organization circumvented agents in order to gain black access to white-owned property. They also lobbied for fair housing legislation, and when laws were passed, they provided critical volunteer support to blacks seeking relief when realtors or owners denied them access in violation of the law.

HCHR, St. Ann's Housing Action Committee, the Heights Community Congress, and city government all used the law to nudge realtors – with both carrots and sticks – to end practices which enforced segregation. They educated realtors about the law, befriended them and rewarded them for following the law. They also, however, collected evidence of them violating the law, helped disenfranchised home seekers file complaints, and filed lawsuits that established the consequences of patterns of discrimination. Several activists even became realtors so buyers could have access to properties without consideration of race. They also focused on the political reality that electing supportive city leaders was necessary to secure policies that advanced their goals.

To activate enforcement of the law, any party who experienced discrimination had to file a complaint and provide evidence; HCHR volunteers helped with that process. The Heights Community Congress went a step further, filing and winning a lawsuit that established substantial consequences for realtors who violated the law. Both of these roles were essential in using the laws to curb discrimination. Through enforcement and realtor education, realtor behavior slowly changed. Fair housing became more likely, and the speed of wholesale population change decelerated.

Successful integration depended on residents overcoming their racial fears, curbing their impulse to flee, and welcoming new neighbors. During this period, HCHR, CICR, Forest Hill Church, and HCC organized activities that helped residents confront racist attitudes and unnecessary fears and develop tolerance. At the same time, they built neighborhood organizations to solve problems and strengthen personal relationships. In addition, they formed task forces to identify issues and advocate policies that would improve the community as a whole.

Realtors and popular narrative had once promoted the idea that racial mixing would destroy property values. Forest Hill Church directly confronted this issue by creating the Forest Hill Church Housing Corporation to address the real threat to property values: discrimination by lenders that limited access to funds needed to finance home ownership and maintenance. FHCHC helped first-time homebuyers maintain the aging housing stock. The City's point of sale inspection ordinance, that prevented homeowners from selling a faulty product to an unsuspecting buyer, also addressed the critical need to maintain property.

Each of these efforts to engage residents made Cleveland Heights a more interesting and durable community. Engagement solved problems, generated pride in and loyalty to Cleveland Heights, strengthened ownership for the fate of the community, and produced a willing cadre of ambassadors for integrated living.

Stable integration depends on continued demand for housing by all racial groups. Typically, the population of a community is in constant flux. Its stability depends on both those who move out and those who replace them. HCHR focused on bringing blacks into their all-white community. They joined with regional projects to connect blacks with housing throughout the suburbs to take pressure off of integrated communities and guarantee a truly open housing market.

They also tackled the challenge of maintaining white demand for housing in integrated spaces. Cleveland Heights is rich with amenities which made it easy to market to all potential residents. City government and the HCC partnered to market the community to black and white buyers and helped to create a new regional housing agency, the Cuyahoga Plan, to open new suburbs and reduce the pressure on already integrated communities.

Cleveland Heights activists believed in integration and fought for it. They created an integrated community from the ground up and organized neighbors to support it. They then actively marketed their community along with its impressive assets. They created nonprofit organizations that addressed real problems and nurtured a culture of civic activism and problem-solving that both made the community attractive and supported diversity. They demanded state and local government involvement and elected representatives who were in tune with changing times and willing to invest city resources in a diverse community.

Grassroots activists and the organizations they created during this period not only adapted effectively to a changing landscape as their community changed, they stayed the course. The most successful and enduring organizations recruited new generations to their work, and both the organizations and their leaders remained dedicated to the cause for decades beyond this pivotal moment. Because of this committed fight, they left behind a vibrant community, a rich civic culture, and an integrated city.

## Integration Progress and Citizen Vigilance

Community activists, starting in the 1960s, fought for housing integration because it was the route to equal opportunity, racial equality, and racial harmony. Integrated living remains a hallmark of a more just and inclusive society. In their 2012 review of the status of housing integration in urban regions, *America's Racially Diverse Suburbs: Opportunities and Challenges*, Myron Orfield and Thomas Luce assert that "integrated communities represent the best policy path for the nation's educational, economic and political success."[4]

Based on their review of 2000 and 2010 census data for America's 50 largest metropolitan areas, the authors conclude that more communities are integrated and a larger portion of the population is living in racially diverse communities. In reviewing data for 52 central cities, 4,332 suburbs, and 2,147 exurbs, they determined that while nonwhite residents of the 52 cities in the study experience nearly "apartheid levels of segregation," there were 1,376 "diverse" suburbs where between 20% and 60% of the population is nonwhite.[5] These communities are home to 31% of the population of these metropolitan areas.

Despite substantial growth in black access to integrated suburbs in the 21st century compared to the 1960s, stable integration is not secure. According to an analysis by the National Commission on Fair Housing and Equal Opportunity, integration is jeopardized by realtors and lenders who continue to discriminate.[6]

Orfield and Luce share this concern: "Most currently diverse communities are in the process of resegregation, but have no real plans to do anything about it. The truth is that most diverse suburbs have no idea of how to address resegregation."[7]

When Cleveland Heights activists and community leaders in hundreds of neighborhoods across the country began to resist segregation in the 1960s, they did not have a roadmap for success. That is no longer the case. Integrated suburbs today may lack knowledge of how to preserve diversity, but there is experience to draw on. These scholars point to the organized, proactive, citizen-driven activists in Cleveland Heights, Shaker Heights and Oak Park, Illinois, as models for successful integration. What worked then, works now.

## Activism Works

Cleveland Heights is one of the places that won this fight, and it provides inspiration and direction to a new generation of civil rights activists who are willing to resist segregation. Integration and its stable maintenance require focused activism. Durable integration requires constant vigilance.

Solutions to massive problems demand leadership by communities. If this case study shows anything, it is that citizens are powerful resources for overcoming the status quo. A handful of people who share a common concern and trust each other can launch a meaningful challenge to problems that demand change but appear to be impossible to resolve.

They can work miracles together, despite every hardship, and against great odds.

# NOTES

### Guide to Abbreviations
**ADC** – Archives, Diocese of Cleveland
**CHCRC** – Cleveland Heights Civil Rights Collection, Cleveland State University Library
**WRHS** – Western Reserve Historical Society

## Introduction – Grassroots Resistance to a National Problem
1. Taylor Branch, *The King Years* (New York: Simon & Schuster, 2013), p. 3.
2. The assumption that integration is only temporary is described by Kermit Lind, "Maintaining Residential Integration," *Cleveland State Law Review* (1982): P. 608 and by Morris Milgram in *Good Neighborhood* (New York: W.W. Norton and Co., 1979), p152.
3. National Commission on Fair Housing and Equal Opportunity, *The Future of Fair Housing* (December 2008), p. 59.
4. Charles Lamb, *Housing Segregation in Suburban America Since 1960* (Cambridge: Cambridge University Press, 2005), p. 116. The author reports President Nixon's opposition both to legally sanctioned segregation and to any mandated remedy. He quotes Nixon: "forced integration of housing or education is equally wrong."
5. The history of National Neighbors is described in Chapter 4 of *Good Neighborhood* by Morris Milgram. Chip Bromley named several other organizations that joined the group including Evanston, Oak Park, Bellwood, and Maywood, Chicago suburbs, and Maplewood, East and West Orange in New Jersey.
6. Morris Milgram, 1979, pages 319-330, and Juliet Saltman, *A Fragile Movement* (Westport,CT: Greenwood Press, 1990) document the history of National Neighbors. Chip Bromley, who as a board member became the volunteer director during this period, also described the transition in an interview with the author.

## Chapter 1: Challenging Difficult Odds
1. Transportation is a significant factor in urban and suburban development. Several authors explore this issue: Kenneth T. Jackson, *Crabgrass Frontier* (New York: Oxford University Press, 1985); Marian Morton, *Cleveland Heights: The Making of an Urban Suburb*, (Charleston: Arcadia Publishing, 2002); and James Borchert in the "Suburbs" entry in *Encyclopedia of Cleveland History*.

2. Kenneth Kusmer, *A Ghetto Takes Shape, Black Cleveland, 1970 -1930* (Urbana: University of Illinois Press, 1976), P. 31.
3. Ibid., p. 46.
4. Langston Hughes, *The Big Sea* (New York: Oxford University Press, 1985), p. 27.
5. Kusmer, *A Ghetto Takes Shape*, p. 162.
6. Howard Whipple Green, *Census Facts and Trends by Tracts, Special 1954 Report* (Cleveland: Cleveland Real Estate Inventory of Metropolitan Cleveland, 1954), p. 5.
7. *Encyclopedia of Cleveland History*, Real Estate. https://case.edu/ech
8. Andrew Wiese, *Places of Their Own* (Chicago: University of Chicago Press, 2004), p. 41.
9. Ibid., p. 50.
10. Antero Pietela, *Not in My Neighborhood* (Chicago: Ivan R. Dee, 2010). p. 50.
11. "Warrensville Heights Gets Blockbusting Measure," *Sun Press*, July 13, 1961, p.1.
12. "Broad Housing Bias Here, Says Ohio Aid," *Cleveland Plain Dealer*, June 5, 1962.
13. "Why Ohio Needs a Fair Housing Act," *Call and Post*, March 23, 1963.
14. Richard Rothstein, *The Color of Law* (New York: Liveright Publishing, 2017), p. xii.
15. See Jackson, Pietela and Wiese for information on these two federal laws and their effects. According to Pietela, Jackson was the first scholar to describe HOLC and the impact of these maps.
16. Pietela, *Not in My Neighborhood*, p. 62.
17. Jackson, *Crabgrass Frontier*, p. 197.
18. Ibid., p.215.
19. Ibid., p. 203.
20. Home Owners Loan Corporation, *Residential Security Map, Cleveland, Ohio, 1939*. Found at www.guides.osu.edu/maps-geospatial-data/maps/redlining/.
21. Jackson, *Crabgrass Frontier*, p. 205.
22. Ibid, p. 208.
23. Ibid, p. 203.
24. Gerda Freedheim and Martin Bloom. *Homesellers Project Work Sheet*. Unpublished, 1968. CHCRC.
25. Mary Emma Harris and Ruth Mills Robinson, *The Proud Heritage of Cleveland Heights, Ohio* (Cleveland: Howard Allen, 1966), p. 1.
26. Morton, *Cleveland Heights, Making of an Urban Suburb*, p. 26.
27. Ibid, p. 42.
28. Ibid, p. 41.
29. Ibid, p. 46.
30. Rich Exner, "When was your town built?" *Sun News*, July 19, 2018, p.1B.

## Chapter 2: The Movement Inspires Action

1. Manning Marable, *Race, Reform, and Rebellion* (Jackson, MS: University Press of Mississippi, 2007), p. 3.

2. Ibid, p. 9.

3. Ibid, p. 38.

4. Steven Lawson and Charles Payne, *Debating the Civil Rights Movement, 1945-68* (Lanham, MD: Rowman and Littlefield Publisher, 1998), p. 18.

5. Branch, *The King Years*, p. 3.

6. Pat Garling and Norman Melnick, "Seeking U.S. Dream, King Tells Throngs," *Cleveland Plain Dealer*, May 15, 1963, p. 1.

7. Branch, *The King Years*, p. 50.

8. John F. Kennedy Library and Museum, *Report to the American People on Civil Rights*, 11 June, 1963.

9. *Encyclopedia of Cleveland History*, "United Freedom Movement," https://case.edu/ech/article/u/united-freedom-movement-ufm.

10. Charles Price, "As Thousands Brave Rain to Join Freedom March," *Call and Post*, July 20, 1963, p. 1A.

11. Robert Peters summarizes the conflict in a letter after the death of Rev. Bruce Klunder. This is also the focus of research by Leonard Moore, "The School Desegregation Crisis of Cleveland, Ohio, 1963-64," *Journal of Urban History* (January 2002).

12. Leonard Moore, p. 136.

13. Charles Sanders, "Operation Bus Lift Goes Without Hitch as Schools End Relays," *Call and Post*, February 3, 1962, p. 3A.

14. "The Tragic Lesson of Murray Hill," *Call and Post*, February 8, 1964, p. 2B.

15. Moore, p. 154.

16. "School Site Pickets Set, CORE Says," *Cleveland Plain Dealer,* April 5, 1964, p.51.

17. "Arrest 20 CORE members at Lakeview School," *Call and Post,* April 11, 1964.

18. Frederick Heuser, "Presbyterians and the Struggle for Civil Rights," *Journal of Presbyterian History*, Spring, 2012, p.15.

19. "Death the harvest of official prejudice," *Call and Post*, April 11, 1964, p.1A.

20. "Our School Problems Cannot be Fenced In, A Statement by Members of the Faculty and Staff of University Circle Institutions," *Cleveland Plain Dealer*, April 12, 1964, p.28.

21. Ken Temple, "McAllister Threatens to Jail Parents Who Participate in School Boycott," *Call and Post*, April 18, 1964, p. 9A. Leonard Moore provides many details about the Freedom Schools on p. 153. Bob Williams reported in the April 25, 1964 *Call and Post* that students get "an A for all-day attention and

attentiveness," and learned lessons about "liberty and justice for all."

22. Jonathan Entin, *A Civil Rights Life: Nathaniel R. Jones Answers the Call* (New York: New Press, 2016). Available at https://scholarlycommons.law.case.edu/caselrev/vol68/iss2/10.

23. Author interview with Joan Dowling, 14 May, 2013.

24. Robert Madison interview. 11 June 2013. Cleveland Regional Oral History Collection.

25. *HCHR Newsletter*, October 1965, and CH-UH Board of Education Minutes, March 8, 1965.

26. CH-UH Board of Education Minutes, December 20, 1965.

27. Letter from Joan Dowling and Dorothy Schiff to Mrs. Sherman Dye, February, 1964.

28. Marion Kelly, "Human Relations Policy Delayed to Study Queries," *Sun Press*, November 17, 1966.

29. "Human Relations Policy Passes," *Sun Press*, Dec. 15, 1966, p. 5A,

30. Cleveland Heights-University Heights City School District, *Proposed Human Relations Policy*, December 5, 1966. CHCRC.

31. Author interview with Lee Blons.

32. Author interview, Phyllis Brody. 14 May 2013.

33. *HCHR Newsletter*, June 1964.

34. Ibid.

35. HCHR founders lived in the Cleveland Heights-University Heights school district. Because they were concerned about both schools and the communities they served, they worked on change in both communities. This project focuses on Cleveland Heights which is where they made the most headway.

36. Barbara Roderick, *President's Report*, HCHR Annual Meeting, May 4, 1966. CHCRC.

**Chapter 3: Activists Open Up a White Suburb**

1. Harris and Robinson, *The Proud Heritage of Cleveland Heights*, p. 152.

2. Ibid, p.155.

3. Heights Citizens for Human Rights, *Statement of Objectives*, 1966. CHCRC.

4. Barbara Roderick, *President's Report*,1966.

5. Ralph Brody, Minutes, August 24, 1964, HCHR Neighborhood Committee. Unpublished.

6. *HCHR Newsletter*, December, 1965.

7. *HCHR Housing Policy Statement*, October 17, 1967. CHCRC.

8. Freedheim and Bloom, *Homesellers Project Work Sheet*, 1966, p. 12. CHCRC.

9. *HCHR Newsletter*, June 1965.
10. Barbara Heald, *Problems of Housing for a Negro Teacher*, Unpublished report of the Human Relations Advisory Committee, 1965. CHCRC.
11. Fair Housing Inc., *Code of Regulations*, Fair Housing Inc. collection, WRHS, Container 1, Folder 13. The board included Charles Gard whose Cleveland Heights home was bombed when he listed it with FHI. Other members were Cleveland Heights lawyer Burt Griffin, a common pleas judge who served on the Warren Commision, HCHR activist Barbara Heald, who later directed Fair Housing Council, and Carl Stokes, who was later elected mayor of Cleveland.
12. *HCHR Newsletter*, February 1968.
13. *Fair Housing Inc. Brokers Report*, June 25, 1965. FHI collection, WRHS, Container 1, Folder 16.
14. *Encyclopedia of Cleveland History*, Fair Housing Inc.
15. Author interview with Joyce Collins.
16. *HCHR Newsletter*, May 1965.
17. *HCHR Newsletter*, October 1965.
18. *HCHR Newsletter*, June 1966.
19. Ibid.
20. Freedheim and Bloom, *Homeseller Project Work Sheet*, 1966.
21. *HCHR Newsletter*, "Integration in Our Community, Winter 1966-67." CHCRC.
22. *HCHR Newsletter*, December, 1968.
23. *HCHR Newsletter*, February 1968.
24. Welcoming new black residents was an ongoing activity that is frequently described in HCHR newsletters.
25. Author interview with Gerda Freedheim.
26. Ralph Brody, *Statement before Cleveland Heights Council*, June 5, 1967, p. 2. CHCRC.
27. HCHR, *Host Letter Neighborhood Discussion Program*, 1967. CHCRC.
28. HCHR, Promotional Flyer, *Neighborhood Discussion Program*, 1967. CHCRC.
29. *HCHR Newsletter*, June 1967.
30. HCHR Brochure, *The Black Experience in America, 1969*. CHCRC.
31. "Editorial," *Cleveland Plain Dealer*, June 20, 1969.

### Chapter 4: Fair Housing Laws Add Leverage

1. John Combs, "Fair Housing Law Drive Launched by Ohio Group," *Call and Post*, Jan. 26, 1963, p. 16C.
2. Gerda Freedheim, "Letter to the Editor," *Cleveland Plain Dealer*, March 18, 1965, p. 14.

3.   *HCHR Newsletter*, October 1965.

4.   "At Fair Housing Rally Negroes Urged to Seek Housing in White Area," *Call and Post*, October 16, 1965.

5.   *Human Progress News*, December, 1965.

6.   *HCHR Newsletter*, "The Ohio Fair Housing Law – Six Months Later," June 1966.

7.   *FACTS, Fair Housing Council Newsletter*, May 1966, p. 1. CHCRC.

8.   Ibid.

9.   *HCHR Newsletter*, May 1966.

10.  *FACTS*, p. 1.

11.  "Fair Housing Council Names New Director," *Call and Post*, April 15, 1967, p. 9A.

12.  Roldo Bartimole, "Equal Housing Plan is Given $405,000," *Cleveland Plain Dealer*, Nov. 3, 1966, p.1; and in "Operation Equality, Urban League and Foundations Start Equal Housing Project," *Call and Post*, Nov. 5, 1966, p. 1A.

13.  Rev. Richard Rangoon, "Operation Equality Project," *Call and Post*, Jan. 27, 1968, p. 5C.

14.  "Operation Equality Phased Out," *Call and Post*, Nov. 20, 1976, p. 18C.

15.  *HCHR Newsletter*, November 1967.

16.  Sally Hunter, Minutes, Fair Housing Council Meeting, June 10, 1966. CHCRC.

17.  *HCHR Newsletter*, February, 1968.

18.  Kenneth Banks, "Whites Help Negro Win Fair Shake on Housing," *Cleveland Plain Dealer*, March 14, 1968.

19.  Author interview with Gerda Freedheim.

20.  *HCHR Newsletter*, July 1966.

21.  *HCHR Newsletter*, May 1966.

22.  Rev. Jack Sersig, personal letter, June 3, 1964.

23.  "Council Increases Property Fines," *Sun Press*, October 28, 1965.

24.  Ibid.

25.  Julian Krowcheck, "Rally Asks Heights Council For Fair Housing Laws," *Cleveland Plain Dealer*, June 29, 1966.

26.  Cleveland Heights City Council, *A Statement of Policy*, November 21, 1966.

27.  Richard Perry, "Barbara Roderick, Defied Threats in Her Work to Integrate Housing," *Cleveland Plain Dealer*, October 31, 2004.

28.  Marion Kelly, "Fair Housing Drive, Heights Chamber Latest Group to Blast 'Maniacs,'" *Sun Press*, May 18, 1967.

29.  Ibid.

30.  "Heights Clergymen Issue Declaration For Open Housing," *Call and Post*, May 27, 1967, p. 1A.

31.  *HCHR Newsletter*, June 1967.

32. Ralph Brody, *HCHR Statement to City Council of Cleveland Heights*, June 5, 1967. CHCRC.
33. City of Cleveland Heights, *Open Letter to the Citizens of Cleveland Heights, Ohio*, April 30, 1968.
34. *HCHR Newsletter*, February 1969.
35. Marion Kelly, "Haggins to Reopen Heights Office as Support Swells," *Sun Press*, February 20, 1969.
36. Ibid.
37. "Editorial," *Sun Press*, February 20, 1969.
38. *HCHR Newsletter*, December 1970, p.2.
39. April 12, 1971 letter from Gerda Freedheim to Mrs. William Kiraly.
40. HCHR Housing Committee, *Position Paper, Cleveland Heights Housing Office*, March 29, 1971. CHCRC.
41. Barbara Roderick outlined these options during a meeting with the HCHR board. They are noted in the minutes of the February 17, 1971 meeting.
42. Gerda Freedheim references the July adoption of the policy and offers her critique in October 1971 *HCHR Newsletter*.

## Chapter 5: Forest Hill Church Grapples with Race

1. Author interview with Diana Woodbridge. 13 August, 2014.
2. The Forest Hill Church history is documented on the church website, http://fhcpresb.org/history. Marian Morton provides important details in *Cleveland Heights Congregations* (Charleston: Arcadia Publishing, 2009).
3. Sharon Gregor, *Forest Hill, The Rockefeller Estate* (Charleston: Arcadia Publishing, 2006) p.59.
4. Marian Morton, in "Deferring Dreams: Racial and Religious Covenants in Shaker Heights, Cleveland Heights and East Cleveland, 1925-1970." www.teachingcleveland.org. Morton explains that unlike some restrictive covenants that specifically excluded African Americans, Forest Hill covenants "did not mention any specific racial group, but required that a property could not be re-sold without consent of the developer or surrounding neighbors… the context meant Jews and African Americans."
5. Forest Hill Homeowners Association website has a detailed history of the neighborhood and its developers. http://fhho.org.
6. "Minister to Be Installed Here," *Sun Press*, May 2, 1963.
7. Email correspondence with Rev. Ned Edwards, 7 December, 2017.
8. Allen Howard, "2000 Hear Dr. King in Cleveland Heights Challenge Churches to Lead," *Call and Post*, May 18, 1963.

9. Frederick Heuser, "Presbyterians and the Struggle for Civil Rights," *Journal of Presbyterian History*, Spring, 2012. Online at https://www. history.pcusa.org/topics-note/Presbyteriansand_civil-rights, P. 11.

10. Nathanial Moore describes their leadership.

11. Email correspondence with Rev. Ned Edwards, 4 December, 2017.

12. "A Non-Segregated Church in a Non-Segregated Society, Presbyterians and the Civil Rights Movement," *Journal of Presbyterian History*, Spring/ Summer 2012, p. 25. Found at: www.history.pcusa.org/history-online/ topics-note-presbyterians -and-civil-rights.

13. Frederick Heuser, "Presbyterians and the Struggle for Civil Rights," *Journal of Presbyterian History*, Spring/summer 2012, p. 11. Found at: www.history.pcusa.org/history-online/exhibits/commission- religion-and-race-page11.

14. Forest Hill Church, Vol. II, *Minutes of Forest Hill Session*, "Non-Segregated Society," June 15, 1964, p. 334.

15. Reflections by Ned Edwards, January 20, 2004. CHCRC.

16. Presbyterian Church USA, *Book of Confessions*, Part II, Section 4, Paragraph 9.44. 1967.

17. Email correspondence with Rev. Ned Edwards, January 10, 2018.

18. Email correspondence with Rev. Ned Edwards, December 6, 2017.

19. Rev. Ned Edwards, Palm Sunday, April 7, 1968 sermon. CHCRC.

20. Forest Hill Church, *Vol. III, Minutes of Forest Hill Session*, "Open Housing," May 20, 1968, p. 454.

21. Email correspondence with Rev. Ned Edwards, November 30, 2017.

22. Forest Hill Church, *Vol IV, Minutes of Forest Hill Session*, "Mission Statement of Forest Hill Church," March 27, 1972, p. 32-33.

23. Forest Hill Church Flyer, "Operation Open Mind," 1968. CHCRC.

24. Email correspondence with Rev. Ned Edwards, November 30, 2017.

25. Forest Hill Church Brochure, "Dynamics of Community Change," October 1969. CHCRC.

26. Forest Hill Church, *Vol. III, Minutes of Forest Hill Session*, Sept. 22, 1969.

27. Rev. Ned Edwards, "The Sacrament of Mind Opening," Sermon delivered October 5, 1969. CHCRC.

28. Rev. Ned Edwards, Letter to Parents and Sisters, October 29, 1969. CHCRC.

29. Ibid.

30. Ibid.

31. Email correspondence with Rev. Ned Edwards, December 4, 2017.

32. Forest Hill Church, *Vol. III, Minutes of Forest Hill Session*, January 18, 1971, p. 567.

33.   Forest Hill Church, *Vol. IV, Minutes of Forest Hill Session*, June 28, 1971, p. 2.
34.   Author interview with Diana Woodbridge.
35.   Ibid.
36.   Ibid.
37.   News Release, "Ecumenical Workshop to Focus on Community Needs," September 19, 1974.
38.   Email correspondence with Rev. Ned Edwards, January 29, 2018.

## Chapter 6: African Americans Lead the Way

1.   Author interview with Betty Nelson, 2013.
2.   Carl Campbell, *CICR Newsletter*, December 15, 1975. CHCRC.
3.   "Neighborhood Harassment Must Be Stopped," *HCHR Newsletter*, August, 1970.
4.   Author interview with Doris Allen.
5.   "Your Urban League at Work," *Call and Post*, June 4, 1977, p.11A. Many details about Bernice Lott's activism are described in her October 5, 1983 obituary in the *Call and Post*.
6.   Minutes, HCHR Meeting, February 14, 1971. CHCRC.
7.   Committee to Improve Community Relations, *What's It All About*, No date. CHCRC.
8.   Ibid.
9.   Committee to Improve Community Relations, *CICR, It's Purpose*, 1975. CHCRC.
10.   Author interview with Carl Campbell.
11.   Ibid.
12.   *CICR Newsletter*, December 1975. CHCRC.
13.   *CICR Newsletter*, April 1977. CHCRC.
14.   Author interview with Doris Allen.
15.   Correspondence from Cornelius Edwards to Chief of Police Gaffney, June 2, 1971. CHCRC.
16.   Matt Smith, "Editorially Speaking," *CICR Newsletter*, October, 1975. CHCRC.
17.   "Disciplinary Action Promised on Heights School Fight," *Cleveland Plain Dealer*, January 30, 1972, p. 21.
18.   James Coleman, "School Staff to Review Black Student Concerns," *Sun Press*, March 21, 1974.
19.   "Blacks Protest Against Heights School Policies," *Cleveland Plain Dealer*, June 11, 1974.
20.   Ibid.
21.   Marion Kelly, "CICR Reps to Press Black Holiday Demand at Monday Meeting," *Sun Press*, June 13, 1974.
22.   "Reach Agreement on Blacks' School Complaints," *Sun Press*, April 3, 1975.

23. The terms of the consent decree are spelled out in *Agreement between CH-UH Board of Education and the Committee to Improve Community Relations*, April 1, 1975. CHCRC.
24. CICCR Newsletter, December 1975.
25. Author interview with Carl Campbell.
26. *Amended Agreement between CH-UH Board of Education and the Committee to Improve Community Relations*, 1982. CHCRC.

**Chapter 7: Housing Audit Documents Discrimination**
1. Suzanne Nigro, *The 1972 St. Ann Audit, Personal Reflections*, 2006. The audit report can be found at ADC, Folder: Community Organizations General – HCC.
2. Author interview with Suzanne Nigro.
3. Jean McCann, "A Congregation Divided, Some at St. Ann Unhappy About Housing Study," *Cleveland Plain Dealer*, January 13, 1973, p.17.
4. Second Vatican Council, www.religion.wikia.org/wiki/second vatican council. Accessed online on 9/15/2017.
5. Several news sources reported on the 50th anniversary of Vatican II. It is described in "Why is Vatican II So Important," *NPR*, October 10, 2012 and "Vatican II Changed the Catholic Church – and the World," *Huffington Post*, October 11, 2012. Both accessed online on 9/15/2017.
6. Randy Cunningham, *Democratizing Cleveland, The Rise and Fall of Community Organizing- 1975-85* (Cleveland: Arambala Press, 2007), p. 16.
7. Several concept papers and proposals outlining the program can be found at ADC, Issenmann papers, Folder Church: CCCA: Action for a Change Correspondence 1970.
8. Richard Kelley describes the early success of Action for A Change in his March 15, 1971 letter to Joseph McSweeney. ADC, Issenmann Papers, Folder Church: CCCA: Action for a Change Finances – 1970-71.
9. *Action Directory*, p.1.
10. The program is described by Rosemary Kovacs, "Catholics Push Social Justice," *Cleveland Plain Dealer*, February 23, 1971. Information about the second installment is reported in "Diocese Social Action Program Returning," *Cleveland Plain Dealer*, October 23, 1971.
11. *St. Ann's Action for a Change Newsletter*, May 11, 1971.
12. "Open Housing Sub-Committee," *St. Ann's Action for A Change Newsletter*, March 13, 1972. These newsletters are found at the Catholic Diocese Archives, Folder: Community Organizations- General – St. Ann's Program 1971-73.
13. Author interview with Suzanne Nigro.

14. National Committee Against Discrimination in Housing, Inc.
"'Testing'- A basic Tool," *Trends in Housing*, March-April, 1973.

15. Nigro, p. 15 and 16.

16. Nigro is quoted in the *Sun Press* coverage of the presentation to Cleveland Heights City Council on September 7, 1972.

17. The complete list of findings is described in the *St. Ann Social Action Housing Committee, Housing Audit I: Assessment of Real Estate Housing Practices in the Eastern Suburbs of Cleveland.* Unpublished. September 1972.
ADC, Folder: Community Organizations General – St. Ann's Program.

18. Author interview with Suzanne Nigro, 2014.

19. Nigro, p. 27.

20. Ibid.

21. Author interview with Suzanne Nigro.

22. Ibid.

23. Author interview with Jeanne Martin, 2017.

24. Author interview with Suzanne Nigro.

25. McCann, *Cleveland Plain Dealer*, January 13, 1973.

26. Nigro, p. 25.

27. Nigro, p. 26.

28. McCann, *Cleveland Plain Dealer*, January 13, 1973.

29. Tom Reim, *Evaluation report on Action for A Change,* April 1973.
ADC, Folder: Community Organization General – St. Ann's Program.

30. Nigro, p.11.

31. Author interview with Suzanne Nigro.

## Chapter 8: Institutes Unite to Support Integration

1. Gerda Freedheim, *HCHR Newsletter*, January 1970.

2. Author interview with Jack Boyle.

3. Author interview with Mary Boyle.

4. Morton, 2002, p. 121.

5. "Show of Community Action," *Cleveland Jewish News*, September 3, 1971.

6. Jerry Barch, "Cleveland Heights, Can it Remain Jewish?"
*Cleveland Jewish News*, January 29, 1971.

7. "First Loans Approved," *Cleveland Jewish News*, September 3, 1971.

8. Jerry Barch, "Individuals Called Key to Success," *Cleveland Jewish News*, October 27, 1972.

9. Thomas Brazaitis, "Five Heights Pupils Attacked by Gangs,"
*Cleveland Plain Dealer*, January 29, 1972.

10. "Disciplinary Action Promised," *Cleveland Plain Dealer*, January 30, 1972.

11. Cristine Jindra, "Unity Urged at Heights High to End Racism,"
    *Cleveland Plain Dealer*, February 4, 1972.

12. Cindy Cooper, "Heights High Administrators Trying to Preserve 'Good Image,'"
    *Call and Post*, February 5, 1972, p. 6A.

13. The attendance sheet for the February 22, 1972 meeting lists all participants.
    ADC, Folder: CCCA-HCC 1972-73.

14. HAC position statement. Ibid.

15. Heights Action Committee letter to Bishop Cosgrove and Mr. Caldwell,
    March 15, 1972. Catholic Diocese Archives. Folder: CCCA-HCC 1972-3.

16. Harry Fagan, "200% Problem," June 6, 1972. ADC, Folder: CCCA-HCC 1972-73.

17. Ibid.

18. Memo about August 10, 1972 meeting from Oliver Schroeder, in
    Cleveland Heights City Manager Collection, WRHS.

19. Minutes, Heights Action Committee Meeting, September 21, 1972.
    ADC, Folder: CCCA-HCC 1972-73.

20. "Presidents Report," *HCHR Newsletter*, December 1972.

21. Minutes, Heights Action Committee Meeting, September 21, 1972.
    ADC, Folder: CCCA-HCC 1972-73.

22. Ibid.

23. Steering Committee Heights Community Congress, "Resolution,"
    September 27, 1972. ADC, Folder: CCCA-HCC 1972-73.

24. "Heights Congress receives $48,500 Foundation grant," *Sun Press*,
    March 22, 1973, p. 1.

25. "Heights Congress: Coalition for an Integrated Community," *Sun Press*,
    March 21, 1974.

26. Author interview with Jack Boyle.

27. Minutes, February 18, 1973 Housing Task Force. ADC,
    Folder: CCCA–HCC 1972-73.

28. *HCHR Newsletter*, September, 1974.

29. "Cooperative Realtor Plan Voted," *Sun Press*, October 19, 1972.

30. "Heights Congress Suit Alleges Steering, Seeks $1 Million," *Sun Press*,
    November 21, 1974.

31. The Rosenblatt case took nearly two years to resolve. The *Cleveland Plain Dealer*
    covered the case as it progressed. Details are documented in Katherine
    Hatton, "Realty Firm Will Answer $1 Million Race Bias Suit," December 31,
    1974; "Community Congress Charges Bias," March 12, 1975, p. 46;
    "Class Action Against Realtors Continued," August 19, 1975, p. 6; and
    "Real Estate Firm Settles Bias Suit," May 27, 1976, p.4A.

32. Author interview with Chip Bromley and personal correspondence with Donalene Poduska.
33. Marion Kelly, "Cleveland Heights Housing Pact Angers Black, White Realtors," *Sun Press*, May 2, 1974.
34. Ibid.
35. Ibid.
36. Author interview with Jeanne Martin Diamond.
37. Author interview with Suzanne Nigro.
38. Ibid.
39. Tom Gaumer and Katherine Hatton, "Tight Money Helped Out," *Cleveland Plain Dealer*, November 30, 1975.
40. Nigro, p. 41.
41. Author interview with Susanna Niermann O'Neil.
42. Ibid.
43. Kristen Mott, "AJC Cleveland Celebrates 50 Years of Isaiah Award," *Cleveland Jewish News*, January 27, 2014.

## Chapter 9: City Government Steps Up

1. Author interview with Jack Boyle.
2. Gene Maeroff, "Opinion," *Cleveland Plain Dealer*, July 25, 1970 describes the closed, self-perpetuating governance tradition. Karen Rubin, *Partisanship and Non-Partisanship: Changes in Cleveland Heights Politics 1920-1979*, January, 1980 documents 25 consecutive elections starting in 1921. During this period only one person was elected who had not been an incumbent (p. 39), and between 1921 and 1948 only ten men (all white) filled 7 council seats for 27 years. CHCRC.
3. The campaign flyer, "Four Can Make the Change," outlines the agenda for four challengers to the status quo: Satillo, Chapin, Brooks and Sklar. CHCRC.
4. *HCHR Newsletter*, November 1971.
5. Author interview with Jack Boyle.
6. Ibid.
7. "Realtors Oppose Any Phone Ban," *Sun Press*, March 23, 1972.
8. "Applings Supported," *Sun Press*, September 21, 1972.
9. Ibid.
10. Ibid.
11. Pippa Kiraly, *HCHR Newsletter*, October 1972.
12. Bruce Melville, *Operation Equality Activity Report*, July 18, 1973.
13. "HCC," *Sun Press*, April 15, 1974.

14. Author interview with Jack Boyle.
15. City of Cleveland Heights, Resolution 26-1976.
16. Author interview with Kermit Lind.
17. David Burwasser, "Housing Legislation," *Coventry Village News*, April 1976, p. 6.

## Chapter 10: Democracy in Action

1. Juliet Saltman, *A Fragile Movement*, (Westport, CT: Greenwood Press 1990).
2. Author interview with Gerda Freedheim.
3. Author interview with Susanna Nermann O'Neil.
4. Myron Orfield and Thomas Luce, *America's Racially Diverse Suburbs: Opportunities and Challenges*, 2012, p. 2.
5. Ibid.
6. Report of the National Commission on Fair Housing and Equal Opportunity, *The Future of Fair Housing*, December 2008, p. 6.
7. Orfield and Luce, p. 3.

# BIBLIOGRAPHY

### Guide to Abbreviations

**ADC** – Archives, Diocese of Cleveland
**CHCRC** – Cleveland Heights Civil Rights Collection, Cleveland State University Library
**WRHS** – Western Reserve Historical Society

"A non-segregated church in a non-segregated society: Presbyterians and the Civil Rights Movement," *Journal of Presbyterian History*, Spring/Summer 2012. Found at http://www:history.pcusa.org/history-online/topics-note/Presbyterians-and-civilrights.

Ad Hoc Open Housing Committee. *A Comprehensive Open Housing Program for Cuyahoga County.* Nov. 6, 1973.

*Agreement Between the Cleveland Heights-University Heights Board of Education and the Committee to Improve Community Relations.* April 1, 1975. CHCRC.

*Agreement Between the Cleveland Heights-University Heights Board of Education and the Committee to Improve Community Relations.* Updated, 1980. CHCRC.

*Boyle-Huston-Phillips for Cleveland Heights City Council.* Flyer, 1971. WRHS.

Borchert, James. "Suburbs," *Encyclopedia of Cleveland History.* Access 4/13/2019. https://case.edu/ech/articles/suburbs.

Branch, Taylor, *The King Years, Historic Moments in the Civil Rights Movement.* New York: Simon & Schuster, 2013.

http://www.fhho.org/what-we-do/ Access on 12/12/2017.

*CICR Newsletter.* June – February, 1975. CHCRC.

*CICR, What's It All About.* No date. CHCRC.

City of Cleveland Heights, Ohio. *A Statement of Policy by Cleveland Heights City Council.* November 21, 1966. Kenneth S. Nash Mayor. CHCRC.

– – – *An Open Letter to the Citizens of Cleveland Heights, Ohio.* April 30, 1968. CHCRC.

– – – *Resolution No. 26-1976 of City of Cleveland Heights,* by Councilman Schroder. Passed: March 15, 1976. CHCRC.

"Commission on Catholic Community Action." *Encyclopedia of Cleveland History.* https://case.edu/ech/a/commissionon-catholic-community-action. Access 3/31/2017.

Culp, Elizabeth. "The Cuyahoga Plan." In *Cleveland Historical.* https://clevelandhistorical.org/files/show/642.

Cuyahoga Plan. *The Cuyahoga Plan Annual Report, 1975.*

Cleveland Heights-University Heights City School District. *Documents for Annual Meeting with the Committee to Improve Community Relations and the Cleveland Heights – University Heights City School District.* March 21,1985. CHCRC.

Cleveland Heights-University Heights Public Schools, Human Relations Advisory Group, Minutes November 4, 1965 Meeting, December 20, 1965. CHCRC.

Cunningham, Randy. *Democratizing Cleveland, The Rise and Fall of Community Organizing – 1975-85.* Cleveland: Arambala Press, 2007.

Edwards, Rev. Ned. "Reading the Palms," Sermon At Forest Hill Church, April 7, 1968. CHCRC.

– – – "The Sacrament of Mind Opening," Sermon at Forest Hill Church, October 5, 1969. CHCRC.

– – – "In Defense of the Church," Sermon at Forest Hill Church, April 19, 1970. CHCRC.

– – – Letter to Parents, October 29, 1969. *Recollections.* January 20, 2004. CHCRC.

– – – Email correspondence with Susie Kaeser. November 30, 2017. December 6,2017. January 10, 2018. January 11, 2018. CHCRC.

Emergency Committee on Clergy for Civil Rights. *Peace, Justice and Public Education, A Statement of Religious Concern.* Cleveland, March 3, 1965.

Entin, Jonathan. *A Civil Rights Life: Nathaniel R. Jones, Answering the Call, An Autobiography of the Modern Struggle to End Racial Discrimination in America.* New York: The New Press, 2016, 68 Case. W. Res.L.Rev.651(2017). Available at https://scholarlycommons.law.case.edu/caselrev/vol68/iss2/10.

*Encyclopedia of Cleveland History.* https://case.edu/ech

*FACTS*, Fair Housing Council Newsletter, May 1966. CHCRC.

Fagan, Harry. *200% Problem, Maintain an Integrated Community.* Unpublished. June 6, 1972. ADC.

Fogelson, Robert. *Bourgeois Nightmares, Suburbia, 1870-1930.* New Haven: Yale University Press, 2005.

Foner, Eric and John Garraty, editors. *The Readers Companion to American History*, 2009. http:llwww.history.com/topics/blackhistory/civil-rights. 1/25/2016.

Forest Hill Church, Presbyterian, Session. *Minutes*, Vol. II, p. 334; Vol III, p. 454; Vol. IV, p. 32-33. Vol V, p. 1-3.

– – – Presbyterian website, https.//wwwfhcpresb.org.history.

– – – *Operation Open Mind – A Festival of Change*, 1968. CHCRC.

Forest Hill Homeowners Association, https://fhho.org.

Freedheim, Gerda and Martin Bloom. *Homesellers Project Work Sheet.* Unpublished, 1966 and 1968. CHCRC.

Goering, John (ed). *Fragile Rights Within Cities.* Lanham, MD: Rowman & Littlefield, 2007.

Green, Howard W. *Census Facts and Trends by Tracts, Special 1954 Report.* Cleveland: Cleveland Real Property Inventory of Metropolitan Cleveland, 1954.

Gregor, Sharon. *Forest Hill, The Rockefeller Estate.* Charleston: Arcadia, 2006.

Harris, Mary Emma and Ruth Mills Robinson. *The Proud Heritage of Cleveland Heights, Ohio.* Cleveland: Howard Allen, 1966.

Hayden, Dolores. *Building Suburbia, Green Fields and Urban Growth, 1820 to 2000.* New York: Pantheon Books, 2003.

Heald, Barbara. "Problems of Housing for a Negro Teacher," Unpublished Report, Cleveland Heights-University Heights Board of Education Human Relations Advisory Committee, 1965. CHCRC.

Heights Citizens for Human Rights. *A Statement of Objectives,*1964. CHCRC.

– – – Flyer, *The Black Experience in America.* 1969. CHCRC.

– – – *Position Paper, Cleveland Heights Housing Office*, March 29, 1971. CHCRC.

Heuser, Frederick. "Presbyterians and the Struggle for Civil Rights," *Journal of Presbyterian History*, Spring, 2012. Online at https.//www.history.pcusa.org/topics-note/Presbyteriansand_civil-rights.

Home Owners Loan Corporation. *Dictionary of American History.* http://www. encyclopedia.com/topic/Home_Owners_Loan_Corporaton.aspx Access 8/12/2014.

– – – *Residential Security Map, Cleveland, Ohio, 1940.* https://library.osu.edu/documents/redlining-maps/195-HLCS_Cleveland_&Cuyahoga_OH-15Mar_1940-68-5-1-Bjpg.

www.guides.osu.edu/maps-geospatial-data/maps/redlining

*HOLC Residential Security "Redlining" Map, Area Descriptions, Cuyahoga County, Ohio 1939.* http://library.osu.edu/documents/redlining-maps-Ohio/area-description/Cuyahoga County. Explanation_and -A4-A31_Area_descriptionpdf

Hughes, Langston. *The Big Sea.* New York: Alfred Knopf, 1940.

Jackson, Kenneth T. *Crabgrass Frontier.* New York: Oxford University Press, 1985.

John F. Kennedy Library and Museum. "Report to the American People on Civil Rights," June 11, 1963. http://www.jfklibrary.org.

Keating, W. Dennis. *The Suburban Racial Dilemma.* Philadelphia: Temple University Press, 1994.

Keating, W. Dennis, Norman Krumholz & David Perry, editors. *Cleveland A Metropolitan Reader*. Kent: The Kent State University Press, 1995.

Kelley, Richard and Fr. Neil Conway. *The Social Mission of the Church Through Action for a Change*, October 26, 1970. ADC, Action for A Change folder.

http://kirwaninstitute.osu.edu/wp-content/uploads/2015/06/The-History-of-Race-Real-Estate-Cuyahoga-County-Final-Report-February-2015.pdf Access: 12/12/2017.

Knots, Dave. "National Commission on Neighborhoods Case Study." September 1978. ADC, Action for A Change folder.

Kusmer, Kenneth. *A Ghetto Takes Shape, Black Cleveland, 1870-1930*. Urbana: University of Illinois Press, 1976.

Lamb, Charles. *Housing Segregation in Suburban America since 1960*. Cambridge: Cambridge University Press, 2005.

Lawson, Steven F. and Charles Payne. *Debating the Civil Rights Movement, 1945-1968*. Lanham, MD.: Rowman & Littlefield Publishers, 1998.

Levine, Naomi. *The Mythos of Racial Integration*. New York: American Jewish Committee. WRHS, Barbara Heald collection.

Lewis, Joanne and Richard Karberg. *In Our Day: Cleveland Heights Its People, Its Places, Its Past*. Cleveland Heights: Heights Community Congress, 1978.

Lind, Kermit. "Maintaining Residential Integration," *Cleveland State Law Review 607*, 1982.

Marable, Manning. *Race, Reform, and Rebellion*. Jackson, MS: University Press of Mississippi, 2007.

Massey, Douglas. "Origins of Economic Disparities: the Historic Role of Housing Segregation," in Carr, James and Nandinee K. Kutty. *Segregation, The Rising Cost for America*. New York: Toutledge. 2008.

Milgram, Morris. *Good Neighborhood, The Challenge of Open Housing*. New York: W.W. Norton and Company, 1979.

Moore, Nathaniel. "The School Desegregation Crisis of Cleveland, Ohio, 1963-64" in *Journal of Urban History*, January 2002. https://academic.csuohio.edu/tebeaum/courses/urban_school desegregationpdf.

Morton, Marian J. *Cleveland Heights Congregations*. Charleston: Arcadia Publishing, 2009.

– – – *Cleveland Heights, The Making of An Urban Suburb*. Charleston: Arcadia Publishing, 2002.

– – – "Deferring Dream: Racial and Religious Covenants in Shaker Heights, Cleveland Heights and East Cleveland, 1925-1970." https://www.teachingcleveland.org./deferring-dreams-racial-and-religious-covenants-in-shaker-heights-and-cleveland-heights-1925-to-1970-by-marian-morton/ (Accessed 12/12/2017)

National Committee Against Discrimination in Housing. "'Testing'- a basic tool," *Trends in Housing*, March-April 1973.

National Commission on Fair Housing and Equal Opportunity. *The Future of Fair Housing.* December 2008. https://nationalfairhousing.org/wp-contentuploads/2017/Future_of_Fair_Housing.pdf.

Nigro, Suzanne. *The 1972 St. Ann Audit, Personal Reflections.* 2006. CHCRC.

Orfield, Myron and Thomas Luce. *America's Racially Diverse Suburbs: Opportunities and Challenges.* July 20, 2012. www.law.umn.edu/metro. 1/20/2019.

Peters, Robert Jr. *The Crisis in Cleveland, Ohio Public Schools, An Interpretive Statement.* Unpublished letter, April 16, 1964, WRHS Klunder collection.

Pietila, Antero. *Not in My Neighborhood.* Chicago: Ivan R. Dee, 2010.

Presbyterian Church USA. *Book of Confessions, Part II, Section 4,* 1967.

Presbyterian Church USA Historical Society, https://www.history.pcusa.org/topics-note/presbyteriansand civil-rights.

Rothstein, Richard. *The Color of Law, A Forgotten History of How Our Government Segregated America.* New York: Liveright Publishing, 2017.

– – – *The Making of Ferguson.* Economic Policy Institute: Oct.15, 2014.

– – – City Club of Cleveland Presentation. February 18, 2015.

Rubin, Karen E. *Partisanship and Non-Partisanship: Changes in Cleveland Heights Politics 1920-1979.* January, 1980. Unpublished. CHCRC.

Saltman, Juliet. *Open Housing, Dynamics of a Social Movement.* New York: Prager, 1978.

– – – *A Fragile Movement, The Struggle for Neighborhood Stabilization.* Westport, CT: Greenwood Press, 1990.

Saphire, Richard B., "Bringing Brown to Cleveland," in *Justice and Legal Change on the Shores of Lake Erie*, Paul Finkelman and Roberta Sue Alexander eds., Athens: Ohio University Press, 2012.

Satter, Beryl. *Family Properties: Race, Real Estate, and the Exploitation of Black Urban America.* New York: Henry Holt and Company, 2009.

"Second Vatican Council." *Wikipedia.* Accessed 4/18/2017.

Sidney, Mara S. "National Fair Housing Policy and Its Perverse Effects on Local Advocacy." In *Fragile Rights Within Cities.* Lanham: Rowman & Littlefield, 2007.

Social Action Housing Committee of St. Ann Church. *Housing Audit I: Assessment of Real Estate Housing Practices in the Eastern Suburbs of Cleveland.* September, 1972. ADC.

*US Census of Population and Housing, 1900 to 2010.*
https://www.census.gov/prod/www/decenial.html

U.S. Department of Justice, Community Relations Division. *Agreement Between the Cleveland Heights-University Heights Board of Education and the Committee to Improve Community Relations.* April 1, 1975. CHCRC.

Wiese, Andrew. *Places of Their Own: African American Suburbanization in the Twentieth Century.* Chicago: The University of Chicago Press, 2004.

**News Sources**
Samford, H.L. "Two Suburbs Consider 'Blockbusting' Laws." *Sun Press*, June 22, 1961.

Simon, Todd. "Broad Housing Bias Here, Says Ohio Aid." *Cleveland Plain Dealer*, June 5, 1962.

Sweeney, Mr. "Jim Farmer Brings CORE Into the Cleveland Area." *Call and Post*, June 9, 1962.

"Warrensville Heights Council Gets Blockbusting Measure." *Sun Press*, July 13, 1961, p. 1.

Sanders, Charles. " 'Operation Bus Lift' Goes Without Hitch as Schools End Relays," *Call and Post*, February 3, 1962, p. 3A.

"Equal Rights Realty Sales Office Set." *Cleveland Plain Dealer*, May 1, 1962.

Combs, John. "Fair Housing Law Drive Launched by Ohio Group." *Call and Post.* Jan. 26, 1963.

"Why Ohio Needs a Fair Housing Act." *Call and Post*, March 23, 1963.

Garling, Pat and Norman Melnick. "Seeking U.S. Dream, King Tells Throngs." *Cleveland Plain Dealer*, May 15, 1963.

Howard, Allen. "2000 Hear Dr. King in Cleveland Heights Challenge Churches to Lead." *Call and Post*, May 18, 1963.

"Rhodes Showered With Praise for Order Banning Race Bias." *Call and Post*, July 13, 1963.

Price, Charles. "As Thousands Brave Rain to Join Freedom March," *Call and Post*, July 20, 1963, p. 1A.

Robertson, Don. "UFM Set to Picket Board of Education." *Cleveland Plain Dealer*, September 25, 1963.

Gleisser, Marcus. "Realty Firm Plans Sales to Minorities." *Cleveland Plain Dealer*, October 15, 1963.

Gleisser, Marcus. "Fair Housing Pressures Grow Here." *Cleveland Plain Dealer.* January 25, 1964.

Howard, Allen. "In a Wave of Passion, Hate-Filled White Mob Attack C-P Newsmen." *Call and Post*, Feb. 8, 1964, p. 1A.

"The Tragic Lesson of Murray Hill," *Call and Post*, Feb. 8, 1964, p. 2B.

Skinner, Ann. "Too Small Parents Say." *Cleveland Plain Dealer*, March 23, 1964."

"Core Schedules Demonstration." *Cleveland Plain Dealer*, April 4, 1964, p. 1A.
"It's Ballot or Bullet, Answers Malcolm X." *Cleveland Plain Dealer*, April 4, 1964, p.20A.

"School Site Pickets Set, CORE Says." *Cleveland Plain Dealer*, April 5, 1964.

Bariman, George. "Schools Siege." *Cleveland Plain Dealer*, April 9, 1964, p.1A.

Temple, Ken, "Rev. Klunder's Valor Hailed by Rights Groups." *Call and Post*, April 11, 1964.

"Death the Harvest of Official Prejudice." *Call and Post*, April 11, 1964.

"Who Owns the Public Schools." *Call and Post*, April 11, 1964.

"Arrest 20 CORE Members at Lakeview School Site," *Call and Post*, April 11, 1964.

"Louis Lomax – Malcolm X Speeches at CORE Rally Shake Up the City." *Call and Post*, April 11, 1964, p. 1A.

Statement by Members of the Faculty and Staff of University Circle Institutions.
"Our School Problems Cannot Be Fenced In." *Cleveland Plain Dealer*, April 12, 1964.

Temple, Ken. "McAllister Threatens to Jail Parents Who Participate in Schools Boycott." *Call and Post*, April 18, 1964, p. 9A.

Temple, Ken. "UFM Issues Call! Keep School Kids Out, Monday." *Call and Post*, April 18, 1964, p. 1A.

Williams, Bob, "School Boycott Proves to be 92% Effective." *Call and Post*, April 25, 1964.

"Suspects in Stoning of Negro's Home Say They Receive Threats." *Sun Press*, June 18, 1964.

"5 'Night Riders' Are Convicted In Stoning of Negro's Home." *Sun Press*, July 30, 1964, p. 1A.

Blum, Willard. "'For Sale' Sign Bans Gain in East Suburbs." *Sun Press*, October 22, 1964.

Gleisser, Marcus. "Fair Housing Pressures Grow Here." *Cleveland Plain Dealer*. December 25, 1964.

Freedheim, Gerda. "Letter to the Editor." *Cleveland Plain Dealer*, March 18, 1965.
"Fair Housing Law is Needed." *Cleveland Plain Dealer*, March 18, 1965.

"Rhodes Keeps His Promise by Signing Fair Housing Bill." *Call and Post*, August 7, 1965.

"At Fair Housing Rally Negroes Urged to Seek Housing in White Area." *Call and Post*, October 16, 1965.

"Bomb Pieces May Solve Blasts at 2 Heights Homes." *Sun Press*, October 21, 1965.

"Council Increases Property Fines." *Sun Press*, October 28, 1965.

Ostrow, Al. "Ohio 'Fair Housing' Law Now in Effect; Realtors Weigh Policy."
*Sun Press*, November 4, 1965.

"Fair Housing Law is Effective this Month." *Call and Post*, November 6, 1965.

Krowcheck, Julian. "Rally Asks Heights Councils for Fair Housing Laws."
*Cleveland Plain Dealer*, June 29, 1966.

Williams, Bob. "Seek Hate Combine in Heights Bombing." *Call and Post*, July 2, 1966.

Kelly, Marion. "Heights Council Pledges Fair Housing Law Study." *Sun Press*, July 7, 1966.

"Fair Housing Council's Job To Help Enact Law of Ohio." *Call and Post*, August 13,1966.

Schroeder, Oliver and William Walker. "Down the Big Road, 'Negro Votes, Black Power
and the Republican Party." *Call and Post*, September 17, 1966, p. 8B.

Bartimole, Roldo. "Equal Housing Plan is Given $405,000." *Cleveland Plain Dealer*,
November 3, 1966.

"Urban League and Foundations Start Equal Housing Project." *Call and Post*,
November 5, 1966.

Kelly, Marion. "Human Relations Policy Delayed to Study Queries." *Sun Press*,
November 17, 1966.

"Human Relations Policy Passed." *Sun Press*, December 15, 1966, p. 5A.

"Fair Housing Council Names New Director." *Call and Post*, April 15, 1967, p. 9A.

Kelly, Marion. "Fair Housing Drive, Heights Chamber Latest Group to Blast 'Maniacs.'"
*Sun Press*, May 18, 1967.

"Federation Leaders Assert: Bombing of Hill Home Demands Immediate Fair
Housing Law." *Cleveland Jewish News*, May 19, 1967, p. 1.

"HEIGHTS CLERGYMEN ISSUE DECLARATION FOR OPEN HOUSING."
*Call and Post*, May 27, 1967.

Young, Whitney, "To be Equal: The High Cost of Housing Discrimination."
*Call and Post*, June 3, 1967, p. 4B.

Rangoon, Richard. "Report, Operation Equality Project." Call and Post, Jan. 27, 1968, p. 5C.
"Heights Realtors Hear Open Housing Confab." *The Cleveland Press*, March 1, 1968.

Banks, Kenneth. "Whites Help Negro Win Fair Shake on Housing."
*Cleveland Plain Dealer*, March 14, 1968.

"Suburbanites Pledge Open Housing Fight." *Call and Post*, June 8, 1968.

"Hate Killed Folksinger, Police Feel." *Sun Press*, Aug., 1968.

"Realty Clearing House Opens in C.H. City Hall." *Sun Press*, August 8, 1968.

Kelly, Marion. "Haggins to Reopen Heights Office as Support Swells." *Sun Press*, February 20, 1969.

"Civic Groups Rally Behind Isaac Haggins." *Sun Press*, February 20, 1969.

"A Cowardly Act." *Call and Post*, February 22,1969, p. 4B.

"Police Search Clues in Heights Bombing." *Sun Press*, Feb. 29, 1969.
"Stormy Battle For Cleveland Heights Council Seats." *Sun Press*, October 2, 1969.

"Cleveland to Provide Stern Test for Ohio's New Fair Housing Law." *Call and Post*, November 29, 1969.

Green, Bernice. "Young Professional Points to Areas Where Agencies Help Social Change." *Cleveland Jewish News*, April 3, 1970.

Maeroff, Gene. "Opinion." *Cleveland Plain Dealer*, July 25, 1970.

"Limping Integration Blamed on Biased Housing Brokers." *Call and Post*, December 5, 1970, p. 8A.

Barch, Jerry. "Cleveland Heights, Can it Remain Jewish?" *Cleveland Jewish News*, January 29, 1971.

"The Heights Assembly." *Cleveland Jewish News*, January 29, 1971.

Zelman, Marvin and Bennett Yanowitz. "Article on Cleveland Heights Picture Distorted, Say CHA Leaders." *Cleveland Jewish News*, February 5, 1971.

"Realtors Back Open Housing." *Cleveland Plain Dealer*, February 13, 1971.

Kovacs, Rosemary. "Catholics Push Social Justice." *Cleveland Plain Dealer*, February 23, 1971.

"Cleveland Heights Citizens! Secret Public Housing Negotiations." *Sun Press*, April 15, 1971.

"Citizens Pick Trio for C.H. Council Run." *Sun Press*, August 5, 1971.

"In Cleveland Heights, Down Payment Assistance to be Provided to Families." *Cleveland Jewish News*, August 6, 1971.

"In Hts. Housing Program, First Loans Approved." *Cleveland Jewish News*, September 3, 1971.

"Show of Community Action." *Cleveland Jewish News*, September 3, 1971.

"Diocese Social Action Program Returning." *Cleveland Plain Dealer*, October 23, 1971.

"5000 Turned-on Catholics Ready to Help." *Cleveland Plain Dealer*, January 29, 1972.

"Disciplinary Action Promised on Hts. School Fight." *Cleveland Plain Dealer*, January 30, 1972.

"Heights High Report Due Tonight." *Sun Press*, January 3, 1972, p. 1A.

Jindra, Christine. "Unity Urged at Hts. High to Fight Racism." *Cleveland Plain Dealer*, February 4, 1972.

Moore, George Anthony. "Heights Meets Race Trouble." *The Cleveland Press*, February 4, 1972, p. 8A.

Cooper, Cindy. "Heights High Administrators Trying to Preserve 'Good Image,'" *Call and Post*, February 5, 1972, p. 6A.

"Realtors Oppose Any Phone Ban." *Sun Press*, March 23, 1972.

"Integration Need Not Fail, Says Panel." *Cleveland Jewish News*, March 24, 1972, p. 10.

"Realtors Face 'Test.'" *Sun Press*, April 6, 1972, p. 1A.

"CH Acts Quickly After Telephone Ban Passage." *Sun Press*, May 4, 1972.

"Blacks, Whites Being 'Steered' in Housing Here, Audit Shows." *Sun Press*, September 7, 1972.

"Steering Must Stop." *Sun Press*, Sept. 7, 1972.

Jindra, Christine. "Subtle Racism Alleged in Eastern Housing." *Cleveland Plain Dealer*, September 7, 1972.

"Applings Supported." *Sun Press*, September 21, 1972.

"Cooperative Realtor Plan Voted." *Sun Press*, October 19, 1972.

Barach, Jerry. "Individual Called Key to Success of Hts. Effort." *Cleveland Jewish News*, October 27, 1972.

Kelly, Marion. "'You're All Right, We're All Right." *Sun Press*, December 14, 1972, p. 1 A.

McCann, Jean. "A Congregation Divided, Some at St. Ann Unhappy About Housing Study." *Cleveland Plain Dealer*, January 13, 1973.

"Heights Congress Received $48,500 Foundation Grant." *Sun Press*, March 22, 1973.

"Heights Group on the Move." *Sun Press*, May 3, 1973, p. 1A.

"Operation Equality: Providing Access To Decent Housing for Black Community." *Call and Post*, September 8, 1973, p 9B.

Coleman, James. "School Staff to Review Black Students' Concerns." *Sun Press*, March 21, 1974, p. A7.

Rex, Marguerite. "Heights Congress: Coalition for an Integrated Community." *Sun Press*, March 21, 1974.

"HCC." *Sun Press*, April 15, 1974.

Kelly, Marion. "Cleveland Hts. Housing Pact Angers Black, White Realtors." *Sun Press*, May 2, 1974.

Kelly, Marion. "Heights Human Relations Get Boost." *Sun Press*, May 30, 1974, p. A 1.

"Blacks Protest Against Heights School Policies." *Cleveland Plain Dealer*, June 11, 1974.

Kelly, Marion. "CICR Reps to Press Black Holiday Demand at Monday Meeting." *Sun Press*, June 13, 1974.

Hatton, Katherine. "Realtors Ask Probe of Heights, Shaker Housing Services." *Cleveland Plain Dealer*, June 19, 1974.

"CICR Will Respond to Board Response." *Sun Press*, July 18, 1974.

"CICR says Cleveland Heights School Response Inadequate." *Call and Post*, August 3, 1974, p. 1A.

"First Black Is Appointed to Heights School Board." *Call and Post*, November 16, 1974, p. 4A.

"Heights Congress Suit Alleges Steering." *Sun Press*, November 21, 1974.

Hatton, Katherine. "Realty Firm Will Answer $1 Million Race Bias Suit." *Cleveland Plain Dealer*, December 31, 1974.

Kelly, Marion. "Seek to Ease Tensions at Heights." *Sun Press*, January 30, 1975.

"Community Congress Charges Bias." *Cleveland Plain Dealer*, March 12, 1975, p. 46.

"Reach Agreement on Blacks' School Complaints." *Sun Press*, April 3, 1975.

Sands, Barry and Eva. "Letter to the Editor." *Sun Press*, April 10, 1975.

"Step in the Right Direction." *Call and Post*, April 12, 1975, p. 2B.

"An Agreement Has Been Reached Between Hts. Bd. of Education," *Call and Post*, April 12, 1975, p. 12A.

Campbell, Carl. "CICR Rebuttal." *Sun Press*, April 17, 1975, p. 4A.

Gaumer, Thomas. "Schools Kept Segregated, NAACP Says." *Cleveland Plain Dealer*, May 17, 1975.

"Class Action Against Realtor Continued." *Cleveland Plain Dealer*, August 19, 1975, p.6.

Robert McGruder and Kathrine Hatton, "Tight Money Helped Out." *Cleveland Plain Dealer*, November 30, 1975, p. 37.

"Campaign Launched for Housing Stability." *Sun Press*, March 18, 1976, p. 1 A.

"Heights Makes All-America." *Sun Press*, April 15, 1976.

"Harry Fagan Named New CCCA Director." *Cleveland Catholic Bulletin*, April 23, 1976.

Burwasser, David. "Housing Legislation." *Coventry Village News*, April 1976.
"Real Estate Firm Settle Bias Suit." *Cleveland Plain Dealer*, May 27, 1976, p. 4A.

Funk, John. "Real Estate Program, City Future Linked." *Sun Press*, June 24, 1976.

Funk, John. "Housing Service Demise Decried." *Sun Press*, July 1, 1976.

"Folk Singer's 'Little Light,' Now Extinguished, Recalled." *Sun Press*, September 2, 1976.

"Operation Equality Phased Out." *Call and Post*, November 20, 1976.

"Your Cleveland Urban League At Work, Spotlight." *Call and Post*, June 4, 1977, p. 11A.

Gleisser, Marcus. "Resident-City Effort Works in Hts." Sunday *Cleveland Plain Dealer*, May 28, 1978.

Ganger, Ted. "Making Integration Work in the Heights Area." *Cleveland Jewish News*, July 5, 1983.

"Bernice Lott Dies." *Call and Post*, October 6, 1983, p. 1A.

Peery, Richard. "Barbara Roderick, Defied Threats in Her Work to Integrate Housing." *Cleveland Plain Dealer*, October 31, 2004.

Teicher, Jordan. "Why is Vatican II So Important?" NPR, October 10, 2012.
"Vatican II Changed the Catholic Church – and the World." *Huffington Post*, October 10, 2012.

Joseph, Peniel. "Kennedy's Finest Moment." *New York Times*, June 10, 2013.

O'Donnell, Patrick. "School That Fueled Unrest to be Razed." *Cleveland Plain Dealer*, September 1, 2013.

Exner, Rich. "When Was Your Town Built?" *Sun News*, July 19,2018.

**Oral History Interviews**
"Arthur Brooks Interview. 11 June 2013."(2013) Cleveland Regional Oral History Collection. Interview 990017. https://engagedscholarship.csu.edu/crohc000/471/

"Bruce Melville Interview. 18 November 2014."(2014) Cleveland Regional Oral History Collection. Interview 999122. https://engagedscholarship.csu.edu/crohc000/736/

"Doris Allen Interview. 4 August 2013." (2013) Cleveland Regional Oral History Collection. Interview 990052. https://engagedscholarship.csu.edu/crohc000/422/

"John J. Boyle III Interview. 3 July 2014." (2014) Cleveland Regional Oral History Collection. Interview 500005. https://engagedscholarship.csu.edu/crohc000/605/

"Juanita Storey Interview. 14 April 2013." (2013) Cleveland Regional Oral History Collection. Interview 990027. https://engagedscholarship.csu.edu/crohc000//

"Kenneth H. Cooley Interview. 21 March 2014." (2014) Cleveland Regional Oral History Collection. Interview 990027. https://engagedscholarship.csu.edu/crohc000/529/

"Robert Madison Interview. 11 June 2013." (2013) Cleveland Regional Oral History Collection. Interview 990015. https://engagedscholarship.csu.edu/crohc000/473/

"Susanna Niermann O'Neil Interview. 25 June 2013." (2013) Cleveland Regional Oral History Collection. Interview 990028. https://engagedscholarship.csu.edu/crohc000/461/

### Interviews Conducted by Susan Kaeser

Betty Nelson. 2013.

Carl and Mary Ann Campbell. 20 March 2013.

Cathy Wherley. 2014.

Charles Bromley. 18 April 2013.

Diana Woodbridge. 13 August 2014.

Doris Allen, 23 January 2014.

Gerda Freedheim. 6 March 2013.

Howard and Judith VanKleef. 2015.

Jeanne Martin. 2017.

Joan Dowling. 24 April, 2013; 14 May 2013.

Joe Hunter. 2014.

Joyce Collins. 2013.

Judy Heyer. 2014.

Kermit Lind. 11 April 2013; and August, 2013.

Lana Cowell. 2013.

Lee Blons. 2017.

Mary Boyle. 12 August 2013.

Marjory Phillips. 2014.

Nina McLellan and Walter Nichols. 5 June 2013.

Phyllis Brody. 14 May 2013.

Richard Obermanns. 2013.

Robert and Nancy Klein. 2014.

Suzanne Nigro. 4 April, 2013.